THE INFAMOUS KING OF THE COMSTOCK

William S. Shepperson Series in Nevada History

UNIVERSITY OF NEVADA PRESS ▲▲ *Reno & Las Vegas*

MICHAEL J. MAKLEY

The
INFAMOUS
KING *of the*
COMSTOCK

William Sharon
and the Gilded Age
in the West

Wilbur S. Shepperson Series in Nevada History
Series Editor: Michael Green

University of Nevada Press, Reno, Nevada 89557 USA
www.unpress.nevada.edu
Copyright © 2006 by University of Nevada Press

All rights reserved

Manufactured in the United States of America

Design by Louise OFarrell

Library of Congress Cataloging-in-Publication Data

Makley, Michael J.
The infamous king of the Comstock : William Sharon and
the Gilded Age in the West / Michael J. Makley.—1st ed.
    p. cm.—(Wilbur S. Shepperson series in Nevada
history)
Includes bibliographical references and index.
ISBN 978-0-87417-630-8 (hardcover : alk. paper)
1. Sharon, William, 1821–1885. 2. Legislators—United
States—Biography. 3. United States. Congress. Senate—
Biography. 4. Capitalists and financiers—Nevada—
Biography. 5. Comstock Lode (Nev.)—History.
6. Nevada—Biography. 7. Virginia and Truckee Railroad
—History. 8. San Francisco Stock and Exchange Board—
History. 9. West (U.S.)—History—1860–1890—
Biography.
I. Title. II. Series.
E664.S53M34 2006
979'.02'092—dc22

                                        2005020436

The paper used in this book meets the requirements
of American National Standard for Information
Sciences—Permanence of Paper for Printed Library
Materials, ANSI/NISO Z39.48-1992 (R2002). Binding
materials were selected for strength and durability.

University of Nevada Press Paperback Edition, 2009

ISBN 978-0-87417-779-4 (paper : alk. paper)
ISBN 978-0-87417-669-8 (ebook)

For my mother, who paints portraits

Contents

Illustrations

Acknowledgements

I RECEIVED A SIGNIFICANT amount of assistance in developing this book, which is reflected in the fact that the first draft of the manuscript was over eight hundred pages long. A considerable debt is owed both to those who helped me accumulate that amount of information and to those who helped me reduce it to publishable size. I was assisted in innumerable ways by the skilled staffs at a host of institutions: The Bancroft Library at the University of California, Berkeley; the California Section of the California State Library; the Alpine County Library at Markleeville, California; the Douglas County Library at Minden, Nevada; the Nevada State Library; the Nevada State Archives; the Getchell Library at the University of Nevada, Reno; the Special Collections Department at the University of Nevada, Reno; the Nevada State Historical Society; and the Storey County Records Department.

In addition I would like to thank a number of professionals who were particularly generous with their time and energy: John Hedger at the National Archives Records Administration; Mary Woods at the Alpine County Library; Guy Rocha, Nevada State Archivist; archivist Jeff Kintop; Michael Maher at the Nevada Historical Society; Robert Blesse, head of Special Collections, University of Nevada, Reno; Special Collections staff members Jacquelyn Sundstrand and Addison White and curator Kathryn Totten; and Sara Vélez, managing editor at the University of Nevada Press. California Superior Court Judge David Devore assisted me in finding the numerous *Sharon v. Sharon* court decisions. Eric Moody of the Nevada Historical Society clarified several of my misinterpretations of early Virginia City and waded through the manuscript's first draft. Daniel Makley and Eric Beavers each contributed books and discussed parts of the developing manuscript. John Brisenden coordinated a meeting I had with William Sharon III. I am particularly grateful to Mr. Sharon for devoting an afternoon to discussing his family history with me.

Margaret Dalrymple guided the manuscript through the jury and editing process at the Press, informing and encouraging me throughout. Michael S. Green read the manuscript twice, analyzing and offering extensive recommendations for rewriting it the first time and thoroughly editing it the second. His contribution was invaluable, and, needless to say, the book would not have appeared in its current form without his involvement.

Michelle Filippini was informative and gracious in administering the final stages of the editing process. I am indebted to Sarah Nestor, the line editor, for her exhaustive effort. Everything from the accuracy of citation page numbers and dates to the text's sequence of events was scrutinized and questioned, resulting in a greatly enhanced manuscript.

I am also grateful to Dan Jones, McAvoy Layne, and Stephen P. Ledyard, who, through their achievements and encouragement, inspired the project. And I owe special thanks to Matthew Makley, who advised and assisted me from the project's inception to publication.

Finally, I would like to thank Randi Lee Makley for her help and support, which sustained me during the lengthy process.

THE INFAMOUS KING OF THE COMSTOCK

PROLOGUE

ON AUGUST 27, 1875, WILLIAM CHAPMAN RALSTON swam out into San Francisco Bay and drowned. Earlier that day the Bank of California's board of directors had asked Ralston to resign his position as president. Because of his reckless speculations, the once invincible bank had failed. Fortunes, large and small, were lost. But his heroic stature was too firmly established to be undone, and the entire West mourned his death. San Franciscans filled the street for a mile behind his hearse as it wound its way to Lone Mountain Cemetery. Within six weeks Ralston's partner, Senator William Sharon, saved the people's fortunes by reestablishing the bank. Like Ralston, Sharon also earned recognition. In 1966 a historian noted that although grudging tributes were paid him, "It is probably impossible to find a really kind word that was ever said about Sharon and preserved in print."[1]

William Sharon's associates and adversaries were the most prominent individuals in the West during the Comstock era. They included Nevada's first full-term senator, the father of federal mining laws, William Stewart; Adolph Sutro, who conceptualized and engineered the great Comstock tunnel; the Bonanza Kings: John Mackay, James G. Fair, J. C. Flood, and William O'Brien; renowned Virginia City newsmen Joseph Goodman, Dan DeQuille, Alf Doten, and Rollin Daggett; U.S. Supreme Court justice and author of the "Ninth Circuit Law" Stephen J. Field; legendary African American entrepreneur Mary E. "Mammy" Pleasant; southern cavalier David S. Terry, the California Supreme Court chief justice who killed U.S. senator David Broderick in a duel; and William Chapman Ralston, the man who built San Francisco.

But no one matched Sharon in the variety and scope of his achievements on the Comstock. Those who mined the Comstock Lode are generally associated with strikes on a single property or perhaps two: John O. Earle and George Hearst with the Gould & Curry mine; Alvinza Hayward and John P. Jones with the Crown Point and the Savage; E. J. "Lucky" Baldwin with the Ophir; and John Mackay with the Kentuck and, with his associates, the Hale & Norcross and the Big Bonanza. Between 1864 and 1874 Sharon controlled more than a dozen of the greatest mines, including the Yellow Jacket, the Kentuck, the Hale & Norcross, the Ophir, the Belcher, the Chollar-Potosi, and the Savage.

A visionary capitalist, Sharon regenerated exploration of the largely untapped Lode when others were abandoning it. He built the Virginia & Truckee Railroad, insuring that all the territory's ore would be milled. At the same time that he directed mine production, he controlled speculation, driving prices on the San Francisco Stock and Exchange to serve his purposes. And, in what deserves to be remembered as one of the great feats in American commerce, he revived the collapsed Bank of California.[2]

The era in which Sharon prospered, 1865 to 1885, is labeled the Gilded Age, because wealth and society's glitter camouflaged massive poverty, moral decay, and corruption in politics and commerce. Sharon epitomized the era's powerful barons. His genius built the notorious "Bank Ring." He acquired enormous wealth while disguising the devious schemes required to gain it. Winning the exalted title of "Senator," he did not serve. For the last ten years of his life, his homes were the world-renowned Belmont estate, twenty-two miles south of San Francisco, and a suite of rooms in his elegant Palace Hotel in the city. Their lavish facades hid the decadence of numerous paid liaisons and trysts that reputedly included wives of associates. Still, in William Graham Sumner's system of social Darwinism, the turn-of-the-century philosophy in which winning served as the cardinal virtue, Sharon was a champion.

Remarkably, there has been no biography of Sharon. Those who have written about Adolph Sutro identify Sharon as a scoundrel whose intrigue blocked the Sutro tunnel project. Biographers of William C. Ralston compare Ralston's generous, civic-minded, and heroic nature to Sharon's aloof, cold persona, portraying Sharon as a Judas who betrayed Ralston and drove him to his death.[3] Still, it should be acknowledged that the corporate revolution of the 1880s, which shifted America from agrarian republicanism to urban industrialization—giving rise to Carnegie Associates, John D. Rockefeller's Standard Oil Trust, and the American Sugar Refining Company—employed strategies anticipated by Sharon. He created a vertical monopoly to control activities from the collecting of raw materials through the shipping of the final product. This book seeks to place Sharon's feats in historical context and to demonstrate how the same characteristics that earned his business success spawned the dissipation that embittered and hastened the end of his life.

Sharon was not a one-dimensional Mephistopheles, leading Ralston to ruin. Mrs. M. M. Matthews, who lived for a time in Virginia City, wrote that Sharon's heart went out to the poor. She and a friend visited him several times requesting help for Virginia City's needy, and they were never turned away. She commented: "Senator Sharon is one of the best men that ever lived in Virginia City. He had a heart for every poor person who went to him, and I think most of his charities were given in secret." In 1864 the leading Comstock newspaper, the *Territorial Enterprise*, mentioned Sharon's donating one hundred dollars to the Sisters of Charity, and he donated "goodly sums" to a theater company attempting Shakespeare.[4] But, perhaps lending credence to Mrs. Matthews's perception of secret charities, during the years of his residence in Nevada there were no other comments regarding Sharon and altruism.

Sharon paid his employees well and treated them with consideration. The manager of the Sharon-owned Palace Hotel commented that most of those hired at the hotel's opening remained in its employ at Sharon's death ten years later, possibly indicating a compassionate bent in Sharon. Ex–superior court judge John Currey, who served as an attorney for Sharon and spent several years as Sharon's neighbor, said: "If a faithful servant became sick or disabled for any cause, involving no derilection as to habits, such servants were continued in service at their regular salary."[5]

Reuben Lloyd, an attorney who worked with Sharon rejuvenating the collapsed Bank of California, commented that Sharon grasped ideas quickly and knew how to handle problems. "Only for him [reestablishing the Bank] would never have carried at all." Charles C. Goodwin, who worked as an editor for Sharon and later served as a district judge, wrote a mostly hagiographic account of Comstock personalities. He pointed out that Sharon's strength of character sustained the development of the Comstock Lode when it appeared barren for several years. "Mr. Sharon had held things together, and made the great discoveries in the Belcher and Crown Point possible. Not one man in a thousand comprehended the work he had performed, but he was called king." In 1883, in a Department of the Interior–sponsored book, *Comstock Mining and Miners,* Eliot Lord added another perspective on Sharon's role, saying he embodied a new period of organization on the Comstock where "cool calculation" and self-interest were the basis of action.[6]

Sharon's obvious self-interest prompted many in Nevada to see his actions as nefarious, leading them to call him "king"—often a disparaging term in the 1860s. They saw him as cold and hard, focused only on corporate goals. People on the street considered his bank's foreclosure policy, his shadowy stock deals, and the assessments levied on stockholders of mines under his control to be simple robbery. An anecdote about Sharon's miserliness was said to be oft repeated: A Comstocker walked into a San Francisco saloon and tossed a twenty-dollar gold piece onto the bar, inviting the boys to share a drink. "A tiny, old Irishman . . . picked up the gold piece, bit it hard between tobacco-stained teeth, sent it ringing, singing down upon the hard wood of the bar, and then, with the unmistakable leer of the saloon wag, the alcoholic king's jester, asked, 'Say, did Sharon know ye had that'?"[7]

Sharon denied a $2,500 loan to cattleman Alexander Toponce, who visited Virginia City in 1867. Toponce told of getting even. Day after day he caught Sharon on the street and raced his pair of trotting horses against the banker's. A crowd would gather to cheer when Toponce's team raced ahead. "Sharon would get mad and touch his team up so hard they would break gait and then he would jerk and saw and lash them and get red in the face. And the madder he got the louder the people would cheer.

"Finally Sharon got so sore he would not order out his team and after a few days I got a tip that he would send a man around to buy my span from me. So I saw him coming first and held the price stiff for $3,000 . . . and got it."[8]

Thompson and West's History of Nevada, published in 1881 as an eight-by-eleven inch, 680-page book, is the first history written about the state. Sharon is mentioned in it mostly in passing. His political and financial efforts are generally criticized, and his personal history is composed of only two sentences. The first is a lengthy statement about his background. The second states simply: "Like all the other operators [Sharon's] career shows a combination of energy, tenacity of purpose and close fistedness, which will win if it is possible."[9]

William Wright, known by his pseudonym Dan DeQuille, arrived in Nevada in 1859 and lived in Virginia City until the late 1890s, when broken health forced him to leave. He wrote for the *Territorial Enterprise* during the years it maintained a prestige unequaled in the western frontier. His mining reports were authoritative; his satires gained him fame across the country. In 1876 DeQuille published his book *The Big Bonanza.* The *Enterprise* had vilified Sharon so mercilessly when he ran for the U.S. Senate in 1872 that he bought the paper before running again in 1874; consequently, DeQuille worked for Sharon while writing about him in *The Big Bonanza.* In chapter LXIX, "Millionaire Proprietors," DeQuille writes short biographies of Comstock kings, including Sharon. In a page and a half he describes Sharon's background then says:

> Mr. Sharon is the father of the Virginia & Truckee Railroad, undoubtedly the crookedest railroad in the world, and a wonderful road in many other respects. In building this road Mr. Sharon secured a subsidy of $500,000 from the people of Washoe in aid of the project, constructed as much of the road as the sum would build, then mortgaged the whole road for the amount of money required for its completion. In this way he built the road without putting his hand in his own pocket for a cent, and he still owns half the road—worth $2,500,000 and bringing him in, as Mr. Adolph Sutro says, $12,000 per day.[10]

The oft-quoted "crookedest railroad in the world" is a play on words, describing the winding roadway as well as the way in which Sharon financed it. A significant number of Nevadans believed that Sharon duped them into paying for the centerpiece of his monopoly. The mention of Sutro's estimation must have been intended to prick Sharon, for the two were bitter enemies. But DeQuille continued, balancing his article by describing the road and other Sharon actions as good for the country.[11]

Sharon's name appears in another place in the book, although it is not listed in the index. Chapter LXVIII is called "Some Interesting Creatures." On the page facing the chapter opening is the picture of a foraging bear, under which is the caption "The Man Eater" (in that era a term that commonly referred not only to carnivorous beasts but also to humans who preyed on others). The chapter's first three paragraphs briefly describe Silver City and Virginia City, listing their mills and mines. But the list includes an incongruous sentence: "The Eureka mill, of the Union Mill and Mining Company, of which company Mr. Sharon is a principal stockholder, is one of the finest mills on the river." While this chapter mentions thirteen mills and eight mines, no other stockholder's name appears in reference to them, nor are Sharon's partners in the Union Mill and Mining Company recognized. Only Sharon. A brief description of Carson City follows the list before the chapter begins to deal with the "creatures" of the title, none of which is the pictured "Man Eater." The beasts include lizards, some whose bite is fatal; scorpions; stinging centipedes; tarantulas with fangs the length of a rattlesnake's, projecting from "blood red" mouths; and wasps that sting the tarantulas, depositing eggs that, when hatched, "devour [the tarantula's] vitals."[12]

The structure of the chapter is peculiar. It begins by discussing mines and mills rather than the topic suggested in its title. The only human name in the chapter is Sharon's, introduced in a superfluous clause. On the page opposite Sharon's name is the picture of "The Man Eater," with no mention of it in the text. Wright's skill as a man of letters suggests something other than carelessness in chapter LXVIII. Unable to openly ridicule his employer, he appears to have used a literary device, revealing his feelings by placing Sharon among the interesting creatures.

Ambrose Bierce, the sardonic San Francisco journalist, felt no compulsion to disguise his feelings about Sharon. He wrote a 107-line poem about his contemporary, addressing the last few lines directly to him:

> Sharon, some years, perchance, remain of life—
> Of vice and greed, vulgarity and strife;
> And then—God speed the day if such His will—
> You'll lie among the dead you helped to kill,
> And be in good society at last,
> Your purse unsilvered and your face unbrassed.[13]

For a number of years Bierce's golden pen made an illustrated weekly, *The Wasp,* the most read magazine on the West Coast. But even before Bierce's association with it, Sharon was a favorite target of *Wasp* cartoonists. He was featured on the cover of its first issue, August 5, 1876, complaining that San Francisco's tax rate would force him back to Virginia City. The magazine periodically ridiculed celebrations such as his daughters' weddings, and when he became embroiled in a divorce scandal late in 1883, his torment was chronicled in a steady stream of caricatures.[14]

William Stewart held the reins of power on the Comstock before Sharon's arrival. An attorney who represented the richest of the mine owners, Stewart would serve as the state's first elected U.S. senator (succeeded by Sharon after his second term). Stewart defended Sharon, at the end of Sharon's life, in a divorce case of nationwide notoriety. Stewart rarely mentions Sharon in his 358-page reminiscence (the litigation occupies 3 pages). At one point he remonstrates against the manner of building the Virginia & Truckee Railroad—using assessments on the mines and bond monies furnished by local governments. He protests that it made millions for its owners in San Francisco and New York (Sharon and his partner, D. O. Mills), leaving nothing for Nevada.[15]

Several years after Sharon died, his archenemy, Adolph Sutro, wrote: "William Sherron. That man is dead—I would not like to say much about him. I think Sherron is a thoroughly bad man—a man entirely void of principle, honesty and gentility . . . capable of doing anything—committing any crime to accomplish his ends . . . and I think everybody will agree with me that knew him."[16]

Francis Newlands, Sharon's son-in-law, adamantly disagreed. Later a nationally prominent U.S. senator from Nevada, he was interviewed regarding Sharon for H. H. Bancroft's 1891 *Chronicle of the Builders.* The interviewer wrote to Bancroft describing how, after the death of Sharon's daughter, Newlands married the daughter of Hall McAllister—dean of the San Francisco bar. Although a statue of McAllister stood before the city hall, built on McAllister Street, in comparing the two Newlands noted, "In whatever goes to make men great among their fellows, Sharon was far the greater man."[17]

The descriptions of those who knew Sharon reveal him as an individual respected and admired or feared and hated. With a longer perspective, how should he now be judged? Instances of moment filled his life. Responsible for many of the era's accomplishments, he also played a leading role in several of its most notorious incidents. His ruthlessness and need to prevail were apparent in his business and social life. He built an empire, often at great cost to those around him. He fought government regulations until, realizing how they might be used, he tailored them to his advantage. His achievements made up a large part of the development of the Comstock Lode. But as the historiographic slights intimate, his was an infamous success.

Chapter One

BLACK BROADCLOTH

WILLIAM SHARON WAS BORN IN Smithfield, Ohio, on January 9, 1821, his ancestors having helped settle William Penn's Philadelphia at the end of the seventeenth century. The family tree included a lieutenant who served in the New Jersey campaign in 1776, a Presbyterian minister, and a state legislator. South Carolina senator John Calhoun was a distant relative, and Samuel Sharon, a brother of his great-grandfather, married Sarah Davis, a relative of Abraham Lincoln.

Sharon's father, also named William, married Susan Kirk, a Quaker of Scotch descent. When Sharon was twelve, his mother died giving birth to her seventh child. His father, grave and determined but kindly, owned a tannery and farmed. For the last twenty years of his life he served as justice of the peace and sat on the board of directors of the First National Bank of Smithfield. He died in 1875 at the age of eighty-three.

Although small and sickly, with a nervous temperament, William Jr. inherited his father's force of character. According to Bancroft's *Chronicle* he was a leader among his peers, but a pronounced individuality and pugnacious temperament kept him from being popular. Three incidents helped form another aspect of his disposition. The first occurred when Sharon, seventeen years old, used savings to buy an interest in a flatboat hauling cargo down the Ohio and Mississippi Rivers. The boat wrecked in falls near Louisville, and the salvaged goods were transported to New Orleans to be sold. There his partners stole the profits, and he returned home defeated. Sharon was to lose his entire stock of merchandise again in a flood at age twenty-nine and was duped out of his life savings at forty-three. His other personal traits, mixed with a shrewdness born of his having suffered nature's vagaries and the economics of the street, formed the personality of a man who would build an empire.

Sharon also possessed an intelligence that brought order to chaos. He honed his aptitude during three years of study at Athens College. Instead of paying expenses, his father gave him the use of a small farm that he worked, and the profits paid his way. He then studied law in the office of Edwin M. Stanton, the mercurial Democrat who became Lincoln's secretary of war. In about 1845 illness prompted Sharon to move west to St. Louis, where he passed the Missouri bar examinations and briefly practiced law. But his health did not improve, so—reluctantly giving up his dream of the law—he moved to Carrollton, Illinois. There he lived with his brother, Dr. John K. Sharon, whose sons ran a mercantile while their father engaged in his medical practice. William joined the merchandise business as a partner, working as much as his health allowed over the course of the next four years.

Finally in 1849, hoping the West would be a panacea, he joined the 49ers. John D. Fry, who remained Sharon's friend throughout their lives, accompanied him. The Fry family was prominent in Illinois. Fry, two years older than Sharon, had already served as a county sheriff, earning him the popular appellation "Colonel," and was completing the second of his terms as an Illinois legislator. The two men left Carrolton on May 1, at the adjournment of the legislative session.[1]

In St. Louis the partners invested in general merchandise and a frame building that could be easily assembled. Sending their goods around Cape Horn to San Francisco, they headed out with a wagon train. Leaving three young aides with their wagons, they departed from the main train on saddle horses, leading two pack animals. Sharon and Fry made the arduous one-thousand-mile trek over the Rockies to Salt Lake City in fifty days. There they rested until the train caught up with them, then they traveled with it across Utah Territory's alkaline plains. Following little more than a trail through the unbroken forest of the Sierra Nevada, the wagons used "Cock-Eye" Johnson's Pass to come out on the American River. Finally, crossing California's Central Valley, they collected their goods in San Francisco. In mid-August of 1849 they recrossed the valley to Placer County, where they opened a store in a tiny mining settlement that came to be called Frytown, presumably after Colonel Fry. A few months later they moved the store to the flats of Sacramento, where they began to prosper.

On the evening of January 8, 1850, a violent rain began pouring onto ground already saturated from a heavy winter, and the Sacramento and American Rivers both overrunning their banks. The resultant flood drowned some people in their beds and trapped others, many of whom died from the effects of exposure.[2] Goods worth tens of thousands of dollars, including Sharon and Fry's tent-house business, were swept away. At age twenty-nine Sharon had to start over once again, but this time he may have welcomed the opportunity. "[Sharon] was a remarkably good business man," Colonel Fry commented years later, saying that they did well until the flood. However, "Mr. Sharon did not have a very good opinion of Sacramento," continued Fry, "and I am half inclined to think that he was secretly glad that the accident by flood occurred, as he then dissolved our partnership and came down to San Francisco."[3]

Fry followed Sharon to San Francisco and was appointed a special agent of the U.S. Post Office. Resigning in 1860, he went on to make a career of working for Sharon. He served as president of three of Sharon's mines and was on the board of trustees of twelve others.

San Francisco in 1850 was a teeming village port, built out over the bay. Waters rose and fell beneath it. Originally, a narrow levee of pilings had marked the boundary of the tide, where ships used a small wharf; then, with the gold rush, vessels began to fill the harbor. Builders drove rows of piles from the wharf and erected stores over the water. At high tide cargoes could be unloaded. Plank walks, four feet wide, without handrails, were laid to connect the various buildings, some of which also became used for housing. By 1850 as many as one thousand people lived over the water or in the hulks of ships run aground for use as waterfront buildings. On land, dwellings were constructed of brushwood, tarpaulins, canvas sails, and boards of deck cabins from ships.

When, in the winter of '49, storm had followed storm, streets turned into treacherous rivers of mud. Stories of wagons and horses being lost in the mire were common.[4] Even worse than the physical difficulties were problems associated with social disorganization and crime. In 1849 two thousand people lived in San Francisco; in 1850 it rose tenfold, to twenty thousand. Ruffians and thieves poured in from around the world. The worst, who were ex-soldiers of Colonel J. D. Stevenson's California Volunteers and were called the "Regulators" or "the Hounds," spread terror from their headquarters, a tent known as "Tammany Hall." When they finally perpetrated a ferocious attack against Little Chile, a tent community, in July of 1849, 230 volunteers formed companies to move against them. Two dozen Hounds were arrested and a week later convicted of conspiracy, riot, robbery, and assault with intent to kill. Despite demands for hanging, the miscreants were merely run out of town.[5]

Sharon was the type of citizen the rough community hoped to attract. The City Directory of 1850, which began with a disclaimer regarding its accuracy since a large portion of the inhabitants lived in tents or places that could not be described, listed Sharron, Wm., as a broker living at the corner of Union and Mason. He worked first with realtor Beverly Miller in 1850 and then in 1851 with Henry S. Fitch, a realtor and auctioneer.[6] After a year with Fitch, Sharon began his own real-estate business. He quickly earned a reputation as a visionary. Realizing before others that California's shipping interests would be concentrated in North Beach, he bought land, erecting one of its first buildings at Chestnut and Taylor.[7]

Sharon immediately became influential in politics, winning election as an assistant alderman on the first city board in May of 1850. As would occur later in Virginia City while he was dealing with affairs that hampered his ability to earn money, Sharon took action that spurred development. Because the Treaty of Guadalupe Hidalgo promised to respect Mexican landowners' rights, disputes arose concerning whether titles should issue from the federal government, California's land grants, Spanish land grants, or Mexican colonization law. Sharon helped secure passage of an ordinance to study the archives of former authorities and laws relating to titles, and the information became the basis of subsequent determinations.[8] In another action Sharon voted with the majority, passing a bill to pay aldermen six thousand dollars a year. The cash-strapped community's hue and cry forced a veto of the bill and its reduction by a third.

In August 1850 Sharon and seven others, including future mayor John W. Geary and future U.S. senator David C. Broderick, formed a group to assist beleaguered immigrants. Twenty thousand had arrived on the overland route to California, and twenty thousand more were still struggling across the Sierra Nevada. By nightfall the committee collected provisions and about six thousand dollars in cash to distribute to the sufferers.[9]

Although its frontier nature was apparent (on June 22 a five-hundred-pound grizzly bear had been captured near the city's Mission Dolores), San Francisco was becoming a metropolitan center. Fire departments were organized, and on September 9, 1850, California became a state. More than sixty thousand men and two thousand women had arrived during the past year (although many proceeded on to the goldfields); 626 vessels lay in the bay.[10] As building in the city became frenzied, Sharon prospered.

In 1852 Sharon married Maria Malloy, the daughter of a noted sea captain from Quebec, Canada. She had come to San Francisco with her mother and stepfather. Less than twenty years old, cultured and refined, she bore Sharon five children, three of whom survived to adulthood.[11]

Early in 1854, robberies, riots, and two murders were laid at the feet of the city's "squatting rascality." On June 5 Sharon helped organize property owners into the Association for the Protection of Property. In 1855 the editors of the *Annals of San Francisco* reported on the organization's activities: "As we close [the spring report], inquests are being held over the murdered bodies, and various rioters are detained for trial in the hospitals and prison."[12]

Between 1850 and 1864 Sharon bought and sold land and amassed a fortune of $150,000. A businessman later noted, "I came here in 1859 and it was then acknowledged that the opinion of William Sharon in anything relating to real estate was of more value than that of four or five men put together. As a business man he had no competitor; he was clear and concise; and he rapidly made up his mind, and in every instance that I am aware of he was right."[13]

Early in 1861 the secession of Southern states created discord. In the election of 1860 Lincoln carried the state of California by one thousand votes, Republican electors garnering thirty-nine thousand, Democrats thirty-eight thousand. But soon, fueled by the dissolution of the Union, opinion swung heavily behind Lincoln.[14] The shelling of Fort Sumter in 1861 caused a great anti-Confederate demonstration in San Francisco. People feared Southern elements would attempt to wrest the Pacific Coast from the Union. Sharon, never comfortable speaking before crowds, was one of several speakers who addressed a "vast assemblage" in front of the old city hall. Although what he said was not recorded, it was noted that "For pungent invective and withering denunciation [Sharon's speech] was worthy of a veteran orator."[15]

The San Francisco Stock and Exchange Board was organized in the fall of 1862. In 1863 it doubled in size, its forty associates electing the new members. Among those chosen were Fry and Sharon, Sharon being elected in October. The same year, along with a friend, Charles H. Wakelee, Sharon began investing in the mines of Nevada's Comstock Lode.

In Gold Canyon near Virginia City, two adjoining mines, the Uncle Sam and the Overman, overlapped each other and also extended into the North American mine, causing litigation. Sharon believed the North American would gain control of the other two, putting an end to the lawsuits. E. P. Peckham, who served three terms as president of the San Francisco Stock and Exchange, reported that a man sold him North American stock before attending the exchange: "Well, when the list was called I offered 100 shares of North American at $290. 'Take it,' said Sharon. One hundred more was offered. 'Take it,' said Sharon; 'but haven't you got any more . . . ' 'Here's 500 [shares],' I replied. 'I'll take 500 more if you have it.'

'Here's 500 more.' 'Take it,' he said. 'Here's 500 more if you want it.' 'Take it,' he said and left the room."

Sharon later told Peckham he believed he had been cheated. He marked his stocks with red ink in the letter O in North American. When the stocks were checked, 1,000 of the 1,700 shares were marked. Sharon had purchased his own stock. Peckham said that Sharon gave him all the money he had on hand without flinching and promised to pay the large balance.[16]

William Sharon and William Chapman Ralston had become acquainted sometime around May of 1858, when Ralston married Lizzie Fry, the niece of John Fry.[17] Fry, accompanied by Sharon's associate Wakelee, went to Ralston on Sharon's behalf. The banker agreed to buy whatever real estate Sharon owned to cover the rest of his stock-market debt. Sharon was left penniless. Shortly therafter, Ralston began to advance Sharon $250 a month and took action that changed both their lives as well as the history of Nevada and California. He made Sharon his partner and appointed him the Bank of California's representative in Virginia City, Nevada.[18]

Sharon did not fit the image of the western capitalist. He wore a big brimmed, slouch hat and quoted the classics. He dressed in black broadcloth, giving him a clerical or ministerial appearance. Unlike brawny Bonanza millionaires, Sharon weighed perhaps 135 pounds and seemed reserved to the point of aloofness. He laughed but rarely smiled. While others might seek to be in the foreground, he blended in with a crowd— although always acting with purpose. His distinguishing feature was his eyes. Detractors said they were black and beady, sly and devious; to friends they were searching, projecting intelligence. According to Goodwin's description: "His face was lighted by a pair of cold gray eyes, a glance into which made clear that any one who dealt with him should understand from the first that no bluff would ever carry with him, that no matter what the crisis would be it would be met without fear."[19]

On the other hand, Ralston was stocky and powerful. People frequently described him as handsome. From the time he founded it in 1864 until his death in 1875, he ran the Bank of California, making him the most powerful man in San Francisco and thus in California and the entire West. Ralston, previously associated with financial stalwarts C. K. Garrison and Cornelius Vanderbilt Sr., was a partner in the San Francisco banking firm of Donahoe, Ralston, and Company, connected with the powerful Eugene Kelly of New York. Because of his affiliations and connections, Ralston handled much of the Comstock Lode's wealth. But Kelly became dissatisfied with Ralston's management in two areas. The first of these was the attitude that allowed Ralston's overwhelming success: his insistence that money made in the West be invested there. The second would be a primary determinant in Ralston's downfall: he used bank resources to lend money to a friend without proper securities.[20]

Early in 1864 Ralston began preparations to break away from Donahoe and Kelly and open a new bank. On June 30 Donahoe, Ralston and Company disbanded and Ralston took most of the firm's clients. On July 5 the Bank of California opened.[21] Darius Ogden Mills, a circumspect Sacramento banker, carried the title of president of the new bank but served only as a figurehead, enlisted to lend an air of repute to the venture. He spent much of his tenure engaged in his own affairs and traveling. Ralston, the cashier, ran all practical aspects of the bank.[22]

The Bank of California dominated financial circles from the time it opened. Ralston enlisted power brokers, so that the first board of directors included Thomas Bell, who made a fortune gaining control of the quicksilver trade; Louis McLane, president of the Pioneer Stage Company; James Whitney Jr. and William Norris, chief officers of the state's primary shipping company, the California Steam Navigation Company; lumber magnate A. J. Pope; and an original Comstock investor, John O. Earle. The bank began with over $2 million in capital, an amount unsurpassed in the West and topped by only two of the fifty-five banks operating in New York City. Within three weeks of the bank's opening, the U.S. Bureau of Internal Revenue named it the depository for money payable.[23]

Ralston took risks. He listened to people with plans for advancing San Francisco and the West. Every day, at an appointed hour, he met with inventors, schemers, and promoters to entertain their ideas. He bought hundreds of patents and provided money for everything from planting the first northern California vineyards to creating a California wool industry and building San Francisco's California Theater.[24]

Not only associates but employees and even acquaintances regarded Ralston as a friend. He made it a point to visit the myriad concerns in which he held an interest, talking with the workers about their jobs and families. They felt as though they knew him and he held them in high regard. When he made Sharon his partner, he allowed him to escape bankruptcy. Naming him the bank representative in Virginia City earned Ralston and his corporations millions of dollars.

The phenomenon of Virginia City mushroomed above the Comstock vein on the side of Mount Davidson, six thousand feet above sea level. To the west, beyond a string of three valleys, rose the escarpment of the Sierra Nevada. To the east lay three hundred and fifty miles of alternating barren hills and desert: the Great Basin. The wealth of the vein ensured that the most advanced technology would be imported, as would amenities and certain urban comforts. But social institutions, laws, and mores proved to be situational.

Mark Twain described the Virginia City he experienced in the early 1860's as "the liveliest town for its age and population that America ever produced." He spoke of swarms of people and endless streams of vehicles. He also recited what became a famous list:

> There were military companies, fire companies, brass bands, banks, hotels, theaters, 'hurdy-gurdy houses,' wide-open gambling palaces, political pow-wows, civic processions, street-fights, murders, inquests, riots, a whiskey-mill every fifteen steps, a Board of Aldermen, a Mayor, a City Surveyor, a City Engineer, a Chief of the Fire Department, with First, Second, and Third Assistants, a Chief of Police, City Marshal, and a large police force, two Boards of Mining Brokers, a dozen breweries, and half a dozen jails and station-houses in full operation, and some talk of building a church.[25]

By 1877 the wife of the publisher of *Leslie's Illustrated Weekly,* Miriam Squire Leslie, noted the town's progress (with an unacknowledged nod to Twain): "Virginia City boasts of forty-nine gambling saloons and one church." She went on: "To call a place dreary, desolate, homeless, uncomfortable and wicked is a good deal, but to call it God-forsaken is a good deal more." But for every account by a Miriam Leslie, a New York reporter would laud the restaurants and saloons as the equal of any in the world and shops and stores "which are dazzling in splendor."[26]

The 1870 Nevada census tallied 16,243 Indians, 23 of whom lived "out of tribal relations" and thus were considered civilized.[27] Washoes and Paiutes lived in the vicinity of Virginia City. Periodically the newspapers would report their activities, the items generally marked by derisiveness or cruelty. The *Gold Hill News* of 1872 issued a call to keep the Indians properly subjugated: "The policy of conciliation has proved a failure. . . . Let them fully understand that they are safe while on their reservation, but when they absent themselves therefrom they are liable to be shot down like deer."[28] The means of survival of the Native cultures were in ruin; the practices of the Euro-Americans—fencing the forage of deer and antelope, clear-cutting the forests, and poisoning the streams with mining waste—were methodically destroying game habitat.[29]

Half of the Comstock's citizens were foreign born. They came from every European country, including the British Isles and Scandinavia, as well as from Mexico and China. Because Chinese immigrants, brought to Nevada in 1852 to dig a ditch from the Carson River to Gold Canyon for mining purposes, proved industrious and worked for far less than others, they were later recruited in larger numbers to build Nevada railroads. In 1870, of the 58,711 residents of Nevada, 3,152 were Chinese. (Only 306 of the Chinese were women.)[30] In Virginia City they eked out a living doing laundry, acting as servants, cooks, or dishwashers, or selling scavenged wood. They lived below D Street at the foot of town, their residences, stores, and restaurants filling the quarter from which emanated smells of unusual foods and burning opium.[31]

In 1863 35 African American men lived in Nevada Territory. By 1870 there were 82 (only 6 of whom had been there in '63). One was a doctor, another owned a saloon, and there were a tailor and 2 women milliners. But the mines as well as skilled trades were closed to them, so other African Americans worked as janitors or servants or porters.[32]

One other segment of the population lived on D Street, below the businesses of B and C Streets. On early maps, "Female Boarding" designated a string of tiny houses for "women of the town." The white cabins were described as "gaudily-furnished rooms, at whose uncurtained windows the inmates sat, spider-like, waiting for flies."[33] An 1876 mining-review journal commented that one could see the worst of society in Virginia City and nearby Gold Hill. While disputing the claim that more mistresses and public women resided there than wives, it noted that there were enough of both.[34]

A madam named Cad Thompson operated a "boarding house" on North D Street. The place, known as the Brick, was considered "a whorehouse of a superior class."[35] In November of 1866 newsman Alf Doten wrote in his diary that some fellows ran out engine no. 1 at 4 o'clock in the morning, using its hose to "wash out" the Brick. "Gave [Cad Thompson] hell—created quite a consternation among the law & order portion of the Community—Not the end of it yet—We shall see who rules the city now, the roughs or decent men." A few weeks later Doten noted that he and H. H. Bence, a member of the assembly from Ormsby County, visited Cad Thompson's, confirming what his entry had intimated: the law-and-order element supported the brothel. It was the "roughs" who had washed it out. Widow Thompson remained a member of the Virginia City community until she sold her house in 1892.[36]

The nature of the Sabbath's observance, or more accurately nonobservance, was another issue offensive to those from more reputable environs. The mines and mills (and saloons) ran twenty-four hours every day, causing auxiliary businesses to remain open seven days a week. Inside houses of worship, sermons and hymns were punctuated by the clanking of metal in the distance and drivers' oaths in the streets outside.[37] In 1874 the Reverend H. Richardson, a distributor of biblical literature, asked rhetorically if there was any other place with so little regard for religious observance, "such heaven-daring profanity, such common drunkenness, such un-blushing licentiousness, and such glorying in shame?"[38]

Sharon, at forty-three, was older than most of Virginia City's denizens. Dressed in black broadcloth, at a glance he looked like a misfit. But it soon became apparent that shrewdness and certain worldly habits made him decidedly a fit. In fact, it was just a matter of time before innocents and sharps alike came under his sway and he would be known, for better or worse, as "King of the Comstock."

Chapter Two

GAMBLING

EARLY IN 1864, mines in the Nevada boomtown of Aurora dried up, and its stocks crashed on the San Francisco Exchange. In Virginia City four hundred wildcat mining companies, most of which had been formed the previous year, were proving unsuccessful and being deserted. Flooding at the lower levels of the developed mines often stopped work. Ore bodies showed signs of exhaustion. The great Comstock boom ebbed. Money became scarce; debts mounted. Between April 1 and July 30, 1864, Savage mining stocks dropped from $2,600 per share to $750. That spring and summer, Ophir mine shares fell from $1,580 to $300. In thirteen months the Gould & Curry mine, which had produced $8 million in two years, lost $5,400 per foot.[1] The *Virginia Daily Union* lamented: "Merchant and miner, banker and broker, lawyer and doctor join in the chorus and echo the oft-made assertion that never since 1860 has Virginia been so dull as during the last few weeks. . . . Stocks are down; money is high, and almost impossible to obtain even at the highest rates."[2]

Eight banks operated in Virginia City and Gold Hill in the spring of 1864. Without warning the J. W. Stateler and N. O. Arrington bank, secured by Ralston in San Francisco, failed. Stateler and Arrington's primary client was the giant Gould & Curry Company (which started its dozen partners, including George Hearst and several men later associated with Ralston and Sharon's Bank Ring, on their way to millionaire status). The mine, which needed vast amounts of coin to pay employees at the beginning of each month, would draw coin from Wells Fargo and Company and promptly repay the overdraft. Stateler, described by a fellow banker as "conceited and unscrupulous," dominated his alcoholic partner, Arrington. That spring he cashed a larger-than-usual draft, and a few days later he drew another. Wells Fargo and Company paid both. Ralston saw something was amiss and refused to cover the second draft. Stateler closed his bank's doors, using the drawn cash to repay depositors. The Stateler and Arrington bank defaulted on approximately twenty thousand dollars owed Wells Fargo and Company and thirty thousand dollars owed the soon-to-open Bank of California. The creditors had no recourse in the territorial courts. Inundated by mining litigation, cases took more than a year to reach court dockets.

Ralston needed to recoup the debt from Stateler and Arrington's assets: selecting securities from deeds, promissory notes, and mortgages. He turned to Sharon, who arrived in Virginia City after the Wells Fargo agent had selected from available properties. Sharon chose well from what remained, and the bank eventually recovered nearly all its claims. While doing so, he struck on the idea that it would be profitable for the Bank of California to establish a branch office in Virginia City.[3] Rather than letting the Comstock's depression influence him, Sharon talked to mining engineers. Once they assured him that the continuity of the veins could be assumed, he focused on the disorganization of the industry. Mining, milling, transportation, and lumbering were all inefficient and expensive. In the rush to discover great veins, miners tossed aside lesser ore. Small pumps were not powerful enough to remove underground reservoirs that prohibited deeper exploration. Because of collusion and double-dealing, mills with productive capabilities often sat idle. Wagons transporting ore were slow and limited in weight by the number and condition of their teams. Rain turned the dirt roads into quagmires, restricting movement, and snow shut them down completely. The timber from the surrounding hills had been cut, and there was no organization to log the distant mountains. Sharon believed that, if rehabilitated, the industry could greatly increase profits.

It became his habit to check and cross-check assays of ore, using several assayers on the same samples so he could be certain of a finding.

(Sharon later brought his nephew, G. H. Sharon, whom he recommended to study assaying, to Virginia City as his primary assayer.) The samples Sharon now collected were mixed, although George Lyman, whose father superintended Comstock mines, has said Sharon found that the nearer the water level, the more valuable the samples.[4]

More than a year elapsed before the information on which Sharon based his recommendation became common knowledge. In November 1865 Ferdinand Bacon Richtofen issued a geological report refuting the theory that the Comstock Lode was played out. Richtofen concluded that the Comstock ore was not a gash vein, comprising only one given bed in the formation, but a fissure vein or lode, with a number of parallel fissures filled with deposits extending to much greater depths.[5] His study proved remarkably accurate. William Ashburner, the mineralogist of the California State Geological Survey and a Sharon advisor, concurred. When Richtofen's report appeared, Ashburner wrote: "We have great right to assume that ore exists and will ultimately be found at as great a depth as it is possible to extend underground workings."[6]

Amid the territory's chaos and the despair of 1864, Sharon adopted the scientists' theory. He wrote Ralston that the Comstock was almost certainly not played out and that a real bank in the territory would prosper. Ralston agreed to meet with Sharon to consider the idea.[7]

Sharon argued that the Bank of California's risk could be mitigated if a branch on site better tracked the mining process. He also proposed his appointment as branch manager. The new bank's directors objected to both recommendations. To begin operations in the territory in a period of decline was a great risk. Moreover Sharon was bankrupt, having been tricked out of his fortune, hardly a man with whom to trust bank money.[8]

But Ralston held the power, and he liked the idea of a Virginia City branch. He first offered the post of manager to a protégé, Edney Tibbey. Tibbey had begun working for Ralston in 1856, serving as an accountant and bookkeeper and staying with him as Ralston changed firms. Tibbey reported that Ralston was induced to change his mind about the manager postition:

> Wakelee suggested to Mr. Ralston that Mr. Sharon should go up to Virginia City. He was Mr. Sharon's Partner [*sic*] in stocks, but they had failed and Mr. Ralston did not like the idea of sending a broken man up there. He wanted to know if I would go up there and I told him I would. . . . I had my life policy transferred up there to Virginia City and Wakelee finding out went to Ralston and he and Colonel Fry went security for Sharon and advanced him money privately, advanced him some $15,000; then Ralston went into partnership with Sharon on all stock transactions in San Francisco pertaining to real estate or stocks.[9]

Ralston biographers have followed Tibbey's account. Although Fry and Wakelee's endorsement, reflected in fronting Sharon fifteen thousand dollars as bond, certainly would have influenced Ralston's decision, Peckham, the Stock and Exchange president, thought that Sharon's "manly action" in paying his debt after being cheated "gained for him the active sympathy of Ralston."[10]

Ralston had sound business reasons to select Sharon over Tibbey. The twenty-nine-year-old Tibbey was familiar with bank operations, but his business experience could not compare with Sharon's. A responsible broker in San Francisco for fourteen years, Sharon served on the Board of Aldermen, and he examined the Comstock realizing the advantages of opening a bank branch. Moreover, the immediate task for the Virginia City manager was to continue collecting on Stateler and Arrington securities, something begun by Sharon.

Another factor favored Sharon: he played poker—well. Poker had come to the United States from France about 1800 as a game called *poque,* first appearing in print as *poker* in 1855. Sharon's French heritage may have given him early training in *poque,* and he possessed the traits presumed important for winning: discipline, a strong desire to win, knowledge of probability, an analytical mind, and the ability to judge others.[11] His steadfast demeanor and unflinching poker face, whether he held aces or a busted flush, made bluffing his decided advantage. Ralston's opinion of a "sporting man" as manager became a popular anecdote. A friend warned Ralston that Sharon was an inveterate poker player. Ralston asked if Sharon won or lost. When the friend said that he almost always won, Ralston replied, "He sounds like the very man I want."[12]

The banker's judgment anticipated twentieth-century game theorist John von Nuemann's postulation that poker is analogous to economic competition. He failed to take into account that poker is an affair of "every man for himself"; only one player will win. As Sharon would prove, in dire circumstances a poker player might well disregard a partner to act only in his own interest.[13] But at this early juncture in the bank's existence, Ralston declared that he would be personally responsible for Sharon's decisions. With such an understanding, the bank directors could not disagree. But Ralston hedged his bet. When the bank opened, his brother James served as cashier—the same position that William held at the home office.

At the end of October 1864, advertisements in Comstock newspapers announced the opening of the Bank of California in Virginia City. On October 31 President Abraham Lincoln proclaimed Nevada a state.[14] A week later, the election provoked a volatile twenty-four-hour period on the Comstock. On November 7 Alf Doten wrote in his journal, "Politics ran higher than ever—several fights on B Street." On November 8, with the new state's vote going heavily for Lincoln, Doten noted: "After voting was over at 6 PM, everybody got drunk—several little fights—one man shot in hand and left thigh & put in Station House."[15]

The Virginia City branch of the Bank of California was already investing in the thirty-sixth state, loaning money to businesses in need. Its offices were temporarily housed on the second floor of a recently purchased building on the southwest corner of C and Taylor. On November 17 a newspaper announcement proclaimed the agency "now prepared to receive deposits of coin or bullion, with Wm. Sharon as general agent."[16]

The completion of the bank's offices on the first floor allowed Sharon to move his residence to the second. Located above one of the town's busiest corners, the rooms featured tall windows, providing sweeping views past the future site of Father Patrick Manogue's St. Mary's Cathedral, across the hills surrounding Six Mile Canyon, to the valleys and ranges beyond.[17] The mines and their works literally enveloped the town. Shafts and piles of tailings, visible from the windows, pressed against the town in each of the four directions. Overhead, steamy air pulsated day and night to the pounding of stamps and humming of engines. The earth beneath the town was honeycombed with tunnels. (There was evidence of them in June 1867, when the earth collapsed and a store fell into the Chollar-Potosi mine.)[18]

Having left his former life and family in San Francisco, Sharon had moved into the middle of the gold-induced melee. He was older than most Comstockers, with more formal education. He knew how to listen to experts and observe, to formulate a plan and follow it. Moreover, bilked earlier in the year, he was desperate to succeed. A friend of Ralston's commented that Sharon had "no pet hobbies to interfere with accumulating money."[19] He was mistaken. Sharon's days were devoted to affairs of the bank and the Comstock Lode, but his personal traits included what one newspaper termed a "nervousness and excess of mental energy." He gained immediate recognition for hosting after-hours card games in his rooms, with large sums riding on each hand. He also was known for fiddle playing. Comstock newsman Wells Drury commented: "Anybody who is industrious can learn to be a violinist but only a gifted few can be fiddlers. . . . [Sharon] could fiddle a man's shirt off."[20] Sharon brought something else few on the Comstock had: a valet. Ah Ki, a Chinese immigrant, had come to America ten years earlier. Ki, as small in stature as Sharon, was polite, affable, and loyal. He maintained his position for twenty-three years, until Sharon's death.

Once established, Sharon reserved a stage box for opening nights at the Opera House.[21] The theater hosted every repertory company and star that came to the West Coast, from Shakespeare troupes and Adah Isaacs Menken starring in *Mazeppa* to Tom Thumb with Commodore Nutt. Sharon also took part in some of the town's more ignoble amusements. Alexander Toponce reported that Virginia City was crazy about cockfighting, with the leading bankers and businessmen attending fights. He related how his rooster killed a "fancy cock" owned by Sharon. Then Toponce bought a blind rooster for a dollar and entered it in the "Battle Royal" against all comers. Frightened, the blind rooster flapped wildly about, causing the other birds to fly out of the pit and leaving his rooster the sole survivor. As Toponce collected the eighty dollars in gold from the floor, Sharon picked up the rooster and examined him. "Look at this," said Sharon. "That damn Mormon cattleman has licked us all with a blind rooster."[22]

The bank building (including Sharon's second-floor rooms) was purchased from the concern of Arnold and Blauvelt. Beginning in 1863 this agency had acted as correspondent and agent for Ralston's bank in San Francisco; they suspended operations once Sharon was to open the Bank of California office. Blauvelt took a position with the bank and, when it expanded to Gold Hill, became its agent, retaining the position through its years of operation.[23] When the banking firm of Paul, Bliss, and Barnes, in business at Gold Hill since 1862, was appropriated, D. L. Bliss, too, went to work for the new bank. A short time later he served on the board of the Sharon-controlled Yellow Jacket mine and became general supply agent of Sharon's Virginia & Truckee Railroad.[24]

Mines and mills paid employees with checks to be cashed at the bank. Sharon arranged a regular payday for each of the large companies, and hundreds of miners would form a line out the Bank of California's door and up the street. Teller Charles William Wendte remembered: "The hours were long and the work exhausting practically consuming the entire day and most of the evenings of the week. . . . I paid the checks thus presented, hour after hour, with a brace of half-cocked revolvers under the counter ready for service."[25]

The other Virginia City banks formed an association in August of 1863. Because they undercut each other on loans, they established interest rates at 5 percent per month.[26] But even after establishing the rate, the banks operated inefficiently. In 1864, with mine production faltering, they found themselves unable to collect payments and without the resources to foreclose and run the businesses. The Bank of California shouldered its way into the market, loaning money to mills at 2 percent interest per month. The indebted mill owners changed their accounts to the new agency. The bank's rate, although substantially lower than that of the others, was still 24 percent per year.

In the Comstock's early years mill builders had flocked to the area, but as ore faltered the mills could not stay busy. In those early months of the bank's operation, Sharon was seen as a savior, pumping money into mills, giving owners a second chance. He loaned amounts from one-tenth to one-sixth of the value of a property. These loans appeared strictly businesslike in the beginning, although Sharon must have seen what was coming. Exorbitant expenses could be met when mills ran full time; when they sat idle, monthly interest added up. The depression afflicting Comstock mines continued for more than a year, and few—if any—mills were run at capacity. By 1869 Adolph Sutro would be calling attention to the fact that "the poor victim taking that money [from Sharon] signed his death-warrant."[27]

In the middle of the depression, April 1865, the news arrived that Lee had surrendered and the Civil War was over. The joy was extinguished five days later with the report of Lincoln's assassination. In his journal on April 15, 1865, Alf Doten wrote: "Everything dark and gloomy, as stores and saloons were all closed—went home before 10 O'clock—gloomiest evening Virginia ever saw." The mourning in the Union's newest state lasted through April 19, when—with the Comstock draped in black—2,700 citizens took part in a funeral procession through Virginia City; another 2,000 assembled at Fort Homestead on the heights above Gold Hill. Church bells tolled from ten o'clock to four, with a gun fired every half hour from sunrise to sunset. When a man named Posey Coxey remarked it was a pity Lincoln was not killed years ago, a crowd grabbed him, laid on ten lashes, and paraded him over the divide wearing a card inscribed "A traitor To His Country." The provost guard subsequently took Coxey to prison.[28]

During 1865 thousands of people abandoned Virginia City. Although annual bullion production by the end of the year was $15,833,720, the value of stocks on the San Francisco Stock and Exchange fell to $4 million. "The mines are turning out bullion more richly than in early summer; but they are spending large sums for explorations for new deposits, with results that are, on the whole disheartening," observed a visitor, who added: "Dividends are decreasing and stopping; assessments coming."[29] C. C. Goodwin later remarked, "In '63 and '64 the first rich deposits were pretty well dug out all along the Comstock and in '65 the impression got out that the old lead was about worked. . . . I do not know what might have happened had not Mr. Sharon kept his nerve and kept work going."[30]

The Swansea, in Gold Canyon, built for forty-five thousand dollars in 1862, was among the mills that borrowed from the bank. Within months it fell in arrears. Unlike mines, there were no stockholders for the mills to assess. The reducing equipment could not be sold, because rates to ship it were prohibitive. On May 1, 1865, the Bank of California foreclosed on the Swansea. Other mills also came into Sharon's sights. Once they were beyond their means, the bank demanded payment. By May 1867 the bank would own seven mills, in some instances paying one-fifth a mill's actual value.[31]

The mines were working in barren rock, and people worried that if the fissures did not produce soon, a collapse of the industry was inevitable. Directors in the Bank of California lost what little confidence they had had. They proposed closing the Virginia City branch.[32]

Bank president D. O. Mills took the lead, insisting that Sharon and Ralston account for money expended—seven hundred thousand dollars in loans. A meeting was called. Some sources have Sharon traveling to San Francisco, while others say Ralston and Mills went to Virginia City; all versions agree on the general content and outcome of the discussion. Mills spoke first, expressing shock at the figures of the bank's Comstock dealings. He saw the use of bank capital to promote seeking and developing ore as an intolerable risk. Mills demanded that the branch close and the bank return to pursuing traditional business.[33]

Sharon argued that closing its branch would accelerate Virginia City's depression and greatly damage the mother bank. Ralston realized more fully than Mills the intricate relationship of the bank and Comstock capital. His industries were sustained by it; the San Francisco Stock and Exchange was built upon it. Sharon explained that extravagant spending and wasteful mining precipitated much of the loss in dividends. Working systematically could reduce costs. He brought mining superintendents into the meeting to sustain his points.

Rather than pull out, Sharon proposed that they take control of the most promising mines and mill the ore themselves. Mills insisted the bank could not take the risk. This spurred Sharon to say he would take the mills at what they cost the bank; Ralston again declared that he would take responsibility for losses the bank might incur. Mills, reportedly impressed with Sharon's presentation and without jeopardy to himself or the bank, consented. The directors fell into line.[34]

Sharon now devised a strategy that the Ralston-Sharon partnership would follow. In November 1865 state mineralogist Ashburner, who also served as a consultant to Sharon, wrote a letter that was published in a book in 1866. He stated that the wide space between the Comstock's eastern and western walls had never been systematically exploited and that many valuable deposits were overlooked. Before publication of his assessment, Sharon took action. All Ralston-controlled mines were reworked to claim overlooked ore. Sharon also sought to push exploration in the Yellow Jacket mine, which Richtofen had mentioned in his 1865 report because of its "continuous sheet of ore."[35] Located in Gold Hill, a mile below the Virginia City mines, it was less affected by water than other mines. In 1865 "a sudden impoverishment" above the 360-foot level afflicted the Yellow Jacket.[36] It proved a boon to Sharon and Ralston: plummeting prices allowed them to gain control at a minimal investment. Ralston, demonstrating unreserved faith in the Comstock Lode, opened the second Comstock branch of the bank in Gold Hill.[37] For a year the Sharon strategy produced negligible profits, although the systematic reworking and controlled methods of mining stabilized expenditures.

John B. Winters, a key member of the reorganization plan, supervised the Yellow Jacket for seven years. He had come to the territory in 1859, and after statehood he served as brigadier general in the Nevada state militia. Winters became a member of Nevada's first Territorial Council, running unsuccessfully in 1865 for U.S. representative, in 1866 for governor, and in 1867 for U.S. senator.

Winters was managing the mill in Como when the camp failed in 1864. Some accused him of double dealing, saying Comstockers united to crush the rising young camp: "It is said, [Winters] raised the mullers [grinding pan] so that the ore, would not amalgamate and the result was—collapse." These accusations may be related to grievances against Winters rather than to fact, since subsequent revivals in Como revealed no bonanzas.[38]

After returning from Como, Winters became president of the Yellow Jacket mine. He received five hundred dollars a month, joining three unpaid trustees in advising and directing the mine superintendent. The superintendent earned five hundred dollars a month, lived at the mine, and ran its daily operations.[39]

In 1864 there were 742 shares of Yellow Jacket stock. Among the shareholders at the meeting of August 4 were men soon to become Bank Ring members: Thomas Bell, who owned 15 shares; Alvinza Hayward, 15 shares; C. H. Wakelee, 3; and William Sharon, 14. The Yellow Jacket listed liabilities of $197,038.58 and assets of $82,319.23, for an indebtedness of $114,716.35. Ralston was appointed to collect company assessments.[40]

Sharon began developing a strategy of controlling the Yellow Jacket that he later applied to other mines. He attended the February 11, 1865, meeting of trustees, but it was noted: "In compliance with law [Sharon] took no part in the proceedings of the meeting." At the meeting the treasurer resigned, and J. A. (James) Ralston was elected in his place. Three weeks later Sharon was elected a trustee. At the April 1 meeting, held at the Bank of California office in Virginia City, Winters and two trustees formed a committee to examine mills for purchase. The following week the company purchased the Morgan mill at Empire, Nevada, on the Carson River.[41]

Later in 1865 the Yellow Jacket struck the Crown Point mine's west dipping vein. In July Sharon stepped aside as a trustee. Although he owned only 8 shares of stock and no longer had a vote on the board, he continued to increase his power, controlling proxy votes for 285 of the 711 shares. J. A. Ralston, reelected treasurer, moved the company account to the recently opened Gold Hill branch of the Bank of California.[42]

On January 1, 1866, while other mines continued to falter, the Kentuck, a tiny mine between the Yellow Jacket and the Crown Point, struck the ledge running through them. Spending what he could, Sharon bought into the Kentuck and the Crown Point and urged Ralston to buy all outstanding shares in them.

At the Yellow Jacket stockholders' meeting in July 1866, Sharon associate D. L. Bliss was elected trustee. This was no surprise, as Sharon now possessed 540 of the 774 total voting shares.[43] Sutro later explained how Sharon controlled so many votes: "Everybody speculates, every miner, or chambermaid, or washerwoman; and as soon as they get into one stock they want to speculate in other stock, and they have to pawn it, and the Bank of California, a regular pawn-broker shop, loans money on them. . . . When the election comes off, all this stock stands in the name of the Bank of California."[44]

Under Sharon's and Winters's direction, the Yellow Jacket sank a new shaft to 360 feet, finding clusters of rich ore in a 350-foot-wide vein. By the end of 1866, prices of Sharon's stocks were rising rapidly. Other mining stocks also began to rise. During 1867 and 1868, the new Yellow Jacket shaft would be sunk to 900 feet, with ore being found on the 425-, 800-, and 900-foot levels. The old shaft was developed to 600 feet. By June 30, 1868, the yield between the upper levels of both shafts was 24,719 tons of ore.[45] The Kentuck and Crown Point mirrored the Yellow Jacket's success.

In 1867 the bank came into possession of mills that defaulted. Sharon's genius now came to the fore: Why not reorganize their business so that they worked the mills themselves? Another of Ralston's brothers, Andrew Ralston, later commented: "Mr. Sharon made a suggestion, and my brother had so much confidence in his judgment that he advocated it, and it was finally adopted by the bank."[46]

In June Sharon, Ralston, and D. O. Mills took the next step toward vertical integration, forming the Union Mill and Mining Company. San Franciscans Alvinza Hayward, Thomas Sunderland, Charles Bonner, Thomas Bell, and William E. Barron joined the venture. These men—stockholders in the bank and several of the most productive mines—comprised what now would be known as the Bank Ring. After buying the mills from the bank, Sharon consolidated the stamp mills. He utilized those on the river, so that water generated power rather than steam (which required purchasing wood for fuel). At the end of 1867 Sharon told broker George Mayre Jr. that through his stock operations and acquiring and developing the mills, he had made $250,000 in six months.[47]

Sharon, Ralston, and the Bank Ring were poised to develop a fortified monopoly. Sam Davis later observed: "There is a vast difference between ownership without a pull and ownership with a dead sure one. And there is where the iniquity began. If the scheme had not been thought of before, the acquisition of these mills suggested a plan by which the whole Comstock could be squeezed like a lemon."[48]

The Gilded Age, in the last part of the nineteenth century, has been labeled a "heedless, rushing anarchy."[49] That aptly describes enterprise in the Far West, which was dramatized by vigilantism and land disputes until the early 1860s, when disorder evolved into oligarchy. Entrepreneurs, elbowing their way to the fore, imitated the Yankee traders and monopolists of the East. "Commodore" Cornelius Vanderbilt's maxim, "What do I care about the law? Hain't I got the power?" reflected the business attitude until the lawmakers were enlisted as allies.[50]

With seemingly limitless land, immeasurable gold and silver, and weak bonds of authority, California heirs to the New York plunderers formulated plans for each side of the Sierra Nevada. They captured the resource wealth of Nevada and built the empire-city of San Francisco through machinations. They swindled and colluded against competition, manipulated officials, procured government subsidies, created monopolies, and used variations of Daniel Drew's handkerchief trick—allowing innocents to believe they acquired inside information while they were fed just enough to be gulled.[51] On the Comstock, William Ralston influenced substantial numbers of senators and congressmen while William Sharon dominated Nevada's judges and state and local officers. Together they controlled the direction and destiny of California and the Great Basin.

Comstock mills received contracts to reduce ore for various reasons, most unscrupulous. Eliot Lord has pointed out that personal friendship between mine and mill management was the least offensive of the determining factors. Others included secret persuasion, secret underbidding, gift giving, and paying a percentage of the charges to the supervisor. On rare occasion contracts were given to the mill that bid the lowest.[52] The scale of corruption grew exponentially when the Union Mill and Mining Company entered the field.

At the July 15, 1867, meeting of the Yellow Jacket Mining Company Sharon held 11 shares and controlled 898 proxy votes. The total of other voting shares was 51.[53] Sharon again became a trustee, to serve with Bliss. Winters was appointed superintendent, while retaining the position of president.

Regarding mining costs, there was a saying: It takes a mine to run a mine. Sharon was struck by a revelation: Why not run mines to feed mills? Seven partners shared in his milling operations, while dozens or even hundreds were stockholders in each mine. Mill earnings, independent of the wealth or paucity of ore veins, were risk free. The trustees now ordered that Yellow Jacket ore be processed at Union Mill and Mining Company mills, even as the Yellow Jacket's own Morgan Mill sat idle. But the plan became more nefarious when Sharon directed Winters to mix waste rock with ore before processing. This allowed the mills to run twenty-four hours a day, being paid by the mine, whose profits diminished in equal measure. Years afterward the *Virginia City Evening Chronicle* reported: "Mr. Sharon being controlling trustee of the Yellow Jacket mine, sent to the mills . . . barren 'Jacket' rock by the thousands of tons, and generously permitted the mills to crush it at $12 a ton. After two weeks run of the stamps on one occasion, *the* [profit] *was* $58,000 LESS *than the milling expenses!* This sum the Jacket stockholders had to pay by assessment."[54]

Comstock historian Grant Smith calls the Yellow Jacket "the worst example of [Sharon's] management." Between 1863 and 1874, it yielded $13,121,176 but paid only $2,184,000 in dividends.[55] Receiving word from miners that they had struck the richest ore body ever seen, Joe Goodman, editor of the *Territorial Enterprise,* bought $50,000 of Yellow Jacket stock. He lost heavily on his investment, later realizing, "It all went to feed the Union Mill and Mining Company's mills."[56]

Other mines controlled by the Bank Ring followed the Yellow Jacket lead, with men friendly to the ring selected as officers and trustees. Sharon's old friend Colonel Fry at different times served as president of the Crown Point, the Belcher, and the Kentuck and was later connected with the Ophir and the Mexican. Years later, an article in the *San Francisco Chronicle* pointed out that during the Bank Ring's reign at least one, and sometimes several, of their operatives served as trustees on twenty-three major Comstock mines.[57] Ring stockholders also exerted pressure on non–Bank Ring trustees of mines in which they owned interest, so they too voted to feed ore to Union Mill and Mining mills. Outside mills starved, and when they could no longer operate, the ring bought them.

The corporation eventually absorbed seventeen mills, funneling profits from the mines to the mills at every opportunity. Calling the Bank Ring "unscrupulous" and noting its complete hold on the Comstock Lode, Sam Davis later observed: "Some of the largest and richest deposits were exhausted without ever paying more than the expense of mining and milling. . . . Everybody was at [the Ring's] mercy." Davis concluded: "People despaired of ever escaping from its relentless grasp."[58]

With the mills now concentrated on the Carson River and its water generating their power, it became imperative that the flow remain uninterrupted. This prompted litigation between the Bank Ring and the ranchers upstream in Carson Valley over water rights. The ranchers were irrigating 3,900 acres on the Carson's west fork and 4,700 acres on the east fork. In 1864 Henry M. Yerington, a mill owner who later became Sharon's right-hand man, filed suit. The federal court in San Francisco found against the mill, ruling that whenever prior possession rights have "vested and accrued," such rights must take precedence. Since ranchers had irrigated their lands nine years before the discovery of the Comstock Lode, subsequent findings upheld the decision.

Sharon outmaneuvered the ranchers by purchasing water rights to ditches in Dayton, the site of Nevada's first mining. Those rights antedated agricultural diversions in Carson Valley. At the same time the Nevada Supreme Court reversed the lower court orders. Despite protests from newspapers that the ruling failed to consider the territory's economic conditions, the court decided that riparian rights—that is, the claims of entities on the river—came before those that would divert water in canals or channels, no matter which claim came first. Ignoring assertions of corruption, it also awarded a superior right to mills between Empire and Dayton—where Sharon's mills were located.[59]

In an area with few officers of the law, ranchers defied the order, saying that "they were poor themselves, and that the mill companies were making heaps of money, and that taking the water from them was an outrage."[60] Sharon's solution exhibited "a crude simplicity." He ordered all upstream diversions to cease and began regulating the water with his own men.[61] John D. Ludwig, "a particularly aggressive water man" sent to Carson Valley, testified: "I was to take absolute possession of the water and send it down the river to the mills. . . . I went to [Judge Bernard C. Whitman] and he said the Courts had decided that the mills had the right to the water, and for me to go ahead and take it, and I did. . . . I would start at Boyd's bridge and go up both streams, one after the other and take out all the dams in my way." Judge Whitman was a respected jurist. He was also a friend of Sharon's, later serving as the attorney and a director on the board of Sharon's Virginia & Truckee Railroad.[62]

William Sharon, not William Ralston, was the strategist behind the Bank Ring's actions on the Comstock. In 1874 the *Virginia Evening Chronicle* claimed otherwise, and its editorial became a source of misinformation in subsequent histories and biographies. Its editor, Robert D. Bogart, attacked Sharon, who was running for the U.S. Senate, accusing him of hoping to buy the election. Calling him "the scrawny little Midas,"

Bogart argued that his partners created his wealth. "[Ralston] it was who planned every operation, devised every scheme, and laid every plan to either control a mine, secure a mill or plunder unsuspecting stockholders. Mills with his private fortune did the respectable and gave tone to the Bank while the agent in this city was the mere clerk, the tool, to do Ralston's minutest bidding." Bogart's employer, General Thomas A. Williams, was Sharon's opponent in the race for the Senate, which goes a long way in explaining the attack. Bogart took a different tack in earlier editions, calling Sharon, among other things, "the little King of local rings." In those articles he argued only that Sharon's skill at organizing rings was inapplicable to politics. He also leveled accusations that Sharon "swindled stockholders, ruined mill owners, and by his selfish and heartless manipulation of mine values [drove] many a man to a suicide's grave."[63] These charges illustrate that at least when it served his editorial purpose, Bogart recognized Sharon as behind the Bank Ring's maneuverings.

Early in their partnership, Sharon worked under Ralston's authority and accepted direction from him. Ralston once wrote instructing Sharon not to act in a matter without his direction and at another time advised Sharon to protect himself by acting "outside the law." But Ralston's involvement in these instances is unique. Hundreds of extant Ralston documents reveal no other examples of his advising or directing Sharon. Asked at a deposition in 1881 who managed the business of the Union Mill and Mining Company, D. O. Mills responded: "William Sharon, nearly all of it." Frequently he and Ralston did not know what was being transacted until a deal was complete. Mills concluded: "It was supposed that [Sharon] would buy whatever he thought the Mill Company needed, and sell what he thought they ought to sell."[64] With Sharon directing Comstock activities, each of them earned a fortune.

Independent mill and mine owners feared and hated Sharon, who possessed the advantage of unlimited finances. He gathered the brightest assistants around him and paid them exceptional wages. When stockholders questioned the salaries, he told them he wanted to trust those around him rather than worrying that they might steal to supplement their income.[65]

Partly for this reason, the information Sharon used to make decisions was
better than anyone else's. From 1867 to 1871, Sharon employed expert
mining engineer Caesar Luckhart to issue confidential summaries of the
mines for him. Under Sharon's and the bank's authority, Luckhart moved
unchecked through tunnels, taking out samples to assay.[66] As a result,
Sharon knew before anyone else which leads were promising and which
were dying out. Using Luckhart's evaluations to determine when to buy
and sell, the stock market became an extension of Sharon's monopoly.

In 1867, as mineral production on the Comstock rose from $12 to $14
million, stock sales doubled. The Bank Ring's mines were producing rich
ore, and Sharon took possession of mills and managed resources in a manner to create a monopoly. In the fall he built a two-story house on the street
above the bank. The *Territorial Enterprise* described Sharon's house as
"a very neat two story cottage."[67] The cottage was a Victorian among other
Victorians, on what was soon referred to as "Millionaire's Row." Sharon
was the wealthiest of the town's inhabitants.

To fuel hoisting works and build the immense walls of lumber required
in square sets to shore up the mines, the Bank Ring bought up mountains
of pine in neighboring ranges. Bank Ring employees Yerington and Bliss
incorporated the Carson and Tahoe Lumber and Fluming Company in
1873 and then the Lake Tahoe Railway and Transportation Company, en-
abling them to clear-cut the forests on the east and south sides of the Lake
Tahoe basin.

By 1888 Yerington and Bliss's multimillion-dollar business included
short-line railroads out of the woods to the lake and up Spooner Summit
to their flumes; steamships for transporting timber across the lake; and
three sawmills located so that logs were drawn from the water directly
onto saw carriages.[68]

Lake Tahoe generated 5 million feet of lumber each month, much of it
from "very tall and straight" sugar pines as large as eight feet in diameter.
Newspaper publisher Samuel Bowles described the ancient trees in 1865
as "forests to which the largest of New England are but pigmies." Of what
followed, Grant Smith wrote: "The Sierras were devastated for a length of

nearly 100 miles to provide the 600,000,000 feet of lumber that went into the Comstock mines and the 2,000,000 cords of firewood consumed by mines and mills up to the year 1880." Bemoaning the loss, he commented: "No later visitor could conceive of the majesty and beauty fed into the maws of those voracious saw-mills."[69]

Drinking water represented another element in Sharon's plan to monopolize Comstock wealth. Heavy metals suffused the insufficient natural water supply. The miners joked that a tablespoon of water became safe to drink only when diluted by a tumbler of whiskey. When he first visited in 1860, J. Ross Browne, later the U.S. Commissioner of Mines in Nevada and a renowned writer, commented: "The common drink is water diluted with arsenic, plumbago and copperas, and corrected with 'rot-gut whiskey' warranted to kill at forty paces, generally understood to be composed of strychnine, tarantula juice, oil of tobacco, and other effective poisons, including a dash of corrosive sublimate."[70]

By the mid-1860s wells used for drinking water failed, so streams flowing from mining tunnels became sources. Sharon purchased control in the $250,000 capital stock of the water company. Citizens who had feared that they would run out of water now worried about costs and being at the mercy of the Bank Ring.[71]

The main stream of drinking water flowed through the Santa Rita tunnel, in some years providing as much as 67 percent of the company's total water. In January 1867 work in the Cole Company tunnel struck through the face of a drift and "water gushed out with such force that the men were driven back to the mouth of the tunnel." The Santa Rita stream immediately dried up, as the prospectors created a subdrainage. The incidental subdrainage, unavoidable in mining work, did not allow sufficient grounds for an injunction, so the water company began to lease water from the Cole Company. When the company refused to renew the lease, starting its own water company, Sharon and the Virginia and Gold Hill Water Company fought back. They sued and began excavating the Nevada tunnel directly below the Cole tunnel. The Cole Company won the resultant water war in the courts. There was no increase in water or decrease in price, but the *Territorial Enterprise* reported that the populace was satisfied. The citizens "dreaded lest food, water, wood, ore, and all supplies should be controlled by the Briareus, whose arms were extended over the district; for Mr. Sharon and his friends were the principal stockholders in the Virginia City Water Company and could at any time dispose of the water as they saw fit."[72]

Before the resolution of the case, Sharon "unloaded" the Bank Ring's interest, happy to pass on the problems to "amateurs."[73] The new owners, John Mackay and associates, later known as the "Bonanza Kings," ran the company as it was for a time. In the spring of 1873, with a water famine looming, they began importing water in newly designed wrought-iron pipe from high in the Sierra Nevada. It was a monumental feat: seven miles of pipe, using differing thicknesses of steel depending on the perpendicular pressure needed for hills and lateral curves to circumvent rock outcroppings. It took a year to survey the route and design, manufacture, and lay the pipe. The cost of the works exceeded $2 million; the resulting profits were many millions more. The system continues to supply water to Virginia City today.[74]

An unannounced factor also contributed to Sharon's ridding the ring of the water company. He had decided to build a railroad. In the beginning the Bank Ring was involved, but as was the case with the Union Mill and Mining Company, once it was established Sharon, Ralston, and Mills bought out the rest. Sharon hired a surveyor for the Virginia & Truckee Railroad in December 1868. The first locomotive arrived in Gold Hill on newly laid track from Carson City in November 1869. Up to 1,200 men, mostly Chinese, worked on the twenty-one mile road after Sharon raised $1,200,000 to finance it in less than two months. The Virginia & Truckee would be the keystone in his fortune.

Chapter Three

THE VIRGINIA
& TRUCKEE

IN 1862 HERBERT SPENCER amplified the doctrine of his friend Charles Darwin by discussing the law of evolution and introducing the phrase "survival of the fittest." In the 1870s at Yale University, William Graham Sumner began applying Spencer's postulations and theories to the social order, teaching that social progress depended on survival of the fittest. "Exploitation was nature's way," he explained, "and laissez faire capitalism was its natural manner of expression." Liberty and social progress are retarded, Sumner theorized, when society tampers with the struggle for existence; social equality is a goal that interferes with social progress. Sumner's theoretical system did not regard entities that suffered or lost. Nature knew no pity; neither did his sociology. "If only the fittest survive, those who lost out in the competitive struggle had no cause for complaint. . . . Anything that further interfered with the free development of economic competition was not only unnatural but immoral, since it must inevitably end in the preservation of the unfit."[1]

In early Nevada, isolated from California by the Sierra Nevada and from Utah by unforgiving desert, with an undeveloped government and mining-camp mores, the survival-of-the-fittest creed—although not yet articulated—regulated development. In the 1850s in the East, Daniel Drew positioned himself to gain intimate, insider knowledge of the Erie Railroad and used the information to buy its stock or sell short, thereby advancing his private speculations. In the 1860s William Sharon used the same tactics in building his fortune in the Comstock mining industry. Sharon, experienced in enterprise and in making and losing fortunes, understood that rules in the developing territory were circumstantial, to be manipulated by the "fittest." Moreover, the bank allowed him the means to do so. In 1874 the *San Francisco Chronicle* described Sharon as a king not by divine right, but because he won the right to rule by demonstrating that he possessed "the active brain and shrewdness of intellect that enable him to acquire money and to make it productive." The commentator observed: "The rich in a free country exemplify in a fashion, the theory of the survival of the fittest."[2]

Although Sharon is generally credited with recognizing that building a railroad to the Comstock Lode to reduce transportation costs would allow lower-grade ores to be milled, visionary builder Theodore Judah actually first promoted the idea. Between 1859 and 1862 Judah lobbied Congress and prominent citizens concerning railroads in the West. He argued that traffic from silver mines required them, describing the commonplace occurrence of passing three hundred teams in a day, transporting an average of two and a half tons of ore. But the cost made it practical to work only high-grade ore. A railroad, in his opinion, would enable mills to handle middle-grade ore as well.[3] In December 1864, Professor Benjamin Silliman, a chemist from Yale University, advocated connecting a Comstock railroad with the road coming from California to reduce the cost of transporting goods. Linking it to the Truckee River "would at once reduce the cost of treating the ores more than one-third."[4] In investing in the Comstock, Sharon adopted the theories of scientists and used Luckhart's daily assessments to make decisions about the mines. It follows that he would listen to voices like those of Judah and Silliman. But to initiate the project meant engaging in war.

On April 20, 1860, a letter to the *San Francisco Alta* from a former cigar salesman, just arrived in Virginia City, suggested the idea of a "gigantic tunnel" under the mines providing drainage and ventilation. (Mine temperatures rose as high as 150 degrees Fahrenheit.)[5] The tobacconist built an amalgamating mill at Dayton, on the Carson River, some miles east of

Virginia City in 1861. He continued to talk about the idea of a tunnel and, to that end, explored the mountains and canyons between his mill and the town. He was energetic, aggressive, and egotistical; his name was Adolph Sutro.

Sutro made his mill a great success, for a time earning nearly ten thousand dollars a month. But he found a spot where the valley approached within four miles of the Comstock and in the spring of 1864 began to pursue the idea of the gigantic tunnel as a business venture. On February 4, 1865, the state legislature passed an act "granting to Adolph Sutro, his heirs and assigns the right to construct a mining, draining, and exploring tunnel to and through the Comstock Lode."[6] Senator William Stewart became the tunnel company's president.

On March 1, 1865, Ralston assured Sutro of the support of the Bank of California. In April twenty-three leading mining companies signed contracts with him. The contracts stipulated that mines would pay two dollars a ton for ore and lesser fees for crews, timber, and waste rock transported through the Sutro tunnel. All investment capital would be secured in the East or Europe, allowing the mines to avoid any payments until the tunnel was operative. In May 1866, Ralston wrote a letter commending Sutro to the "courteous attention" of the Oriental Bank Corporation in London, with which the Bank of California dealt extensively. He also collected endorsements from other businessmen, including Sharon.[7]

In July 1866 Sutro traveled to Washington, D.C., where, with Stewart's aid, the Sutro Tunnel Act passed. Congress granted the company construction rights and ownership of veins along its course. From Washington Sutro went to New York, obtaining a letter signed by forty financiers. The letter stated that if Sutro could secure several hundred thousand dollars from West Coast investors, as a show of faith, the East would contribute the rest of the required $3 million dollars. Sutro estimated those signing the letter represented "probably $100,000,000."[8]

Upon returning to the West, Sutro met with Ralston in San Francisco and the state legislature in Carson City. Support for the project remained widespread, with Nevada legislators drawing up a resolution citing the

tunnel's significance to the nation's economy. Mineralogist William Ashburner spoke for Comstock mining experts: "Its importance cannot be
too highly estimated as affording a permanent, economical drainage to
such a great depth."[9] The twenty-three mines that signed contracts now
agreed that they would contribute developmental money.

But in September 1866 Sutro blundered severely, publishing a
pamphlet describing how the tunnel would reconfigure the territory. Its
mouth, in Dayton, would become the center of commerce; as for Virginia
City, "The owls would roost in it."[10] Businessmen expressed outrage. Ralston and Sharon decided that supporting Sutro was a grievous misstep.
Why move ore away from existing mills? Instead of hauling materials and
ore through Sutro's tunnel, *they* might control transportation. It was an
epiphany—the genesis of their vertical monopoly. They went to work. By
January 15, 1868, Sharon and eight mine presidents and superintendents
telegraphed Senators Stewart and James W. Nye in Washington: "We are
opposed to the Sutro Tunnel project and desire it defeated if possible."[11]
Senator Stewart immediately resigned as tunnel president.

When Sharon made his opposition known the mines split their support: eleven continued to favor Sutro's venture; twelve opposed it. By the
end of May 1867, those supporting Sutro subscribed a total of six hundred
thousand dollars. On June 7 the Crown Point mine officials, still favoring
the project, pledged seventy-five thousand dollars. Bank Ring members
controlled the majority of shares, and instead of ratifying the funding, they
replaced the president and superintendent, vetoing the proposed subscription. The other firms that pledged to subscribe soon followed suit.[12]

Sutro knew nothing of the Sharon conspiracy until the mines withdrew
their subscriptions for the tunnel. Throughout his life he maintained that
Sharon's "counter scheme" stole the money the mines and the government had pledged. "[Sharon] argued with his friends and especially with
William C. Ralston, which had been my particular friend, that this was a
fine chance of getting a large sum of money out of Uncle Sam."[13]

In withdrawing support the companies pointed to new tools—pumps,
fans, compressor drills, hoisting machinery, and dynamite—that made it

easier to battle the water and heat, reducing the need for a tunnel. They said the "dangerous water-belt" lay behind them, with drier sections ahead. But Sutro knew Sharon's pressure to be the overriding reason the companies opposed the tunnel. He described periodic chance meetings with Sharon as polite but cold, calling Sharon's opposition underhanded. Testifying before Congress, Sutro described what he called "Ring Rascalities": "They put their heads together then, and said: Let us break up the Sutro tunnel. . . . we will make the mining companies give the money subscribed to the tunnel company towards a railroad, which we will build and own, and that will kill Sutro."[14]

Sutro found himself ostracized. He lamented years later: "Ah! it was a hard thing to see so many old friends in Virginia City and San Francisco actually afraid to be seen talking to me after the fiat had gone forth that I was to be crushed."[15] Unbowed, he demonstrated his tenacity, again traveling east to regain support and financing. He eventually raised the money and built his tunnel, but by then the Comstock Lode was failing.

By 1860 thirty thousand miles of railroad existed in America, and the Pacific Railroad Bill in 1862 spurred construction of the rails to the Pacific Ocean. Construction generally followed a pattern. Land was secured, much of it received from the federal government as grants, and then local governments on the line issued bonds for stocks that were sold to build the road. Sharon, the gambler and sharp-eyed businessman, followed the pattern but ensured its initiation with an interesting sleight of hand.

On May 8, 1867, Sharon and several investors filed organization papers for a railroad with Nevada's secretary of state. The filing proposed building a road north from Gold Hill to the Truckee River. Several previous unsuccessful proposals included running a line south along the Carson River from Virginia City to Carson City, the state capital, then through Washoe Valley. The new proposal ignored Carson City and Washoe to run directly to the Truckee and a connection with the soon-to-be-completed Central Pacific Railroad in Reno. The ore mills already built on the Carson River would go to waste, and the people of Carson and Washoe would be segregated, left out of the progress sweeping the West. Residents of those areas demanded the route be changed. Sharon agreed to reroute the track with a proviso: Ormsby and Washoe Counties would take two hundred thousand dollars in company stock at one dollar per share.[16]

The proposed Gold Hill to Reno route was certainly a bluff used to raise county monies. From the beginning Sharon undoubtedly intended to run the line along the Carson River, since he was in the process of acquiring the bank's seven foreclosed mills for the Bank Ring and consolidating them on the river. Also, a road to Carson City would connect the ring's timber resources with the mines. A line north would do them no good, while one running to the Carson River and Carson City would be a direct link to and from the mines and their businesses.[17]

Thomas Sunderland, a Bank of California lawyer, was the first railroad president. But he was running for the U.S. Senate at the time, and Nevadans questioned his motives. The *Enterprise* observed: "The suspicion was quite generally entertained that [Sunderland's] scheme was somehow more directly designed to elevate himself to the Senatorship than to give the people the railroad they demanded."[18] This lack of public confidence caused Sharon to take charge. "In December 1868, [Sharon] sent for I. E. James, the leading mine surveyor of the district, and said to him curtly, without any preface: 'Can you run a road from Virginia City to the Carson River?' 'Yes!' answered the surveyor with equal brevity. 'Do it, then, at once!' said Mr. Sharon."[19]

On January 9, 1869, common knowledge became formal recognition: Sunderland resigned and Sharon took over as president, with William Ralston as treasurer.[20] As I. E. James surveyed the land, Sharon worked to secure the charter from the legislature, bought the rights of the failed companies that owned previous charters, acquired the right-of-way through state land, and acted as the agent in the issuance of three hundred thousand dollars' worth of bonds to Storey County and two hundred thousand dollars to Ormsby County. (He would concern himself with Washoe County after the first phase, Virginia City to Carson, was complete.) Citizens were told that their counties' gifts to the railroad ensured that prices of goods would be reduced by as much as two-thirds and property values would increase. Sharon assured them that over $1 million would be added to the taxable property of the counties, including the roadbed at $40,000 per mile. Canvassers gathered signatures. "The people of the region enthusiastically responded. The counties of Storey and Ormsby bonded themselves for $500,000, which was made a gift to the enterprise on the promise of largely increased taxes on the railroad."[21]

Sharon was quickly putting into effect a plan that, the *Enterprise* noted, had been "bounding about like a shuttlecock" at the hands of lesser men for years. Sharon, it was argued, was entitled to gratitude for pursuing a project of such public benefit, considering his hectic work schedule. An era of renewed prosperity was at hand, declared the paper, "and no matter who may be profited by the subsidies granted to the enterprise, every dollar advanced by the people of Storey County will be returned to them a thousand fold."[22]

The mines contributed $700,000, part of which was to be returned in reduced freight charges.[23] The Yellow Jacket mine subscribed $150,000 in the same manner as the others, but Sharon's board of directors governed this mine. Years later the *Virginia Evening Chronicle* revealed: "These new trustees were to rescind the contract made with the railroad company and substitute a resolution making the $150,000 subscription by the Yellow Jacket an absolute free gift for which the railroad company were no longer to be under any obligation whatever!"[24] To make up the difference, the board levied an assessment on the oft-abused stockholders.

Sharon and Ralston were unusually daring. On January 10, 1869, Ralston received a letter marked "private" from Senator John Conness of California in Washington, D.C., stating that "Comstock Mines will succumb in the next year or eighteen months and Virginia City will probably go through an experience unlike any that has yet occurred to it. . . . I would stake life on my information and if you think that is worth anything you will shape your affairs so as to avoid loss."[25] Ralston responded by allowing the ground breaking for the railroad to go ahead a month later.

As with all Sharon projects, the railroad was cogently organized. Superintendent H. M. Yerington broke ground on February 18, 1869, before the completion of James's survey. In mid-April 750 men were at work. By the end of the month another 450 were added. (The Central Pacific would meet the Union Pacific at Promontory, Utah, on May 10. As the thousands of Chinese workmen were being laid off, Sharon hired those he needed.) Blasting and tunneling crews preceded the men grading the roadway. Deep ravines were filled. At one juncture, between the Santiago and Vivian Mills, the character of rock was deemed unfit for tunneling, so workers cut a 60-foot-deep road. Across the 350-foot Crown Point ravine, a 90-foot-high trestle was constructed. In the Sierra Nevada laborers hewed ties from massive timbers, while the rails were ordered from England.[26]

On September 28, 1869, the *Gold Hill News* reported that, with substantial amounts of grading completed, H. M. Yerington drove a silver spike to secure the first rail for the railroad in Carson City. The road was entering its final stage. The next day the news was decidedly different: "About 1 ½ o'clock p. m., to-day, the Miner's Unions . . . headed by their respective officers, marched down Main Street, Gold Hill, to the number of about 350, with drum and fife, and out on the line of the Virginia and Truckee Railroad, with the avowed purpose of driving off the Chinese employed as graders."[27]

Comstock miners were not the only laborers unhappy with their plight. In the 1860s workers throughout the country suffered from oppressive working conditions and severely depressed wages. In Jackson, Mississippi, just before the Civil War, workers in a cotton factory earned thirty cents a day, while in the north men made three dollars a week working sixteen hours a day stitching shoes. In the United States 200,000 workers, men and women, joined trade unions. As an antidote Congress passed the Contract Labor Law of 1864, allowing companies to hire foreign laborers who would pledge twelve months' work to pay the cost of emigration.[28]

In Comstock mines, owing to the amount of wealth being produced and the inherent danger of the work, miners earned the substantial wage of $4 a day. In the early sixties, when mining profits sagged, rumors began that the wages of miners were to be reduced from $4 to $3.50. Three to four hundred miners met to organize, vowing never to work for less than $4.

When several mines moved to jointly reduce wages, many hundred miners demonstrated, marching on the mines and, on August 6, 1863, formed the Storey County Miners' League. Six weeks later Governor James Nye, a mine owner himself, called for two heavily armed companies of federal cavalry to protect against what might become "riotous and unlawful proceedings." In the face of such force the union withdrew its demand for a closed shop. By spring of the following year, many of the organizers had lost their jobs and many miners were working for less than $4.[29]

But this time the miners were unwavering. Yielding substantial amounts of ore, the mines paid $4 a day again. The miners were afraid the Chinese, working at minimal wages, would replace them. They chased off two gangs of workers before Virginia City's sheriff and Gold Hill's constable and their deputies convinced them to halt. When a deputy read from the U.S. Riot Act, the miners gave three cheers for the United States ("we certainly hope not in derision," remarked the *News*) and marched on. "Everywhere at their approach the Chinese all left their work . . . many of them taking to the hills."[30]

The *News* proclaimed its disapproval (while also demeaning the Chinese): "The miners certainly have put a check upon the construction of that road even though they have cut their fellow white men out of a steady job. . . . As for the long tailed rice eaters they simply quit work a couple of weeks sooner than they otherwise would have done had they been let alone."[31]

The *Territorial Enterprise* took the opposing view. Editor Goodman said the miners' action was correct. "If they had gone further and hanged some of the men who were trying to introduce servile labor into Nevada they would have been entirely justifiable." This initiated a celebrated row between Goodman and Sharon. Sharon questioned how Goodman could challenge the territory's business interests. The popular editor responded by calling Sharon names described as "illogical but colorful." The disagreement, Miriam Michelson later reported, did not "disrupt their acquaintance."[32]

Road grading stopped for eight days. On October 6 Sharon came from San Francisco to face the miners. He announced a compromise that would allow roadwork to continue. At the 6 P.M. shift change at the Yellow Jacket hoisting works, he spoke to three hundred antagonistic miners. He later gave a similar address to a meeting of the Miners Union at the courthouse in Virginia City. The *Gold Hill News,* October 7, 1869, reported:

> Mounted on a little pile of mining timbers . . . and with the assemblage gathered closely and attentively around him, Mr. Sharon spoke in effect as follows:
>
> Gentlemen: . . . The institution and interests I represent have been vilified and maligned by spiteful, designing men, and I have even heard that threats of assassination have been uttered against myself. This last I care nothing about, for I fear no one, and none of you are afraid of me. I am simply a man of flesh and blood like yourselves, and I, too, have been a working man. I am no demagogue or politician. You are no better than I am, and I am no better than you are. We are all here in this world together and supposed to work for each others' interests as far as possible. It has been charged that I am in favor of introducing Chinese labor into these mines, but that is false. I never have had any such idea; neither have I now. The Chinese are no miners. . . . They have no interest in the country, nor even religion, tastes and ideas in common with us, and we can only employ them at menial service, inferior occupations, railroad grading, and all that sort of thing. There is a wrong feeling of antagonism against the Bank of California, which charges it with being the enemy of the working man, and trying to crush labor and grind down wages, yet this is not so. Can these mines or mills be worked without capital; and is it not this very capital, that pays four dollars a day to you miners? . . . The object in building this railroad is to bring timber and wood from a distance for these mines, at a less cost, thus rendering them more productive and better able to pay you your wages. Besides this, there is plenty of low grade ore which can then be mined and milled at a profit giving additional

employment to hundreds of men. . . . If that railroad was to have
cost $3,000,000 it could not have been built; but as by using the
Chinese it could be built for half that money, it is being built. When
it is completed the Chinese are no longer wanted, and can go. . . .
Never mind what needy and designing demagogues tell you, but
with the good sense you are endowed with, study and work for
your own interest and that of the country. . . .

Three cheers for Mr. Sharon were proposed and heartily given
by the miners.

Sharon's speech quelled the issue of job security and hence the revolt.
It would be the only labor conflict during the years he dominated the
Comstock. (His policy of maintaining the $4 wage, even when mines were
unproductive, went a long way toward eliminating labor's central issue.)
The speech demonstrated not only his self-possession and intelligence
but also his artfulness. In nineteenth-century industry, management established firm lines of authority; employees were expected to act in obedient,
subservient roles. But in his talk Sharon anticipated a modern leadership
device: setting aside authority to present the notion of being part of the
team; no less a man nor better than the miners; all of them working together. When saying that they worked in each other's interest, he avoided
mentioning the disparity in the miners' earnings and his own, later reported from the railroad alone as not less than $2,000 a day.[33]

Sharon also used the speech to dispel damning charges about the bank
and its motives and to assure the workers that they would be protected. At
the same time he attacked the "demagogues" who, if followed, would en-
danger the men's ability to make a living. In addressing their most basic
concern that the Chinese would soon be working in the mines, he played
to the widespread racism of the age. By assuring them that he realized the
Chinese were good only for menial service, that they had no interest in the
country or in religion, he showed that he understood the "inferiority" of
"less developed" races.[34] He omitted the facts that it was he who hired the
immigrants and that the speech was delivered so he might continue to

benefit from their half-wage labor. He concluded with a predictable demagogic plea for patriotism, asking the men to do what was best for them and for the country. In the end he won their approval by endorsing the action the miners sought: he signed the agreement that kept Chinese workers from the vicinity of Gold Hill and Virginia City mines.

Six weeks after Sharon's speech, the road from Carson City to Gold Hill was complete. The last spike was driven with a solid silver hammer weighing forty-three ounces, cast in silver from each mine on the Comstock.[35]

The road was a success. In Virginia City the price of cordwood fell from $15 to $11.50, and it was reduced to $9 a cord when contracts were signed for delivery in the spring of 1870. The price of carrying ore from the mines to the Carson River mills dropped from $3.50 a ton to $2. The cost of shipping other items fell proportionally. As Judah and Silliman had predicted, lesser-grade ore left in the ground or dumped as waste rock was now worth milling. In 1876 trains made twenty-four daily runs each way between Virginia City and Carson. The number later went to thirty (and at times to forty-five) runs.[36]

In July 1870 Sharon directed Superintendent Yerington to run the line to Reno and connect with the Central Pacific. That enterprise cost $1,700,000, but with owners' profits calculated to be as much as $12,000 a day and $1,000,000 in bonds, funding for the connecting line was never a problem.[37]

Less prominent spurs also contributed to the roads' success. In 1870 Sharon approved a two-mile spur to the King's Canyon flume and a one and one-half-mile spur to the Summit flume, abetting the owners' lumber business.[38] In March 1872 the Eureka Mill road was completed. About a mile and an eighth in length, it illustrated the prowess of the line's engineering and construction crews and Sharon's lack of concern about expense when healthy returns were promised. Built on the side of a steep bluff above the Carson River, it cost over twice as much per mile as any other line in Nevada. It was held in place by "a heavy stone wall, more than twenty feet high, for a third of a mile, and crossing two deep cañons on high trestlework, besides deep cuts and heavy fills."[39]

For a number of months Sharon enjoyed renewed popularity. He rode triumphantly into Gold Hill on the railroad's initial run in the early evening of November 12, 1869, gave a short speech, and invited the crowd to partake of free alcohol. At the meeting's adjournment it was said, "Mr. Sharon might have had any office in the gift of his hearers for the asking."[40]

A segment of the population soon realized that they were stuck with the debt on the railroad while Sharon and company pocketed immense sums. The first engines were named after Nevada counties. Critics derisively commented that two of the original engines, "Ormsby" and "Storey," were a fitting salute to areas bilked to build the road.[41]

In January 1870 a new newspaper, *The People's Tribune,* charged that in order to build the road, Sharon had bribed legislators and deceived the populace. The people believed the bonds were to be issued in payment for stock in the railroad or that the counties were merely loaning credit. When the *real* contents of the petition for the bonds became known, *The People's Tribune* reported, a counterpetition was circulated. "But when it was too late to duplicate the paper, THE BEARER OF THE PETITION LOST (!) IT ON HIS WAY TO CARSON!! Treachery came in to cover fraud."[42] It was later claimed that the founders contributed $1,500,000 to the railroad treasury in addition to the $1,200,000 raised. But the articles of incorporation showed only $42,000 invested by the group, with nearly $3 million worth of stock being held by them.[43]

In the end Sharon, Ralston, and Mills bought out the other stockholders, Sharon's scheme allowing them to pay next to nothing for the railway to be built. The *Mining Review* of 1876 commented: "The freights collected at the Virginia office run from $60,000 to $90,000 per month, while that at Gold Hill is but little less."[44]

But before the completion of the initial road, Sharon worked to ensure that assessments would not cut into expected profits, even writing to Mark Hopkins of the Central Pacific to enlist his support in lobbying Congress. Sharon's maneuverings succeeded. The road's assessed valuation, which Sharon promised would be $40,000 per mile, was reduced to $14,000 per mile and then to $11,333. In 1872 Ormsby county assessor George W. Chedic declared himself satisfied when county assessments increased to

$313,053.53, "which increase is owing mainly to the building and completion of the Virginia and Truckee Railroad, and the erection of buildings necessary for the successful operation thereof."[45]

Historians later evaluating the railway's maneuverings reached a different conclusion. Grant Smith observed: "The road managed to pay little in taxes, and the counties struggled for years with their bond issue."[46] Bancroft's *History of Nevada* assessment concluded, "That Nevada assessors, sheriffs, legislators, and shareholders have assisted these railroads to oppress the commonwealth cannot be gainsaid."[47] In 1881 Thompson and West's history summarized: "Moral: Let those who would vote to give money to soulless corporations, upon an expectation of beneficial results that will not be a pecuniary benefit to the corporation remember what God said about men who were given over to believe a lie and be damned."[48]

Once "Sharon's iron mules" began hauling shipments, most freighters and quartz-wagon owners realized that their day on the Comstock was done. But some came up with a slogan: "Beat Sharon or bust." The trains, hauling ever heavier loads, set weight records that rose to 112 tons. The stubborn teamsters hitched teams of ten, twelve, and even fourteen horses to drag loads of up to 25 tons in a risky attempt to compete. Finally, a fourteen-horse team fell over the side of steep Geiger Grade, disabling the horses and shattering the wagon. Even the most stubborn freighters now capitulated.[49]

In January 1873 the Comstock bemoaned the loss of wagons. The *Territorial Enterprise* reported that the railroad was being mismanaged, running too few trains: "The hundreds of heavy teams that before the completion of the railroad furnished all the transportation required, have been drawn off. . . . Relief must be found in some quarter." The *Enterprise* also warned, without giving names, that capitalists were investigating the feasibility of starting a rival line. (Surveyors for John P. Jones and his associates were studying the course a new line would take.) It was also reported that a time later John Mackay considered rates out of proportion and asked for a reduction. When a response was slow to come, he threatened to build his own line.[50] But Sharon was too wary to jeopardize his gains. Schedules and rates were adjusted; neither Jones's nor Mackay's plan ever materialized.

English Common Law had condemned monopolies as trade conspiracies as far back as Elizabeth's Tudor regime. Sharon and Ralston's combination was a prelude to Frick and Carnegie's coal and steel merger, Rockefeller's oil and oil-transport trust, and the three hundred other monopolies formed after them in the 1890s. The Virginia & Truckee Railroad secured the Bank Ring's vertical monopoly, adding transportation to their control of the Comstock's timber, mines, and mills.

Chapter Four

THE LAMB

THE BANE OF MINE SHAREHOLDERS was assessments. When they deemed it necessary, mine trustees posted an amount per share levied upon capital stock, payable immediately. A month later, unpaid assessments would be deemed delinquent and advertised for sale at a public auction to be held one month after the advertisement. Comstock papers filled columns with names of those who were delinquent, the number of the certificates, and the number of shares.

There were legitimate reasons for assessing shareholders; whether mines were earning profits or not, wages needed to be paid. The mines needed to explore ever deeper, securing lumber and building frameworks to prevent collapse. They needed to purchase and run equipment to remove water, hoist rock, and cool oppressive tunnel air. Upon striking a vein, they needed to transport and mill the ore. Mine superintendent I. L. Requa, who spent twenty-five years on the Comstock, said finances rendered it impossible to mine the lode any other way.[1] But Sharon, above all others, milked the assessment system. He used it to drive the stock market, assessing mines whose stock he wanted to devalue. Dan DeQuille told of a character named Nat Codrington who was affected by Sharon's intrigues: "Whenever things went wrong with Nat, 'Uncle Billy,' as Nat affectionately called Mr. Sharon, was at the bottom of the business. When Nat bought stock it was sure to go down at once; then he would say: 'That's Uncle Billy, he's turning the crank again!' As soon as Nat sold short on a stock, up it would go, and he would say 'Well, Uncle Billy's at it again—grindin' of 'em the other way this time!'"

Eventually DeQuille wrote: "Nat Codrington is off for California. . . . Sharon—'Uncle Billy,' as Nat affectionately calls him—'turns the crank too much.' Poor Codrington's all was in stocks, and there his all still remains."[2] Money was the primary basis for the era's social prestige, with wealth and power held in heroic regard. DeQuille's anecdotes illustrate how the populace in the West laughed at the acquisitiveness of men of achieve-ment, winking at their unethical means.[3]

H. R. Linderman, in his *Report of the Director of the Mint* for 1875, wrote that the mining industry was succeeding because of the efforts and expenditures of men "of superior energy and business qualifications."[4] Comstock chroniclers of the age subscribed unreservedly to the proposi-tion that looting or corruption by the enriched (the new American nobil-ity) might be overlooked; were their efforts not benefiting all? Eliot Lord noted that Sharon and the Bank Ring "lifted the Washoe Mining District out of a slough of despond." He philosophized: "It is for achievements and not for possibilities that this world is in debt. The bones of mute Mil-tons and guiltless Cromwells rot justly in unmarked graves." He proposed that Sharon, in expending capital when needed, was of "more real service to the working people of the district than a hundred professed charities." In response Sharon demurred, indicating that self-interest was the motive for Comstock speculation.[5]

In 1869 Sharon had rebuilt his fortune and was a man of stature on the West Coast.[6] When members of the Ways and Means Committee of the U.S. House of Representatives came to Virginia City in May of that year, he hosted them. In August, when Vice President Schuyler Colfax arrived with Senator Nye, Sharon again played ambassador. His residence was decorated with colored lanterns, a brass band played, and the principals addressed an appreciative crowd in the street.[7]

But by the end of 1869, the local economy was again faltering: lesser mines shut down, and others were operating with reduced workforces. Sharon's were among the few producing mines. On September 29, 1869, an advertisement in the *Territorial Enterprise* attacked his management of the Yellow Jacket. It requested that anyone dissatisfied with its management meet on October 11 in Virginia City's courtroom and directed San Francisco stockholders to communicate by correspondence. The *Gold Hill News* derided the notice, pointing out that it was published anonymously and that officers had been duly elected only two months earlier. "Every stockholder in that company had a fair chance at the election, and he could vote, according to his interest, just for whoever he pleased."[8]

When nothing came of the meeting, a man stepped forward to take on Sharon, the Yellow Jacket and Virginia & Truckee Railroad management, and the assessment system. He was a most unlikely champion.

Conrad Wiegand was a longtime Comstock resident. An assayer, by avocation he was a street minister for the Humanitarian Christian Society. In February 1868 a notice that he was to lecture appeared in the *Territorial Enterprise*. The piece built in his praise, culminating in a physical description. His large blue eyes, it said, were "full of fire and thought yet impress you as singularly pure and gentle . . . [and he has] a countenance that will irresistibly recall to mind the likeness of the Savior—and that man will be Conrad Wiegand."[9]

The article was a practical joke that climaxed when the rumor spread that Wiegand had written the description himself. This charge prompted him to publish a card in the *Territorial Enterprise* and *Gold Hill News* emphatically denying the "shameful" accusation. He complained that because of the notice the Humanitarian Christian Society, which had heretofore entertained confidence in him and held him in respect, now regarded him with loathing. He and his family were looked upon with derision. Describing his tact in dealing with the abuse, he remarked that he would remain above vindictiveness, shaming those who attacked him with "unmerited kindness."[10]

Ten days later the *Gold Hill News* published a blurb: "Wiegandish.—Anything of a particular egotistical nature is now styled 'Wiegandish.' We believe the word originated in the *Enterprise* office."[11] Wiegand's paid statement had done nothing to dissuade the perpetrators.

A harbinger that Wiegand might engage in righteous battle had been displayed many years earlier in San Francisco. On October 12, 1856, using a pseudonym, "William Carrol," he gave a lecture on "Dr. Scott, the Committee of Vigilance and the Church." Supporting the Reverend William Andrew Scott was a singular act, since the recently dispersed vigilantes consisted of the most powerful citizens in the city, and they had hung Scott in effigy after he denounced their actions from the pulpit.[12]

Wiegand's mettle went unnoticed in Nevada. In the appendix of *Roughing It* Mark Twain described Wiegand as "a lamb": "If ever there was a harmless man, it is Conrad Wiegand of Gold Hill, Nevada. If ever there was a gentle spirit that thought itself unfired gunpowder and latent ruin, it is Conrad Wiegand. If ever there was an oyster that fancied itself a whale; or a jack-o'-lantern, confined to a swamp, that fancied itself a planet with a billion-mile orbit; or a summer zephyr that deemed itself a hurricane, it is Conrad Wiegand."[13] This was the man who, two years after the practical joke, thought to challenge the Comstock's most powerful entities.

Wiegand said that he was roused to act against the Bank Ring after Adolph Sutro exposed its collection of undue mining profits.[14] On the morning of January 13, 1870, Wiegand published the first issue of his newspaper, *The People's Tribune*. It commented: "If [mine management was] done in a similar way in any well governed State of Europe, not only Wm. Sharon but (with only an exception or two) his subservient mining superintendents, secretaries and foremen in the mines, would be promptly consigned to the public galleys or be locked behind the iron gratings of prisoners' cells."[15] At midday, while distributing the paper, Wiegand was attacked by a stranger.

Along with the accusation against Sharon and his managers, *The People's Tribune* promoted women's suffrage and life insurance for miners. A long article described deception and fraud against the masses in Sharon's financing of the Virginia & Truckee. It observed that the community dreaded the Bank of California and charged that legislators were in the pay of Sharon. And it indicted the courts: "The Supreme Court at Carson is alleged to have become Sharonic. . . . With 'friends at court,' both in Carson and in U.S. Chambers, Mr. Sharon ought certainly to have felt able to laugh at the people, while his tax-collectors picked their pockets." Another article developed eleven points that might result from an investigation of the company, including jobbing, collusion, payoffs, overpayments to top employees, and mismanagement, all of which, it argued, should be indictable by the grand jury.[16]

Two letters in the issue incited fervor. One, over the name "A. Miner," questioned expenses charged by the Yellow Jacket Mining Company. The other, by "Silver Struck," attacked Yellow Jacket management for unethical practices. It stated in part that "after striking a body of good ore, *and having been ordered to conceal it and to suppress all information respecting it,*" an underboss spoke out and was fired. "What right [has] John B. Winters, or Wm. Sharon or any one else, to *order* a discovery of that kind to be concealed; or, *while levying assessments,* to allow that body of ore to remain untouched." Under the title "Answer," Wiegand said that President Winters refused to explain Yellow Jacket policies.[17]

That night the *Gold Hill News* carried a story under the headline: "A Strange Case of Public Assault and Battery." It reported that while distributing his paper in Gold Hill, Wiegand was assaulted by one Griff Williams. Williams was arrested, and, after pleading guilty before a judge, fined $7.50 and released. Williams gave as his excuse that he could no longer stand Wiegand's "talking about him."

Wiegand told the *Gold Hill News* that he did not know his assailant or why he was attacked, but "he only knows that he was used mighty rough."[18] Wiegand, speaking of himself in the third person in Victorian style, later described the assault: "With no warning . . . [Wiegand] was dealt a powerful fist blow in the face, which felled him to the ground, his head striking the sidewalk with violence, partially bewildering him. As he scrambled to regain his feet, his assailant, heavily shod, and as is alleged, likewise *secretly armed with a small pointed saw,* if not with instruments which could be more strictly termed weapons, immediately began kicking him in the face."

Wiegand described rising to one knee and grabbing the assailant's leg. But, admitting his strength was not great, he said he was forced to let go—

a fortunate circumstance, since he believed that if he had remained with his back exposed, he might have been stabbed by the jagged saw. A by-stander got involved, shouting at the attacker to stop. Since a crowd was gathering, the man fled, jumping on a horse "which it would seem, had been in waiting and prepared for flight."

Wiegand wrote that he believed either someone hired the man to assault him or he was "made to believe" that Wiegand had spoken offensively about him. "Who hired or deceived, time may show; but the larger and more ALARMING consideration . . . is *that in our community men are to be found who are both base and cowardly enough thugs to procure a brutal, or if needful, murderous assault upon the most peaceably disposed person in the state; and besides, that men are to be found who are* READY TO MAKE *such violent assaults.*"[19]

Once the accusations were printed, Winters, previously uncommunicative, demanded a meeting with Wiegand. Two days after the paper's distribution, Winters sent word for Wiegand to meet him at his office. Wiegand balked. He was still suffering from the assault, and word on the street was that Winters was looking to either kill or horsewhip him. When Winters informed him that he would come to Wiegand's office at 4 P.M., Wiegand asked Sheriff Cummings to be in attendance. Winters did not appear. Instead, at 4:30 P.M. Philip Lynch, publisher of the *Gold Hill News,* came asking Wiegand to meet Winters at the *News*'s offices.[20]

Against his better judgement but reasoning that at least staff members would be there, Wiegand consented. When he arrived he was ushered downstairs to an office, the door was closed and Winters placed himself before it, demanding a written retraction of the "damnably false charges." Wiegand refused. Winters asked if the publisher had recently converted his personal property to the ownership of others to avoid losing it in libel suits. When Wiegand admitted it, Winters said: "Very good, sir. Having placed yourself beyond the pale of the law, *may God help your soul* if you DON'T make precisely such a retraction as I have demanded . . .—you God d—d low-lived s—g lying s—n of a b—h, I'll teach you what *personal* responsibility is *outside* of the law; and, by God, Sheriff Cummings and all the friends you've got in the world besides, can't save you, you G—d d—d, etc.!'"

After a time, with Winters becoming even more outraged, Wiegand agreed to write a retraction, but it actually was a seeming retraction that did not disavow anything. Winters saw through the ploy. Desperate and demonstrating one of the peculiarities that prompted those who ridiculed him, Wiegand attempted to use mesmerism to subdue his captor. Wiegand later said he believed this weakened Winters and perhaps saved his life.

In the end, even asking for time to pray served only to hasten the onslaught: "Prayer! G—d d—n you, this is not your hour for prayer—your time to pray was when you were writing those d—d lying charges." Wiegand stated that the first blow with the whip fell downward over his left ear, "as if to tear it off, and afterwards on the side of the head." A large, strong man, Winters beat Wiegand until he exhausted himself. When he was through, taking the butt of the whip and shaking it in Wiegand's face, he warned him that if the publisher ever introduced Winters's name in print again, he would cut off his left ear and send him home mutilated.

In the *Gold Hill News* on Monday the 17th, Philip Lynch published his account of the attack, *A Case of Slanderous Vilification and Its Consequences*. As suggested by the title, Lynch blamed the trouble on Wiegand for attacking the honesty and integrity of several businessmen, including Winters. Lynch pointed out that Wiegand, although uncertain of the charges in his paper, refused to write a retraction. "General Winters was greatly excited, as was Mr. Wiegand, who suggested that *they both engage in prayer*. The motion not being seconded, there was no prayer meeting— and there being no retraction. . . . Mr. Wiegand was severely handled with a cowhide. Thus ended the latest 'sensation.'"

Lynch went on to say that he regretted the affair had taken place in the *Gold Hill News* offices: "The senior editor, who was the only witness of the affair, besides the parties, themselves, especially feels aggrieved, as the report has been telegraphed all over the State that he was 'cowhided like the devil' on Saturday! When in fact it was all a mistake. Several telegrams have been received by him to-day, from different sections, inquiring after his health, the price of raw-hides, etc."[21]

Wiegand charged that Lynch colluded with Winters in the attack. After Winters left the room, Wiegand reported that Lynch told him Winters was a fine man and noted: "He told me the reason he did not meet you up stairs was to spare you the humiliation of a beating in the sight of others." Wiegand argued that that unguarded remark illustrated that Lynch was privy in advance to Winters's intentions.[22]

Two days later Lynch's mocking tone became more pronounced:

> Neighbor Wiegand, in the prospectus of his *Tribune* says that its mission shall partly be—"An observer and photographist of the Beautiful and the Good—a spirit-like friend." These dissolving views have certainly not proven very popular thus far. The pictures are evidently too highly colored.
>
> But again, neighbor Wiegand says the *Tribune* is to be—"A watchman for rascality in the mines and in public posts—a terrier till able to be a mastiff."
>
> That "dorg" had better be chained at home—as he seems too inexperienced in his calling to be let run at large.[23]

The crusade of *The People's Tribune* lasted only four more issues, through June 1870. The mines, buoyed by Sharon and the bank, though still working in barren ground and fighting water, were sustaining the Comstock economy. They were employing 2,866 hands, with 2,057 working underground. Capital was $32,353,400, and wages totaled $2,900,872.[24] Few locals dared to support Wiegand. (He commented: "Nothing is more common in Nevada than cursing for the Bank of California, though it is usually indulged in behind the door or in whispers.")[25] Attempts to garner national recognition were also to no avail: He sent the paper to influential individuals across the nation, but his solicitations for subscriptions were universally unsuccessful.[26] His work as an assayer, thriving before his publishing venture, was ruined. Businesses influenced by the Bank Ring, which included almost all on the Comstock, took their assaying elsewhere. As his epithet, Wells Drury labeled Wiegand "the most peculiar man who ever tramped the trails through the sagebrush."[27]

On November 7, 1870, after a falling out with Sharon, John Winters resigned from the Yellow Jacket. "Winters is no gentleman," said Sharon. "He is nothing but a lackey, a very bootblack to me, ever since he came on the Lode. Damn him, I'll beggar him and run him out of the state."[28] Wiegand had insisted that nine out of ten people on the street knew his charges were true. Now Winters admitted his and Sharon's guilt. "I've lost my self-respect doing dirty work for [Sharon]," Winters said. "To feed his mills, I've mixed waste rock with the Yellow Jacket ore, till it would scarcely pay for crushing, when the company might have been paying dividends for years; and when he has wished to make a deal, I've smashed the engine and thrown the pieces into the sump, in order to break the price of the stock."[29]

The Sharon-Winters conflict made its way to the courts in January 1873 in a case that the *Territorial Enterprise* said sparked "universal interest." Winters sued Sharon and Thomas Sunderland, charging that the three men together bought 1,507 ½ shares of Kentuck mine stock but that he received only 400 shares while his partners split the balance. "[Sharon] denies that such an agreement was made, and contended, through counsel, that such an agreement was only implied." A hung jury (reportedly deadlocked seven to five for Sharon) was discharged, and jurors' fees amounting to $180 were assessed to Winters, his case unproven.[30] On March 26, 1873, Winters gave expert testimony in a deposition for the Dardanelles' Company, which sought a patent for mining a ledge vein comprised of bonanza ore that the Crown Point mine and Sharon's Belcher mine were working. The testimony did the company no good. The Belcher and Crown Point combined to produce over $30 million in gold and over $26 million in silver during their bonanza days of the 1870s. Over the same period, the Dardanelles Company produced no recorded profit.[31]

The others involved fared far worse. In February 1872, a year and a half after Wiegand's paper failed, Philip Lynch, editor of the *Gold Hill News*, died after suffering several months from "bleeding of the stomach." Alf Doten, his associate editor, replaced him, continuing the *News*'s journalistic support of Sharon and the Bank Ring. On June 14, 1880, Conrad Wiegand committed suicide. Debts and increasing nervous depression were said to be the cause.[32]

Chapter Five

CONFLICTS

Located on two hundred acres at Glenbrook Creek, about a mile from Lake Tahoe, the Glenbrook House was organized as a club for Bank Ring members and other Comstock magnates. Sharon and Charles Bonner started it in 1869; when they later sold it, it became the Glenbrook Hotel. All night poker games were common when the Comstock magnates were on site, and it was there that Will Bliss reported seeing legendary stage driver Hank Monk "so full of liquor that he couldn't stand, but he could drive all right."[1] Monk also played a practical joke on Sharon at the hotel, energetically putting a "mirror-like polish" on only one of a muddy pair of boots left overnight outside Sharon's door. Hurrying to a meeting the next morning, Sharon caused comment, presenting, according to an eyewitness, a ridiculous appearance "when his pedal extremities were compared to his otherwise impeccable broadcloth."[2]

In many aspects of his life Sharon was circumspect. He was conservative in dress and action, and he drank in moderation. But other tendencies regarded as immoral in Victorian society also marked his character. Virginia City's distant environs were ideal for a man wanting to take part in no-limit poker games and cockfighting. Most of his associates, including other business leaders, engaged in similar behavior.[3] But his need for esteem included conduct outside even mining-camp mores; he not only cultivated illicit relationships with women, he flaunted them. On one visit to Glenbrook, he wrote in the hotel register: "Wm. Sharon and lady." When the inscription was entered, Sharon's wife, Maria, was two hundred miles away in San Francisco.

Another incident at Glenbrook gives further insight into Sharon's nature. He and Ralston bet on the quickest route up the mountain from Carson City to the hotel. They would race, one following King's Canyon, the other Clear Creek. Sharon ended up forfeiting the contest. He rode his horse so hard, it went blind from the effort.[4]

As he built his fortune, Sharon lent financial assistance to associates. In several cases he "saved his friends from disaster by carrying their burdens, until a change of the market came."[5] In 1874 Sharon related how he repaid Ralston for taking him in as a partner: "Ralston saved me at that time, but I got even with him. Four years ago I went down and found he had been opening New Montgomery street, spreading out in his big way, and when he came to figure up how he stood he was in debt to the bank $3,000,000. I happened to have a little matter of $4,000,000 in the bank and it is a great pleasure to me to make it possible for him not to make any accounting of how much he had overdrawn."[6]

Some months after an argument with Sharon caused a stammering John Mackay to stomp out of the bank, Mackay told one of the bank's attorneys that he needed sixty thousand dollars or he would lose stocks worth twenty times that. The attorney's partner, Thomas Sunderland, made a memorandum of the stock and asked Mackay to wait in his office. Minutes later, Mackay received Sharon's personal check for the entire amount.[7]

Sharon was a client of stockbroker George Mayre Sr. and his son George Mayre Jr. Mayre Jr. related that when business complications caused his father to become four hundred thousand dollars overdrawn, he went to Sharon telling him he needed another eighty thousand dollars to secure a friend's account. "All right," said Sharon without a moment's hesitation, "make out your note and I will give you a check."[8]

On the street Sharon appeared much different. He was seen as an intriguer, his actions reflected only callous self-advancement. An unsigned note demonstrated the depths to which those holding such perceptions might sink:

> March 10, ____
>
> William Sharron,
>
> Your time and mine is short. I have hoped that the assessment would be rescinded and save me from ruin. To come to poverty and misery, NO, NO, I will die first, you force me to it. The assessment is unnecessary—you and your party are now trying to freeze out the weak ones for 18 months I have held on but now alas the worst is upon me & the Day of Grace is a short one and you shall have it. So help me God.
>
> PS You will not Believe this till you see the muzzle of my Revolver and then it will be too late.[9]

It is generally overlooked that his partner Ralston, a benefactor to many and known for his kindness and charities, was also involved in numerous secret, sometimes underhanded schemes. Ralston's correspondence includes ample evidence of generosity. People wrote to request favors and jobs or charity for themselves and their relations. They thanked him for past kindness, gifts, or thoughtfulness. At the same time, among the pieces of correspondence are letters that proposed schemes and deals, some marked confidential or secret, some written in code. Letters from senators in Washington discussed legislation that Ralston wished passed or blocked. There are letters from officials of the Treasury Department; officials from England, Germany, and Japan; colonels and generals; Charles Crocker, Collis Huntington, Mark Hopkins, Leland Stanford. Throughout the correspondence can be seen Ralston's magnanimous hand, using his own funds as well as the bank's.

But another letter from Ralston to Sharon, published in an exposé by the *Virginia Evening Chronicle,* advised Sharon how to deal with their mine supervisor and associate, I. L. Requa: "You have been entirely too severe on Requa, and I must express my surprise and regret at it. He is here, and is much excited. You must be more careful in the future. Remember he owns too much 'Chollar' for us to make an enemy of him. Give him sugar and molasses at present, but when our time comes give him vinegar of the sharpest kind. He is our friend, and I think will assist us. But go slow in all your operations and do nothing without consulting me." Another Ralston to Sharon letter published in the *Virginia Evening Chronicle* discussed deceiving the Yellow Jacket stockholders so that they subscribed $150,000 as a gift to the Virginia & Truckee Railroad: "It is desirable that the matter should be arranged as quickly as possible. It will not do for you to act as one of the trustees. Therefore I think that you had better put some irresponsible person in your place. REMEMBER THAT IN THIS BUSINESS YOU MUST BE CAREFUL TO PUT YOURSELF OUTSIDE THE LAW!"[10]

Few suspected that Ralston would engage in deceitful dealings; the common perception was that Sharon did. From the beginning of his operations, accusations were leveled against Sharon. In mid-December 1865, William Bourn, owner of the Imperial-Empire mine in Little Gold Hill, was forced to travel from San Francisco across the snow-packed Sierra Nevada to the Comstock. He made the journey because a drift from the Sharon-owned Apple-Bates mine, between the Alpha mine and the Imperial-Empire, cut into the Imperial-Empire mine, stealing ore. On May 16, 1866, Bourn returned to the Comstock to deal with the "dangerous situation." Bourn's trip yielded unsatisfactory results: "Although William Sharon's claim-jumping tunnel, which ran from the nearby Apple and Bates mine was taking tons of ore from their west vein, Bourn could not get the other officers of the Imperial-Empire to react against what amounted to outright theft."[11] Why the mine trustees failed to react is unclear, but Sharon eventually settled the matter in typical fashion. In October 1866, collecting on $60,788.50 in promissory notes, he took possession of Alpha Company land and its steam quartz mill.[12] Soon he bought the Imperial-Empire. Within ten years he acquired all the mines of Little Gold Hill, merging them into the Consolidated Imperial.

Sharon was consistently embroiled in litigation. When the bank foreclosed and took control of its first mill, the Swansea, in May 1866, the owners removed property "appertaining thereto." A year later he was in the Nevada Supreme Court, still attempting to gain possession. Another case of disputed mill property, involving Sharon and A. D. Treadway, began in August 1871 and remained in the court into January 1872.[13]

In August 1866 J. W. Haines built the first flume in the eastern Sierra Nevada—a square-box flume. It ran a mile down Kingsbury Grade from Lake Tahoe, carrying lengths of timber to the valley floor. But it continually jammed. In the spring of 1867, after watching his children throw cobs into a little V-shaped trough used to irrigate the garden, Haines redesigned the flume into a V shape. The new design carried the pine "like arrows from a bow."[14] When others put Haines's design to use, he demanded that they compensate him. Granted a patent for the V flume in 1871, he brought suit: *James W. Haines* v. *William Sharon et al.,* August 7, 1872. Judge Stephen J. Field, a friend of Sharon's who years later would sit in judgment in the sensational Sharon divorce case, heard the suit. Field found Haines's patent invalid, because "the invention had been in common use for two years before an application for patent had been filed."[15]

While Sharon and Ralston were taking control of all elements of the mining industry, they were careful to avoid the inherent risks that lead monopolists to lose power. Although keeping prices of milling, timber, and water (while he ran the water company) high, Sharon did not allow them to become exorbitant. In usurping the transportation element by building the Virginia & Truckee Railroad, he provided lower rates for consumers. This was deceptive, because the real cost included the taxes levied by counties to pay their share of the road's construction. Stock manipulations and schemes to squeeze out opposition mills were hidden during the building of the monopoly. By the time they were publicized, the Bank Ring was too powerful to be challenged.

Sharon did little to avoid public disdain, and after forcing old-time mill owners off the Comstock, there was little likelihood that he could have done so. Assessments on mines working good ore contributed to his reputation for unscrupulousness. His actions reflected a desire for power, not popularity. At the same time the name of his partner, Ralston, was kept free from imputation, and Sharon ensured that the Bank of California, the Comstock's driving force, was perceived as beyond reproof. The *Enter-*

prise reported: "Bejabers! The whole of Virginia is comprised in two blocks, and them two blocks consist of one corner, and that corner is the Bank of California."[16]

Until Sharon came along, William Stewart had dominated the state. When the constitution was drawn, in 1863 and 1864, he insisted that mines not be taxed as other properties were, but only on their net proceeds (his persistence was burlesqued by Mark Twain in communiqués from the capital to the *Territorial Enterprise*). Without his proposal the constitution was defeated; ratification followed its inclusion. The first Nevada territorial legislature authorized a tax of $1.50 for the county and $1.25 for the state on each $100 of valuation. But it limited taxes on mine proceeds to $.50 on each $100 for the county and $.50 for the state and allowed deductions as well. In 1867 Sharon brought his influence to bear, until Storey County's Comstock mines were limited to $.25 on the $100, for county purposes.[17]

By 1871 Sharon and the Bank Ring controlled nearly all the producing mines on the Comstock. Lobbying, and reportedly Bank of California money, led to the passage of legislation to further reduce the taxation of mines. The new deduction allowed an amount per ton equal to the cost of extraction and conversion into bullion. "Under the new law, the owners ... might figure expenses so high as to leave but one dollar per ton liable to assessment."[18]

With such tax-free incentives, intrigues to control ownership of the mines were inevitable. The Hale & Norcross mine, situated between two rich mines, the Savage and the Chollar-Potosi, yielded over $2 million in 1866 and 1867. In January 1868, following an assessment, stocks fell below $300 a share. Sharon's brokers began surreptitiously buying. When the owner, San Francisco businessman Charles L. Low, understood the coup attempt, he fought back. Both sides bought recklessly, driving the market. By February 8, prices rose to $2,925 a share.[19]

People sold short, knowing the stocks were inflated and would fall. When prices continued to rise, the short sellers could not cover, and fortunes were in jeopardy. A foot of stock went to $8,000, then to the incredible price of $12,000. T. C. Sanborn, chairman of the Open Board, made a standing offer of $100,000 for ten feet. There were no sellers.[20]

Just before the March 12 stockholders' meeting, it became known that Sharon had outbid Low, and prices fell to $2,900. When Sharon's board of directors—including Barron, Bell, Hayward, and Sunderland—took charge, the number of stocks was increased from eight hundred to eight thousand. For a time the vein remained strong, then it began to pinch off, and Sharon unloaded his stock. After the other Bank Ring members followed suit, they levied an assessment. Shares plummeted. They ordered two more assessments. By September the price of Hale & Norcross stocks was $41.50 a share. Sharon was employing what was becoming a familiar strategy: He controlled the mine and would be informed at the earliest moment if its prospects changed; at that time he would buy back the deflated stocks to again reap the mine's benefits.[21]

At the end of 1868 and through January 1869, a new group began buying deflated Hale & Norcross shares without being noticed. In February word leaked out that someone was cornering the market. Sharon fought to retain control, buying all available shares. It then became known that John Mackay and his partners—James Fair, J. C. Flood, and William O'Brien— were the opposition. Legend holds that with the balance of the election in doubt, Sharon discovered the name and address of a widow in San Francisco who owned one hundred shares. Sharon used the telegraph operator, a man named Hedger, to send a ciphered message directing Ralston to get the stock. When he finished and left the telegraph office, Mackay stepped in. He asked Hedger what Sharon had sent. Hedger, like most on the street, disliked Sharon. He deciphered the message, which Mackay immediately sent to Flood in San Francisco. Ralston, unsuspecting, waited until morning to send a messenger to the widow, who informed him that Flood had already bought her shares. The *San Francisco Call* said Flood had paid the widow $8,000 a foot.[22]

On February 26, 1869, in its "Mining Intelligence" column, the *Territorial Enterprise* casually announced: "J. G. Fair and John W. Mackay of this city now own a controlling interest in the Hale & Norcross mine. The mine is looking exceedingly well, and the gentlemen named will doubtless shortly become millionaires." On March 10, the Bank Ring's trustees were ousted and O'Brien and Mackay were voted in. Flood was elected president of the company, and Fair became its superintendent. At the conclusion of the election, Sharon patronizingly remarked to Mackay that with Mackay's limited experience, Sharon should continue to manage the mine. Mackay thanked him and declined.[23] The Sharon officers had called for an $80,000 assessment. The new management rescinded it and instead declared a dividend. The mine began to pay. In the next two years it produced seven times the tonnage of 1868 and paid $728,000 in dividends.[24]

In the early spring of 1869, the Yellow Jacket produced high-grade ore on the eight-hundred- and nine-hundred-foot levels.[25] Then on April 7 (a month after Mackay's Hale & Norcross coup), shortly after the day shifts arrived and cages lowered the miners into the Yellow Jacket, fire erupted. Probably started by a candle left near timbers at the eight-hundred-foot level, the blaze quickly spread through the Yellow Jacket's drifts and into those connecting it to the adjoining Crown Point and Kentuck mines.

The first men to realize there was trouble below began to try to rescue those who had descended. Only when Superintendent Winters arrived did the whistles of the Yellow Jacket begin to shriek. Firemen rushed to their station houses then to the mines. Smoke and gasses spewed from the shafts, preventing rescuers from descending. The cages were dropped and jerked back to the surface, but few men came up. "The first man out told a harrowing story of the situation below. In the Crown Point so many men crowded upon the first cage, designed to carry a maximum of sixteen, that the shift boss was afraid to give the signal to hoist. It would have been death to a dozen attempting to cling to the cage. For five minutes it stood in the inferno with men battling in frenzy for places before the hoisting bell was sounded. As the cage started upward several of the men left behind threw themselves to death in the shaft in their panic."[26]

The fires were burning at the seven-hundred- and eight-hundred-foot levels. Men in the Crown Point at the one-thousand-foot level were trapped. J. P. Jones, the superintendent, sent a message down in the cage telling them not to attempt to come up through the poison gases yet but to send word of their location. The message went unanswered.

The *Territorial Enterprise* reported: "Father Manogue and several other Catholic clergymen did all that could be done to comfort the weeping women and children, but even the reverend fathers could find but little to say upon such an occasion. The poor women with their weeping children clinging about them stood about with hands clasped, rocking themselves to and fro."[27]

On April 12 J. P. Jones took a young man named Nagle with him to seal off the tunnel at eight hundred feet. They worked for fifteen minutes before the last of nine candles died out and they were dragged up in the cage, Jones tottering, Nagle insensible.

Reports of the number of deaths ranged from thirty-four to forty-five. Dan DeQuille, who reported at the scene for the *Territorial Enterprise,* used the higher number. In *The Big Bonanza* he tallied the daily body count and added three missing miners known to have been trapped in the tunnels. Even as the fires were being battled, a damning conjecture spread. It was said Sharon had ordered the torching to depress stocks. Based in distrust and hatred and never supported, the charge was repeated into the twentieth century.[28]

The fires smoldered for months, with even upper levels of the mines closed because of smoke and gases. In July 1869 the Yellow Jacket stockholders elected their usual slate of trustees, including Sharon and Winters. On the 19th the trustees voted to donate $2,500 for the relief of the living sufferers of the mining calamity. On the 20th an assessment of ten dollars per share was announced.[29]

In May 1869, with the mines still fighting the effects of the fire, Samuel Hooper of Boston led a contingent of six members of the U.S. House of Representatives to the West Coast. They came to investigate the Central Pacific railroad, and Adolph Sutro pestered them into visiting the mines as well.[30]

There was still support for Sutro's tunnel among experts on the Comstock. In the fall of 1868 Sharon's mining engineer, C. A. Luckhardt, had reported on the status of the Comstock vein to the commissioner of Mineral Statistics. The correspondence listed the mines' yields and prospects as well as problems with hot air and water at great depths. Luckhardt concluded, "The future of the Comstock will depend much on the construction of the tunnel." These ideas were not discussed on the streets of Virginia City.[31]

When the congressional committee arrived in San Francisco in 1869, Ralston entertained them. Beginning at Lake Tahoe, Sharon hosted the Nevada portion of their visit. Hooper later wrote to Ralston: "I do not forget the many kind attentions received from you and your friends, which contributed so much not only to the pleasure of myself and the other members of the committee, but to our information of matters in California. Wm Sharon did every thing in his power to render our journey across Tahoe Lake to Virginia City agreeable to us, and we enjoyed that portion of the journey very much."[32]

Sharon monopolized the committee in Virginia City but "declared in a careless moment that 'this Sutro Tunnel business should be stopped.'"[33] That comment piqued interest, and the committee ventured deep into the mines, where they experienced the heat and suffocating lack of ventilation. When Sharon failed to keep the congressmen from meeting with Sutro, the trip was undone. The *Gold Hill News* issued a sarcastic report: "Adolph Sutro, the originator and projector of the famous Sutro tunnel, managed to corral a portion of [the committee] and took them up to the roof of the International Hotel, in order to give them some idea of the true importance of that great work. From that exalted eminence he showed them the lay of the land."[34]

Despite the *News*'s jibe, the committee reached a consensus in supporting the tunnel. Sutro remarked: "All went down into those mines. They saw it all; and if you ask any of those gentlemen about it, they will express but one opinion, every one of them."[35] Thereafter, Sutro could count on Hooper's and the others' votes when battling the Bank Ring's minions in Congress.

In September Sutro's campaign reached a turning point when he took it to the miners themselves. Sharon's railroad extinguished the hope of transporting ore to mills, but the Yellow Jacket fire reemphasized the danger of working underground with only one way out. The tunnel would still be valuable as a drain and for ventilation; more importantly, it would serve as a fire escape. Sutro addressed the unions and, stressing the safety issue, secured a fifty-thousand-dollar subscription by a unanimous vote. He then sought to win over the entire community. On September 1 he opened a stock-subscriptions office at 76 C Street and began advertising in the *Enterprise*.[36] Broadsides appeared on Virginia City's streets: "Miners! Laboring men! Mechanics! Rally! . . . Great mass meeting . . . Adolph Sutro will address the citizens . . . Subject: 'The Sutro tunnel and the Bank of California!'"[37]

Anticipating Thomas Nast's attacks on Boss Tweed by more than a year, Sutro used oversized cartoon drawings to rally the miners. The cartoons caricatured Sharon and the Bank Ring, showing "Bill Sharon's crooked railroad" and "Bill Sharon's big wood pile" (illustrating the clear-cutting of the forests) and emphasizing the monopoly's grip on the territory. The most spectacular and inflammatory drawing rendered a scene of the Yellow Jacket fire. One side of the poster showed a shaft full of burning ladders and timbers with miners falling headlong into the depths; above ground, wives and children raised their arms in despair. The other half showed a shaft on fire, with the miners below the flames escaping to meet their families through the Sutro tunnel.[38]

The *Gold Hill News* led the attacks against the campaign. On September 18, 1869, it commented that despite all his talk, Sutro had not even begun his work. In an attempt to plant the seeds of ridicule for Sutro's speech before the fact, it compared him to George Francis Train, an eccentric young millionaire renowned for malapropisms.

On September 20 Sutro spoke to a crowd of four hundred:

> Laboring men of Nevada, crush out that hydra-headed monster:
> that serpent in your midst—the Bank of California. . . . The enemy

who has spun his web around you until you are almost helpless
has bribed your judges, packed your juries, hired false witnesses,
bought legislatures, elected representatives to defend their iniquity,
imposed taxes upon you for their private benefit. . . . I do not mean
to incite you to any violence . . . but I do mean to say that you can
destroy your enemy by simple concert of action. Let all of you join
together to build the Sutro Tunnel. . . . They know that the first
pick struck into the tunnel will be the first pick into their graves.[39]

On October 19, 1869, buoyed by the pledge of fifty thousand dollars from
the miners (little of which would actually ever be collected), Sutro finally
broke ground on his tunnel.

The battle to drill the tunnel continued throughout the decade. In mid-
February 1872 in Washington, D.C., the House of Representatives Committee on Mines and Mining held hearings on it. The previous summer
a three-person commission, appointed by President Grant, had visited
the Comstock for five weeks to study the mines. The commissioners—two
army generals and a college professor—concluded that the tunnel was unnecessary. Adolph Sutro immediately assailed the conclusion and asked to
interrogate the commissioners. Bank of California lawyers, led by Thomas
Sunderland, and Sharon's mining experts traveled to Washington for
the hearings. Sutro, without the resources to hire attorneys or expert witnesses, represented his interests alone.

Over the course of several meetings Sutro examined the first commissioner, a Major General Foster, to determine the way in which the report
had been compiled. Foster acknowledged that because of flooding, they
were not allowed in all the mines they wished to visit. Sutro also forced
Foster to admit using superintendents' reports rather than auditing company books. Sutro then used the books of the Ophir mine to prove that
in reporting pumping water, the superintendent had understated costs by
four to six hundred thousand dollars.[40]

Sutro also asked how John P. Jones, of the Crown Point mine, had
evaluated the proposed tunnel.

> *Mr. Foster* . . . I think Jones was a little more favorable, perhaps
> than either of the others. He carefully considered and weighed the
> chances of the tunnel being a benefit to the country.

> *Mr. Sutro.* Do you know why Mr. Jones did not send his statement
> to you?

> *A.* No. We expected an elborate statement from him.

Sutro explained that it was reported on the Comstock that because
powerful interests opposed the tunnel, if Jones submitted a favorable statement he would have no chance in his proposed bid for a U.S. Senate seat.[41]
General Foster stated further that Sharon had informed him he would
"break up this tunnel."[42] Sutro then questioned a second commissioner,
Professor Wesley Newcomb, asking whether Sharon had said anything
about opposition to the tunnel.

> *A.* Well, he expressed himself very strongly when I first saw him in
> the street. . . .

> *Q.* On what grounds did he state he was opposed to it?

> *A.* The grounds were not given; only he would crush it, or some-
> thing of that effect.[43]

Newcomb then discussed Sharon's inordinate influence on the Comstock
(Sunderland, for the bank, repeatedly objected to questions and re-
sponses, but the committee almost always allowed a contested point to be
made):

> *Newcomb.* [One of the miners] stated that if the mining ring knew
> that any intelligence was communicated . . . in favor of the tunnel,
> the parties communicating it would be discharged from employ-
> ment . . .

> *Mr. Sunderland.* I would like, if the chairman please, to have the
> name of that man given. I would like to know what position he
> holds, so as to know whether his information is entitled to respect.

Mr. Sutro. If the man gave his information, and stated it would jeopardize his position to have it known, it would hardly be fair to give it.

Mr. Newcomb. I would decline to give his name, because I promised not to.

The chairman did not require the use of the man's name.[44]

Sutro interviewed the last of the three commissioners, Major General H. G. Wright, on Thursday, February 29. Wright was not forthcoming. When asked whose interests were being served in the working of the mines, he repeatedly avoided answering, claiming that he did not to wish to take the responsibility for saying. Sunderland tried to protect him, but, after much wrangling, Sunderland commented: "I have been objecting so long, that I don't propose to object to anything hereafter." A congressman tried with Wright again:

> What would be regarded as the public sentiment there, the general conviction of the people?
>
> *Mr. Wright.* I think the general opinion, so far as I had occasion to ascertain, is that the mines are not managed exclusively in the interests of the stockholders. I do not give that as my opinion. I have no opinion about it."[45]

In mid-March the committee turned to the mining experts, the first being I. L. Requa. Sutro again took up the questioning. Requa denied that Sharon controlled Requa's mine.

> *Q.* Did you ever communicate with him about the state of the mine?
>
> *A.* Sometimes. He, like a good many other men, would ask me how the mine looked, and I would always give him all the information I had.
>
> *Q.* Is he a stockholder in the mine?

> *A.* . . . There have been times . . . when he owned nearly all the
> stock that the mine consisted of. At the last annual election I do not
> think the Bank of California owned a share, but I think Mr. Sharon
> and others and myself included did. We voted about 26,000 of the
> 28,000 shares.[46]

Requa told how he came from his duties on the Comstock to give testimony before Congress, saying Senator Stewart had sent a telegram causing Sharon to ask Requa to travel to Washington.[47]

A week later, Sutro questioned Sharon's mining engineer, C. A. Luckhardt. Luckhardt testified that for five years he had examined mines to which Sharon sent him. When Sutro asked what in particular his employers' interests were, Luckhardt said that they would buy into mines he recommended. "The injunction was put upon me, when I was employed, to keep all that I saw there for their especial benefit and no one else's."

Under Sutro's questioning, Luckhart agreed that it was commonly understood that the Bank of California manipulated the leading mines' trustees. Sunderland moved to strike the answer but, as a matter of course, was overruled. When asked, Luckhardt testified that his expenses were paid so he could cross the country to testify. Sutro inquired at whose instance.

> *A.* At the instance of a friend of mine in San Francisco.
>
> *Q.* Who?
>
> *Witness.* Have I got to state that? I reckon I might as well state: Mr.
> Sharon.[48]

Sutro had shown Sharon's dominance, his interrogation undermining the integrity of the commissioners' report. He illustrated that they failed to investigate the companies' books, that superintendents understated their costs by hundreds of thousands of dollars, and that the flooding in the mines remained unexamined. Never shy about his achievements, Sutro proclaimed that Sharon's money and legal talent were defeated "by the strength of my will and position."[49]

It was not an idle boast. The House Committee on Mines and Mining reported in favor of $2 million in aid for construction of his tunnel. Although voted down by the Ralston-influenced Senate, the committee's endorsement attracted subscribers. Using investments from Europeans and fought every step of the way by Sharon and the Bank Ring, Sutro completed the tunnel after nine years. It proved an effective drain, and Sutro became a millionaire by selling his interest. But its usefulness was short lived. By the time it was completed, the Comstock Lode's glory days were done.[50]

Another of those Sharon did battle with was John P. Jones. A hero in the Yellow Jacket fire, he superintended the Crown Point mine for the Bank Ring. The mine yielded pay ore in the lode's early years but was drowned in eighty feet of water in 1864. After its connecting tunnels burned in the fire, vast expenses accrued as level after level revealed only barren rock. In November 1870 no one would buy its shares offered at a mere two dollars. But that month Jones, in San Francisco, was summoned to view "a promising development."[51]

He liked what he saw, but as he could not afford to buy the plentiful mine shares, he chose not to notify Sharon or members of the Bank Ring and turned instead to several San Francisco speculators. They bought the stock when he guaranteed their losses in consideration of one-half of possible profits. Shortly thereafter, Jones's daughter fell ill in the East. He told the speculators he would have to sell his stock and visit her. They thought he was running out on them and their investment. Believing Crown Point the real invalid, "Jones's sick child" became their inside joke.[52]

Once he was back on the job, Jones's inspections showed that the vein was becoming fuller. At his urging, Bank Ring member Alvinza Hayward, Jones's relation by marriage, quietly bought almost half the company's stock, 5,000 shares. He paid less than $5 per share. Sharon, who controlled 4,100 shares, was slow to realize what had occurred. By the time he discovered his allies' betrayal, the price per share had rocketed to $340.

It was unfeasible for Sharon to fight Jones and Hayward at that time, as they already held close to a majority of the stock. Sharon could not call on Ralston. His fortune was interwoven with that of the bank. Only Ralston and Sharon knew that $3 million of the bank's $5 million capital was sunk into Comstock-related businesses. The overextended bank put Ralston and his partner in a precarious position and severely restricted their ability to raise money.[53] Sharon, as always, acted decisively.

The Crown Point adjoined the long discredited Belcher mine. Sharon, believing a rich vein in one might run into the other, proposed selling the Crown Point shares at the market price on the condition that Jones and Hayward sell him their interests in the Belcher. On June 7, 1871, Sharon sold his Crown Point stock for $1,400,000, the largest private transfer of mining shares ever on the Comstock. He lost both the Crown Point bonanza and the contract to mill its ore. Like Mackay, Jones understood the Bank Ring's mode of milling, so he and Hayward organized their own company. Sharon later told Eliot Lord that he never forgot Jones and Hayward's action. Lord commented: "To thus outwit the head of the combination either prior and more accurate information must have been obtained by Mr. Hayward, or he must have been the more daring speculator of the two. Mr. Sharon attributed his defeat to the first cause assigned."[54]

In this instance Sharon proved his astuteness. He hired foreman W. H. "Hank" Smith away from the Crown Point to superintend the Belcher. Smith, able and popular among the miners, had made the original discovery of the vein in the Crown Point. Immediate exploration began in Belcher ground adjacent to the Crown Point strike.

Professor Wesley Newcomb, one of the commissioners who had testified at the Sutro tunnel hearings, had been with Sharon when a man rode up with urgent news. "[Sharon] was taking us out in his carriage, very kindly, to show us the mill property, and we saw that this was a matter of considerable importance to him. We rather urged him to turn back, thinking that he might be required at his office. He did so, and telegraphed to San Francisco for the purchase of stock of the Belcher Company."

Ralston and Sharon reportedly bought much of the Belcher stock for $1 a share. Within three months its stock rose to $1,525 a share. Sharon's gamble had paid off: the Crown Point's rich vein extended far into the

Belcher. Between 1871 and 1878, while the Crown Point bonanza pro-
duced $25.8 million, Sharon's Belcher produced $31.8 million.[55] As
Mackay before them, Jones and Hayward had dented Sharon's armor.
There were more assaults to come.

Chapter Six

HURLY-BURLY

AT THE SAME TIME the Sutro hearings were being held in Washington, D.C., Sharon let it be known that he was a candidate for Nevada's U.S. Senate seat. He and Ralston had first considered such a move two years earlier.[1]

On March 10, 1872, the *Territorial Enterprise* reported that although the *Enterprise*'s "unknown candidate" was still in the field, Sharon was to resign from the bank to "[attend] to the Virginia and Truckee Railroad, his large mining interests, and to some little Senatorial matters in which he feels some concern." By the end of 1872 Sharon moved fulltime to California. He felt justified in running for the Senate as a Nevadan, since he retained his business interests and paid taxes in Nevada.

Since Nevada's statehood in 1864, the Republican Party had dominated its politics. Republicans swept the 1866 state elections. In 1869 the state legislature was composed of fifty Republicans and nine Democrats.[2] But in the election of 1870 there was a backlash, because Republicans were seen as the Bank of California party. Sharon was derisively called "the Great King." Regarding the Republican convention and its slate of candidates, the *Elko Independent* editorialized: "The same men who have ruled this State since it was a Territory ruled the convention. Nothing can ever break up the clique but a total defeat at the polls." The paper then listed the nominees: "For Governor—F. A. Tritle, Grand Scribe of the Bank of California. For Lieutenant Governor—J. S. Singerland, Grand Hotel Keeper of the Bank of California." Thirteen men were listed, after each their fanciful relationship to the bank, through "State Mineralogist—Henry Witchell, Grand Bugologist of the Bank of California."[3]

In the voting on November 8, 1870, the Democrats gained their first substantial victories in the state. They won Nevada's lone House seat and the most important state offices: governor, lieutenant governor, treasurer, attorney general, and Nevada Supreme Court justice.[4] Anti-Sharon sentiment was generally cited as the cause of the Republican collapse.

Two years later, Sharon was ready to rectify the poor showing of 1870 by running himself. In mid-1872 two other candidates announced that they would seek the Republican nomination for the U.S. Senate: the incumbent, James W. Nye, and John P. Jones. This was the first of three senatorial races in which Sharon ran, and disturbing amounts of money were thrown around. Although as early as 1869 Governor Henry Blasdel had addressed bribing electors in his message to the state legislature, the three Sharon-contested U.S. Senate races earned the state the designation "the rotten borough."[5]

Early in the '72 campaign, it became clear that Senator Nye would not be a factor. Nye, appointed territorial governor by Abraham Lincoln, had also served eight years as senator from Nevada. The years of service were not enough when opposed by Sharon's unlimited wealth and that of Jones, the Crown Point millionaire. (It proved fortuitous when Nye later showed signs of the onset of senility.)[6]

In February Sharon authorized the bank to loan Alf Doten ten thousand dollars to purchase the *Gold Hill News*. Doten supported his candidacy. As it had been two years earlier, much of the rest of the state's press was antagonistic toward "the King"—especially Nevada's most influential paper, the *Territorial Enterprise*. In May 1870 *Enterprise* editor Joseph Goodman had published a wry column illustrating both his disdain for Sharon and the hard edge of the era's newspaper humor. The column told of a San Francisco letter writer's statement that Sharon would soon be assassinated. The writer owned stocks that, he believed, Sharon suppressed. He or someone else would perform the task, claiming to have recently met a man with a gun who was waiting for Sharon. Although Goodman announced that he had prepared a biographical notice of Sharon, "which, were he permitted to read in advance, would reconcile him to his fate," he protested: "Sharon belongs to Virginia, and our individual right to put an end to him must not be trespassed upon by outsiders."[7]

By 1872 Goodman was poised to take up the battle against Sharon. The *Enterprise*'s "unknown candidate" stepped forward in the person of John P. Jones, immediately dubbed "the Commoner," to emphasize the difference between him and Sharon. That January, when the market sagged, Jones and his partner, Alvinza Hayward, employed a scheme to bull the market that was used periodically through the years. After Hayward bought all available Savage stock at $62 a share (having wrested the mine from Sharon the previous summer), they locked the miners underground, as if they might spread news of a tremendous new strike if they were allowed out.[8]

On February 4, 1872, the *Enterprise* announced widespread stock excitement, with crowds blocking sidewalks outside brokers' offices. The demand for Savage stocks spread to other mines, until "speculation was seen in every eye and Mammon charged up and down the street like a stump-tailed bovine in fly time." Savage stock rose to $310 by February 8. On the 15th, as the market swelled, the *San Francisco Alta* assailed the manner in which Comstock mines were being managed, attacking the Bank Ring. The next day the *San Francisco Chronicle* followed the *Alta*'s lead, exposing the Bank Ring's methods of operation. Its headline shouted: "HOW 'THE MILL RING' GOT CONTROL OF THE MINES—ELECTION OF TRUSTEES BY NON-OWNERS OF STOCK."[9]

On the 18th, another *San Francisco Chronicle* headline proclaimed: "STOCKSHARPS.—HOW THE MILL RING GOT THE MILLS—ASSESSMENTS TO PAY CRUSHING BILLS—THE ADVANTAGE OF BEING ON THE INSIDE." Its exposé warned that owners were playing a "hogging game." Great profits were being extracted from the mines, but none of the money made its way to investors.[10] Stock prices slowed for a time and then continued their dramatic rise. Savage stock inflated to $725 by the end of April. That made the mine worth $12,400,000, almost as much as the richest Comstock properties, the Crown Point and the Belcher.[11]

On May 7 the market reached its high, an estimated $81 million. But the next day, word reached the street that the Savage strike was insubstantial. At the same time, Sharon unleashed a devastating financial attack against Jones, dumping stocks.[12] Savage shares dropped 40 percent, and all stocks plunged with them. Sharon appeared to come out unscathed, recouping perhaps as much as $5 million, while everyone else suffered. George Lyman commented: "The collapse was fearful to behold. Wreckage was strewn all over San Francisco's financial area." The market shrank nearly $49,000,000.[13] The *San Francisco Call* observed: "When [Sharon] got through singeing Jones and Hayward, the former was 'from $700,000.00 to $1,000,000.00 poorer this morning than a week ago and Hayward is set down for double that amount.'"[14]

On May 8, with West Coast finances on the edge of collapse, another accusation against J. P. Jones carried to Virginia City. Sharon let it be known that former mine managers accused Jones of setting the devastating Yellow Jacket mine fire.[15] The May 9 *Territorial Enterprise* printed two versions of a sensational story from that morning's *San Francisco Chronicle:* one by Jasper O'Donnell, Yellow Jacket foreman for eight years, and the other by J. S. Hubbell, an underground foreman at the mine at the time of the fire. The two had apparently told the same story originally, leading to the charge that mine supervisor G. F. Kellog had set the fire and that Jones was involved.

O'Donnell gave the version of the story that Sharon released: Hubbell had visited O'Donnell's house months before and told him that something "was bothering him very much and he wanted [it] brought to light." Hubbell then purportedly stated that G. F. Kellog had intentionally caused the fire in the Yellow Jacket and that "J. P. Jones was privy to the alleged crime." O'Donnell reported Hubbell as saying it was started with explosive powder. Hubbell knew Kellog had set the fire, because "Kellog asked [Hubbell] to go in with him."

Hubbell, though, now gave a much different version—one that sup-

ported Jones. He said Sharon had sent O'Donnell to Carson City to bring
him to San Francisco, insisting that he come to talk about the fire, and that
Sharon would pay him from fifty thousand to one hundred thousand
dollars. Meeting with O'Donnell, Sharon, and Detective I. W. Lees, whom
Sharon introduced as his private secretary, Hubbell told what he knew.
O'Donnell said, "That statement ain't worth a d—n for what we want."
Sharon added, "No; Mr. Hubbell does not say that he saw anybody set fire
to the mine." Hubbell was then told an affidavit would be drawn up for
him to sign. "[Hubbell] became convinced that a false and not a true statement was required. He added many embellishments to the story for the
purpose of ascertaining how far they would go, but with the secret determination in his own mind that he would not only refuse to sign the affidavit, but would in due time inform Jones of the plot against him." After leaving the room, Hubbell sought out Jones.

O'Donnell's story was unsustainable; three years earlier it had been
determined that powder did not start the fire. The *Enterprise* commented:
"The evidence taken before the Coroner at that time concerning that
phase of the fire, and now on record, completely refutes that charge, and
stamps Hubbell's statement to that effect as utterly worthless." The *Enterprise* reported that a time after the fire Kellog had fired Hubbell, who then
threatened vengeance. Further, Kellog replaced O'Donnell as foreman
in both the Yellow Jacket and the Kentuck mines. Because the story did
not hold up and there were motives to slander Kellog, the charges were
quickly dismissed. But the question of how the accusation became public
was not. The *Enterprise* of May 9th charged that Sharon's purpose
was well known: "Since Jones became a formidable rival Sharon has
grown singularly malevolent and indiscreet."[16] The next day the *Enterprise* termed the incident "the Sharon conspiracy." It reported that no one
believed the charges, but that everyone instead condemned Sharon as the
instigator.[17]

Doten's *Gold Hill News* of May 10th dismissed the charges against
Sharon as an attempt at blackmail by O'Donnell and Hubbell. It concluded that it was time to put an end to "the foul story." When the *Enter-

prise sought to expand the investigation, to reveal who sought to use it for "financial or political purposes." Doten undertook a defense of Sharon. The *News* emphasized that Sharon had merely allowed an investigation to advance before discovering the blackmailing scheme. "Hubbell, it seems, gave a statement implicating Jones, but demanded a nice little sum of $50,000 from Sharon before he would sign it and, on refusal, he went to Jones and trumped up the story that Sharon had tried to bribe him."[18]

The *Enterprise* published what it called "a bouquet of Eastern Nevada sentiments," illustrating the venom others directed at Sharon:

> From the Eureka Sentinel, May 10. Sharon never had any show on earth to be elected dog pelter. . . . He is a selfish, narrow-minded and rotten-hearted puppy—fit only to be loathed and spit upon by the generous and high-minded . . .

> From the Humboldt Register, May 11. The more the matter is ventilated the more apparent is it the whole thing is a deep and damnable plot, conceived and matured by Sharon . . .

> From the Reese River Reveille, May 10. Our dispatches to-day state that several brokers who have been cinched by Sharon, threaten to kill him on sight. If he had half the decency of Judas Iscariot, he would save them the trouble by going off and hanging himself."[19]

The *Gold Hill News* came under fire as it continued to defend Sharon. John H. Dennis, editor of the *Reese River Reveille,* was a friend of Doten's from eastern Nevada. But by the end of May, Dennis's paper joined the others in pricking the *News:* "As in the case of the metaphorical bull and the locomotive, we glory in its spunk, but deprecate its judgment." Doten answered in the *News* with a curious disavowal: "All right, Dennis. Have it just as you please. We have been vigorously defending Jones all along, but call him Sharon if you like. . . . Our exchanges may all suit themselves in the matter and suit us at the same time. The Gold Hill *News* is an independent paper and minds its own business."[20]

A few nights earlier Doten had drunk and told stories with the *En-*

terprise's Dan DeQuille "till daylight began to peep."[21] But no matter his friends nor whom he claimed to defend, an editorial by Goodman on May 31 forced Doten to fight. The famous attack appeared in the *Enterprise* under the heading A WELCOME TO MR. SHARON. It read in part:

> You are probably aware that you have returned to a community where you are feared, hated and despised. . . . Your career in Nevada for the past nine years has been one of merciless rapacity. You fastened yourself upon the vitals of the State like a hyena, and woe to him who disputed with you a single coveted morsel of your prey. . . . You cast honor, honesty and the commonest civilities of life aside. You broke faith with men whenever you could subserve your purpose by so doing; you robbed stockholders with an unscrupulousness that would have shamed a highwayman. . . . As Agent of the Bank of California, you converted an institution that should have been a public aid and blessing into an instrument of tyranny and usurpation. . . . Though indignant, the people propose no bodily harm. . . . Your punishment shall be to walk our thoroughfares . . . and feel that you are despised by every honest man; to know that every individual who is prompted by interest to clasp your hand shall feel himself contaminated by its touch, and hasten home to wash away the stain . . . to see the poor man spurn you in pride of honesty, the degraded scorn your lower degradation. . . . To such honors and hospitalities, Mr. Sharon, we cordially welcome you on behalf of the people. If your unlawfully acquired millions can compensate you for such universal contempt and execration, your sojourn may possibly prove pleasant to you; if not, it may happily be mutually unendurable and brief.[22]

Doten answered Goodman in his evening edition. He titled the column "Nauseating," calling Goodman's article "trash." He commented: "It is the silliest and most discredible string of twaddle we ever knew that really talented editor to be delivered of."[23]

During the next ninety days the *Territorial Enterprise* and the *Gold Hill News* engaged in a running battle. Early in June, Doten met privately with Sharon at Sharon's request.[24] Shortly thereafter, Goodman labeled Doten the "Chief Organ Grinder," or "COG," for Sharon. Although Doten responded by calling Goodman the COG for Jones, the debate centered on the monopolist.

On June 15 in Virginia City, Republicans held a meeting on C Street with a band and bonfires. Sharon was one of the dignitaries who, from a platform in front of the post office, addressed the crowd. There were loud calls for him when it was his turn to speak. But as he stepped forward, three "rousing cheers" were given for Jones. The *Enterprise* commented that Sharon's speech lacked coherency and sense: "[Sharon] said so many unmeaning and ridiculous things, that the audience did not know what to think." The paper asked him to use the *Enterprise* or "his own sheet—the Gold Hill *News*" to explain. Instead, Sharon left for San Francisco.[25]

On June 17 the *News* made an inexplicable misstatement: "[Sharon] certainly showed himself to be a man of pluck, conscious of his own right, and equally as ready to face his personal or political foes as he was to face the foes of his country when he served in the Union army during the rebellion." Sharon did not fight in the Civil War, nor did he serve in the army.

The *Enterprise* jumped on the error: "Great heavens! Can it be possible that in our pleasant and sportive mentions of Mr. Sharon we have unconsciously toyed with one of the heroes of the rebellion? . . . But that he was a patriot warrior, we never dreamed until his organ appalled us with the paragraph at the head of this article. We beg to suspend all we have said of Mr. Sharon until we learn the particulars of his illustrious career."[26] Three days later, with Doten unresponsive, Goodman pressed the attack. Did the *News* lie in its account?

> If the suspicion is unjust, give us his war record, that we may make a proper recognition of Mr. Sharon's valor. Otherwise, we shall be compelled to believe that his campaigns exist only in the imagination . . . that instead of sharing the dangers of the field, he was shav-

ing notes in his office; that instead of charging the enemy, he was only charging usurious interest on call loans; that instead of bleeding for his country at Fair Oaks, or Fredericksburg, or Chickamauga, or Chattanooga, he only bled the Comstock lode and the people of Nevada.[27]

Over the next couple of days, the *Enterprise* continued to bait the *News*. On June 21 Doten wrote supporting Sharon but skirting the issue of a war record. On the 22nd Goodman replied: "At length, last evening, it opened its lips and spoke; and as we strained to catch the words that were to relieve our perplexity, we discovered that all our hopes were foiled—the organ had become a driveling idiot."[28] When Sharon came back to Virginia City, Goodman titled his lead column "The Veteran Returned," dubbing him "William Tecumseh Sharon." The article laid nine years of Comstock "spoliation" at the feet of "the warrior."[29]

And so it went for another month. Then, on Friday, August 16, the *News* published a surprising telegram from San Francisco: "Editor Gold Hill News: Please announce to the public that continued ill health compels me to withdraw my name as a candidate for United States Senator. Words cannot express my high appreciation of the numerous friends in Nevada who have stood by me and I hope still to serve them and the State of my adoption in other ways as I shall have opportunity and strength. Wm. Sharon."

During the campaign, Jones investigated starting a railroad line to compete with the Virginia & Truckee. When Sharon's withdrawal became imminent, Ralston wrote to Jones asking his position on the railroad. On August 18, two days after Sharon's announcement, Jones responded that he supported the Virginia & Truckee Railroad and would oppose any change that might hurt Ralston's interests. He went on to comment that he believed the Sutro tunnel "scheme" to be "oppressive, unfair and unjust" and would oppose it in all possible ways.[30] On November 5 voters cast their ballots for legislators who would elect John P. Jones to the U.S. Senate. (Until 1913 senators were elected in state legislative conventions, with the representatives choosing between nominees.)

Wealth generally guarantees political power, allowing the capitalist to dictate public policy by buying politicians and pundits.[31] But even though Sharon controlled Nevada legislators and one of its pundits, Doten, his election hopes had been crushed by Goodman's *Territorial Enterprise.* On February 7, 1874, a year and a half after Jones's election, the *Gold Hill News* made a stunning announcement: Joseph Goodman was selling the *Enterprise,* which would be "published in the interest of William Sharon as a candidate for United States Senator, with Mr. Daggett as editor." Sharon spent twenty-five thousand dollars to buy Lot #10, Block 105, from C Street to D Street, including the *Enterprise* property and building, and another twenty-five thousand dollars for the paper. The fifty thousand dollars was five times the *Enterprise*'s value.[32]

Rollin Daggett was described as resembling a bulldog, with a great moustache and a scar above one eye. He was "rough, uncouth and at times seemed almost brutal," but he also owned a "sunny smile" and could be witty or tender in turn. Years earlier he had edited San Francisco's leading literary journal, the *Golden Era,* and recently he had served as Goodman's associate editor.[33]

Years later C. C. Goodwin related an anecdote regarding the relationship between Sharon and his new editor. As Daggett came from breakfast, Sharon asked him to sit down while he ate. When Sharon began picking at quail on toast, Daggett ordered a plate of ham and eggs. "'I thought you said you had breakfasted,' said Sharon. 'I had, but the way you eat made me hungry,' was the reply. 'Heavens, I would give half my fortune for your appetite,' was Sharon's comment. 'Yes,' said Daggett, 'and the other half for my character and lofty bearing. You see I am richer than you.'"[34]

The *Enterprise* would now begin rebuilding Sharon's public image. Daggett wrote that Sharon had used "nerve, energy and sagacity" to discover Comstock riches when it was too hazardous a venture for others. He noted that Sharon had employed hundreds and provided homes for thousands. And Daggett confronted Sharon's critics, accusing them of attacking him for the crime of being wealthy.

William Stewart, Nevada's first U.S. senator, served two terms, left office for twelve years, and then ran again, serving another eighteen years.

Why he did not run in 1874, when he was still openly ambitious and his legislative accomplishments were widely acclaimed, remains open to speculation. Sharon's decision to run surely influenced him (Gilman M. Ostrander has postulated that he may have withdrawn "upon orders from Sharon"). At the very least, his decision appears to have been a pragmatic reaction to Sharon's desire for the post. The Bank of California and the Central Pacific Railroad, which had supported Stewart in his previous political campaigns, were now behind Sharon. When explaining his decision, Stewart, who suffered from lifelong financial difficulties, did not mention the all-powerful financiers but stated simply, "The means of communication between my State and Washington were slow. . . . I was engaged in mining operations, many of which proved disastrous, and I thought it time to retire from politics and return to the practice of law."[35]

In Washington, D.C., the war between the Bank Ring and Adolph Sutro escalated. Mining companies were refusing to take out land patents, because the patents stated that ownership was subject to Sutro-tunnel royalty fees. Companies preferred to take their chances, holding their claims without patents, rather than pay the royalty. While Sutro's friends in the House of Representatives introduced legislation protecting the rights of the tunnel owners, he turned his attention to Sharon.

Sutro was a Prussian Jew who had immigrated when dislocations in the Revolution of 1848 ruined the family fortune. Prejudice against Jews on the Comstock was less overt than that against African Americans, Chinese, or Indians. This phenomenon can be attributed to two factors: Jews were not subject to the consistent virulence based on skin color, and they generally possessed specific business skills. Prohibited from owning land in large parts of Europe, they became craftsmen and merchants. The Jews in Virginia City were said to take the lead in dry goods and secondhand furniture stores.[36] But there was anti-Semitism beneath the surface. As Sutro challenged Sharon, bigotry was introduced not by Sharon, who would refer to Sutro as "that penniless carpetbagger," but by Sharon's ally, Alf Doten.

On March 29 Sharon made a trip to the Comstock. Mine owners had just held an anti-Sutro meeting, and petitions against tunnel legislation were circulated. Doten published an editorial entitled "Shylock Sutro." A few days later, Sharon met with Doten and reduced the interest rate on his *Gold Hill News* debt to 1 percent. Doten's attacks on Sutro now became more frequent and vicious. He quoted him using phonetic spelling— "mine" for my and "der" for the—and called Sutro: "This emigrant from Assyria . . . backed by certain foreign money lenders," and "A liar . . . a villain . . . a traitor to the people by whose sufferance he lives and urges his nefarious schemes in free America."[37]

Ralston's correspondence in April and May reveals the efforts of politicos working to assist the Bank Ring in suppressing Sutro. S. O. Houghton, in the U.S. House of Representatives, wrote sarcastically, "Why will you persist in 'Hunting Down' this poor devil Sutro and not permit him to gobble up the Comstock Lode, and so be rewarded for his great enterprise." U.S. Senator John S. Hager, heading his missive "*Private* to Ralston," wrote, "I do not think there is much danger of [Sutro's] measure passing in the Senate. . . . California and Nevada, and I think Oregon, will work together *against it.* I am prepared for anything—from an earthquake to a nitro glycerin explosion." Fred McCrellish, owner of the *San Francisco Alta,* addressed a note to Ralston, saying, "Wetmore writes me that the Sutro bill is practically dead, but he wants to crush it out of the possibility of resurrection; as Sutro has so many lives it will not do to let up until his advocacy is utterly powerless—his influence killed forever." On June 10 the director of the U.S. Mint, H. R. Linderman, signing his letter 'The Old Man,' wrote, "The Judiciary Council has put a quietus on the Piractical Sutro.—So much for having able and honest men in the Senate."[38]

On June 1, 1874, the *Daily Independent* newspaper began publishing in Virginia City. John Guinn, a talented newsman previously with the *Virginia Evening Chronicle,* edited it. Its initial issue reprinted the two-year-old Goodman attack, "A Welcome to Mr. Sharon," demonstrating its editorial position. Sutro helped fund the *Daily Independent,* and it supported his views. In the 1874 senate race, the *Gold Hill News* and the *Territorial Enterprise* carried Sharon's banner, while the *Virginia Evening Chronicle* boosted the Democratic candidate.

Candidates were expected to contribute money to their own campaign and to the party for the entire ticket. The money was used to defray expenses: the printing of broadsides, travel, renting halls for rallies. But with the amount of money in Sharon's and others' war chests, they often funded bribery and purchased votes as well. (One well-regarded minister attacked the Republican Party during a sermon and declared the electioneering so "rotten" that he offered to join a vigilance committee to drive the perpetrators from the community.)[39]

Sutro, running as a populist, proclaimed "the paramount dignity and honor of labor." For his trouble he was labeled a communist.[40] General Thomas H. Williams, who made millions as an investor in the Consolidated Virginia mine, campaigned as the lone Democratic candidate until, just before the election, party discord caused him to be rejected for Henry K. Mitchell.

The most serious question regarding candidate Sharon was his residency, as he now lived in California. He postponed his daughter's wedding day—set for a year—until after the election, because he preferred not to call attention to his San Francisco home, where it would be celebrated.

Nor was Sharon gaining in personal popularity. In Nevada he allowed his agents to speak for him, but at times he visited the state to address its citizens. Grant Smith has related how one night at an Opera House rally he defended his wealth, saying: "'You know I can't take my money with me.' Whereupon a voice from the gallery responded 'If you did it would burn.'"[41]

In mid-August Senator Jones returned to Nevada, and in Carson City Sharon, ignoring their bitter fight two years earlier, delivered a welcome speech: "I thank you on behalf of Senator Jones for the reception given him in your fair city this evening. . . . He has been true to the trust of the people reposed in him, and I am happy to add my voice in commending him for it." Myron Angel noted in Thompson and West's *History of Nevada*: "Mr. Jones was helping Mr. Sharon to become Stewart's successor in the United States Senate at the time of the above eulogy; and it makes a world of difference whose ox is being gored."[42]

On August 25 Jones was to receive a welcome on the Comstock. From the balcony of the International Hotel, Sharon addressed a crowd, declaring past differences with Jones forgotten. When somebody yelled, "What about the Chinese?" he answered: "Like the old man I knew in the States who was not able to buy a horse, therefore purchased and did his work with a jackass, there are some kinds of work that may be done by the Chinese. . . . Thus we see them employed as cooks and at certain kinds of labor in households. . . . But I do not wish you to understand from this that I am in favor of inviting an inferior people to our shores—of using all jackasses in place of horses." Sharon, also spoke of his opponent, Sutro:

> I have in my quiet way, for years given thousands of men steady employment, and to every man I have paid every dime of his earnings. I have planted millions in these mines, and at times when the lead was not paying, and even when my own heart failed me. . . . What [Sutro] has done for you and the country I should like to hear. I have expended and caused to be expended millions in your midst—in building mills and hoisting works and in opening our mines and improving the country. In doing this work you have been with me and helped me out and I thank you for it . . . while he was in Washington making his misrepresentations and trying to corrupt the very center of the nation.[43]

Working men in San Francisco expressed their opinion of the candidate. In October 1874 James McGill, president of the Bricklayers' Association, and its secretary, John D. Cavanagh, signed an open letter to the workers of Nevada about their efforts to win the eight-hour day: "[Sharon] announced himself as utterly opposed to the eight-hour law, utterly opposed to associations of laboring men for the purpose of mutual aid and protection." With the views Sharon held, they said, "he is the last man that the working class of Nevada should choose to represent them in the National legislature."[44]

But Daggett, Doten, and Nevada's still powerful Republican politicos supported Sharon. A plank of the Republican platform reflected Sharon's influence. Calling the Sutro tunnel "a great shadow" and "a great danger," it demanded the rout and defeat of the promoters of "this wicked sceme."[45]

If publicity generated is the evaluative tool, one of the best uses of Sharon's cash was his hiring of Tom Fitch, the "Silver Tongued Orator." The lawyer's political career had included many runs at the U.S. Senate. "Fitch was irrepressible," Grant Smith has commented. "When a Republican convention failed to nominate him for Congress, he rose and said: 'Gentlemen: from the bottom of my heart I can now sympathize with Lazarus—I too have been licked by dogs.'"[46] During the summer of 1874 in Virginia City, Fitch wrote "a scathing speech" against Sharon and the Bank Ring. "By some means a knowledge of the existence of this speech came to Mr. Sharon, and then it was that Mr. Fitch [the speech undelivered] left suddenly for San Francisco, with a goodly sized check in his pocket."[47]

The end of October 1874 was filled with snowstorms, but as the election neared, rhetoric warmed the nights. Fitch, suddenly in the hire of Sharon, spoke to packed houses. His speech—"Sutro, His Bore, His Calibre and His Wanderings to and fro upon the Face of the Earth"—intimated that the "Great Bore" referred to the tunnel and the man. The Sharon element praised the talk for its poetry, historical references, and "flights into the blue abusing and ridiculing Sutro." Doten wrote in his diary: "Hall densely crowded . . .—Grand speech—Gave immense satisfaction."[48]

A few nights later Sutro fired back, presenting a lantern-and-slide show that berated Sharon. But it was not enough. The offices of state legislators and state officials were contested on November 3. When the final returns were tallied, Sharon's Republican Party won forty-seven seats and the Democrats twenty-eight. Sutro's Independents were shut out.

November 19 gave rise to San Francisco's premiere social event of the season: Clara Sharon's postponed marriage to Francis Newlands. The papers' description of the event devoted as much space to Sharon and his mansion as to the couple.[49]

Clara was twenty-one; Newlands, Sharon's lawyer, was a twenty-eight-year-old Yale graduate. The wedding and reception were held at Sharon's newly remodeled home. The wedding included only the Ralstons and a few of the city's aristocratic elite. The reception, at eight P.M., included eight hundred guests. The *San Francisco Chronicle*'s Sunday edition ran a headline that indicates the import of the occasion as well as Sharon's stature:

> TWO ENTIRE PAGES DEVOTED TO THE SHARON WEDDING: A BRIL-
> LIANT MATRIMONIAL DAZZLE. SPLENDID CELEBRATION OF THE
> NEWLANDS-SHARON NUPTIALS. A DESCRIPTION OF THE SHARON
> MANSION. HOW A CITY MILLIONAIRE SURROUNDS HIMSELF WITH
> LUXURY. THE MOST ELEGANTLY APPOINTED RESIDENCE ON THE
> COAST. BIOGRAPHY OF THE NEVADA MINING KING. CLIMBING
> THE THORNY WAY TO FAME AND FORTUNE. LOVE IN A PALACE.
> ELEGANT TOILETS OF THE QUEENS OF SOCIETY.[50]

The reception carpet ran to the curb. Chinese lanterns lit the grounds. Chandeliers, crystal fountains, delicate flowers, wreaths, and trailing vines filled the rooms. One orchestra performed in the ballroom, professionally decorated with palms, ferns, orange trees, cedars, and exotic shrubs; another orchestra played upstairs. The banquet began at 10 P.M., and the party continued through the night. It involved revelry and splender "such as the ordinary person would not witness during a lifetime."[51]

Newlands had known Clara for two years. He was so well regarded that there was no hint Sharon's wealth played any part in the courtship, except in the opposition press. Daggett took his journalistic brothers to task for their jibes: "[Sharon] has millions of money, and started the young couple out pleasantly and without fear in life. This is the simple story of an event which envy and ill-nature have prompted not a few journalists to refer to with a lack of gallantry of which they should be ashamed."[52]

Before 1875 Sharon's career in Virginia City had featured an unbridled acquisition of real estate. Six weeks after Clara and Francis Newlands's wedding, days before legislators were to vote for Nevada's U.S. senator, Sharon began to divest himself of it. On January 9, 1875, he deeded twenty-five lots in Virginia City and thirty-seven in Gold Hill to the Virginia

& Truckee Railroad. The following year, in June, he deeded Maynard's Block, a series of brick buildings fronting the road below the divide, to the bank. Each of these transactions was made for the legal-fiction price of one dollar, hiding what consideration was actually involved.[53]

On January 4 the *Virginia Evening Chronicle* implored the legislature to elect someone other than Sharon. It described his arrival "from his home in San Francisco in a special palace car." Pointing out that this was his first appearance since November 3, it commented: "If he is elected next week he will again depart from our gaze, and be lost ... for many months— mayhap many years." In the next column it continued the theme, while tweaking his new coiffure. "As he stood upon the platform ... and sunned his maroon colored hair, his brow became more clouded, in keeping with the change which was taking place in his locks. . . . He was thinking no doubt of his sunny home in San Francisco, of the good things he had left behind."[54] The *Gold Hill News* countered with a description of Sharon by reporter Fred H. Hart, who later wrote *The Sazarac Lying Club*. Using the pseudonym Toby Green, Hart noted that most criticism of Sharon was in general terms. "'Is he dishonest?' you ask. 'No,' is the reply—with the o long drawn out—"can't say that he is.' 'Is he not a man of his word?' 'H—l! His word is as good as his bond ... he just won't do on general principles." Hart concluded: "I expect that jealousy and envy have about as much to do with making some people hate him as anything he has ever done to earn their dislike."[55]

On January 6, when the Republican caucus unanimously nominated Sharon, he hosted the forty-seven members in the parlors of the Ormsby House Hotel. Hangers-on also made frequent visits, "each time coming down with a fresh pocketful of cigars. The champagne was furnished by the lavish hand of Ah Ky."[56]

The galleries and halls of both houses were crowded for the vote on the 12th. In the Nevada assembly, Democratic legislator J. C. Dow of Elko sec-onded the nomination of H. K. Mitchell, observing: "In voting for Mr. Mitchell, Democrats would know that they voted for a citizen of the State of Nevada." This began debate concerning whether Sharon was a citizen or not. Two Washoe independents, H. H. Beck and H. H. Hogan, argued that Sharon was constitutionally ineligible because he lived in California. Asked the meaning of "actual resident," Hogan replied, "Where his domicile and his family are; it is where he goes when he says, 'I am going home.'" Republican Thomas Wren of Eureka argued that although he was forced by his wife's failing health to maintain a residence in San Francisco, Sharon paid his poll tax, registered, voted, and paid his taxes in Nevada. This argument, supported by all Republicans, carried the day. On the 13th, the two houses gave Sharon forty-nine of seventy-four votes, a two-thirds majority.

Sharon's acceptance was a graceful pledge: "I will neither affect indifference to the honor which tradition gives to him who holds the Senatorial office, nor will I disguise the deep sense of responsibility which rests upon me in no small degree, but if an honest desire and unalterable determination to give his best energies and powers to the general service; to guard the interests and develop the resources of his constituents, can arm a citizen who goes from private to public life for a successful struggle with inevitable difficulties, then I am well prepared for every emergency."[57] After the "usual jollification" at the successful candidate's headquarters, Sharon, needing to look after business interests, left in a special car for San Francisco.

At the assembly's adjournment, Dow said: "Out of respect to the burial of State rights and loss of identity of Nevada, I move that the House do now adjourn." The motion was declared out of order. Dow repeated it. Wren replied: "I consider it out of place and unworthy [of] the Assembly that a motion to adjourn should be accompanied by a slur upon the majority here. I now move that the Assembly adjourn."[58]

The *Territorial Enterprise* congratulated the people of Nevada. Others mourned. Sam Davis later contributed an ode:

> On yonder hillside, bleak and barren,
> Lies many a friend of William Sharon,

Who in election's hurly-burly
Voted often, voted early.

.   .   .   .

To take a hand in the election
And hustle back without detection.
As we recall those mem'ries hoary,
Let's bless the graveyard vote of Storey.[59]

While not denying that Sharon contributed money liberally to the party, the *Enterprise* commented: "To achieve success, not one dollar was used corruptly by Mr. Sharon. Not a single vote was purchased by him or for him either at the polls or in the Legislature."[60] Few agreed. Davis subsequently reported that the election caused comment throughout the United States; he claimed that Sharon spent at no less than eight hundred thousand dollars. The *Virginia Evening Chronicle* remarked: "We are told by the Sharon organs that their candidate earned the position . . . by means of his 'influence' and 'labor.' These two plain English words may therefore hereafter be expressed by this sign—$."[61]

Chapter Seven

THE OPHIR
DEBACLE

ECONOMIC HISTORIANS LONG AGO debunked American laissez faire as myth. Jefferson's colonial Virginia philosophy proposed a wise, frugal government that, while preventing men from injuring one another, left them free to regulate their own pursuit of industry. He advocated keeping economic affairs free from government regulations in part to protect Congress from coming under the control of stockjobbers. But the vast resources in America could not be harnessed by private capital. Enterprise became "mixed" as state and federal governments contributed direct aid to assist corporations. States provided funding for plank roads, turnpikes, railroads, and bridges. The federal government donated land, built roads (the Cumberland Road being a prime example), used the Army Corps of Engineers to produce engineering surveys, and protected industry with tariff rebates.[1] Legislative involvement came full circle when groups that gained the upper hand with government assistance dragged representatives into jobbery to protect what they built. Throughout the nineteenth century, the tradition of utilizing the public treasury as a major source of venture capital grew. The Internal Improvements Act of 1841, the Swamplands Act and the Illinois Land Grant Bill of 1850, and the railway acts of the 1860s included giveaways that made magnates of speculators and their corporate associates.[2]

As well as the general public, Ralston's bank clients included the wealthiest businessmen, the most profitable Comstock mining companies, and the U.S. Internal Revenue Service. Ralston used their deposits and his influence to promote his interests: industry and growth in the West. At times his policy benefited himself and his partners, as in blocking the Sutro tunnel and building the Virginia & Truckee Railroad; more often it benefited the populace, developing resources and jobs. In the early years Ralston was cautious regarding examinations of loan applications and proffered collateral.[3] As time passed, he became less prudent.

In 1873 financial institutions east of the Mississippi suffered the greenback panic that culminated on Black Thursday, September 18. Jay Cooke and Company, the most influential of U.S. financiers, failed. Banks collapsed, European investors lost $600 million, the New York Stock Exchange closed for ten days (its first closure since its formation in 1792), and America was plunged into recession.

Earlier that year, tight money had combined with Ralston's extravagances to cause the Bank of California to reel. On February 19, 1873, Ralston announced that companies he financed could pay neither interest nor anything on the principal of their loans. George P. Kimball and Company owed $578,580; the New Montgomery Street Real Estate Company owed $1,971,700; the Pacific Woolen Mills Company owed $967,900. Private funds eased the crisis. John D. Fry and the Bank of California entered an agreement: Fry advanced the bank $3,500,000 in return for the securities indemnifying the debt.[4]

Such was the faith in Ralston's capacity that the directors issued no call for censure and no request for restraint in future dealings. The exception was bank president D. O. Mills. He resigned in July, and Ralston succeeded him. In a confidential statement, fellow banker Henry D. Bacon said: "The general information at the time Mr. Mills resigned the presidency of the Bank, is the Bank was insolvent & that he knew it to be insolvent & he retired because he wanted to get out before it went by the board." Bank director Thomas Bell's assessment of the situation was similar. Bell said that Mills had advised Ralston to rein in his speculations, but instead Ralston had made things worse by beginning to build the Palace Hotel. Unbeknownst to Mills, Ralston kept two hundred and fifty bank shares in his name to retain the Mills association.[5]

Ralston often referred schemes to associates and would offer them financial backing if they wished to become involved. No one knew how many such ventures Ralston engaged in, but one involved a mine at Candelaria. Ralston sent a man needing financing to a friend, George S. Dodge: "In a day or two Dodge had bought and paid for the mine and proceeded at once to erect a great mill, though before that he was not known to have any money. He made a great fortune from it in the succeeding three years and passed for a shrewd operator, while Ralston's name was not mentioned in connection with the enterprise."[6]

In his bookkeeping Ralston used names of associates to head ledger accounts, wholly controlled by him. An attorney, Charles Lee Tilden, did an accounting of Ralston's Bank of California books after the banker's death and reported that one ledger account was headed by Burling Brothers brokerage, another by realtor Maurice Dore; through these accounts, Ralston purchased stocks and real estate.[7] One ledger, headed William Sharon, differed from the others. Since signing the contract in 1864, Sharon and Ralston were full partners in some California properties managed by Ralston and Nevada projects controlled by Sharon.[8]

At the end of 1873, Ralston began construction of a long-planned project entirely under his control, the Palace Hotel. He had already built the Grand Hotel and the California Theater, and his enthusiasm for the Palace Hotel was marked. He visited the site daily during construction. Because the bills were paid from his "William Sharon & Company" account, the press attributed it to Sharon. "Largest Hotel in the United States Now going Up Here" was the title of an item in the San Francisco *Real Estate Circular* at the end of 1873, which stated: "It will be six stories high; it will hold 1,200 guests and will cost about $600,000 . . . William Sharon will be the owner." Another article in the same publication was a dig at the Comstock millionaire headed "Squeezing Sharon." It told of a workman who owned a lot on the property intended for the Palace Hotel. The article concluded: "As it was Mr. Sharon who wanted the property, [the owner] thought he would be easy with him, and therefore let him have it for $30,000—over three times what it was worth."[9]

The purchase price was nothing compared to construction costs. Projected at $1,750,000, that amount was expended before the foundation reached street level. "It was carried to completion as regardless of cost as might an Egyptian king have built a pyramid. Its foundation walls were made twelve feet in thickness, and beneath its huge central court was constructed a reservoir containing 650,000 gallons of water."[10] Ralston used bricks and mortar and created the massive reservoir to withstand fire; to protect it from earthquakes he used iron bars built into the bricks and bolted together, running the length of each wall. Sharon commented:

> Ralston was disposed to scatter. If he got into anything there was no end to it. . . . In building the Palace Hotel he wanted to get some oak planks for it and he bought a ranch for a very large sum of money and never used a plank from it. When he wanted to make the furniture for the Hotel he bought the Kimball Manufacturing Company. I said to him, "If you are going to buy a factory for a nail, a ranch for a plank, and a manufactory to build furniture, where is this thing going to end?" He said, "It does look ridiculous to you." "Yes," said I.[11]

But at the end of 1873, Ralston's overspending was not an issue of concern. The bank and its ring were infused by excitement in Virginia City. In the second week of May, rumors of a rich strike at its lower level prompted a jump in Savage mine stock from $72 to $125. In sympathy all stocks rose. The Bank Ring's Belcher and the Crown Point mines were beginning to produce the best of their rich ore. The Belcher yielded $10,525,000 worth of ore in 1873, the Crown Point $7,307,258 during the year ending May 1, 1874.[12]

Early in the 1870s, John Mackay and the Bonanza Firm used profits from their Hale & Norcross mine to purchase a seemingly barren property between the Ophir mine and the Gould & Curry—the Consolidated Virginia mine. Through the 1860s investors had sunk over a million dollars into the worthless section, so the cost of buying it was perhaps less than $50,000. The original Comstock ore body dipped eastward 40 to 47 degrees, and the Consolidated Virginia was many hundreds of feet downslope. The Bonanza Firm speculated that ore in that section would be found only far beneath the surface. They proposed to use the Gould & Curry shaft and not begin horizontal drifting until thirteen hundred feet.[13]

Sharon, controlling the Gould & Curry, is said to have remarked: "I'll help those Irishmen lose some of their Hale & Norcross money."[14] It was his most spectacular miscalculation. They began operations in January 1872, and by the fall of 1873 took two hundred tons of ore daily. Five mills were run to reduce it. Eliot Lord enthused: "No discovery which matches it has been made on this earth from the day when the first miner struck a ledge with his rude pick until the present."[15]

The day of his election to the U.S. Senate, January 13, 1875, Sharon abruptly returned to San Francisco. Ophir mine stocks needed attending. Like Jay Cooke in New York in the 1860s (and Daniel Drew and Cornelius Vanderbilt in earlier years), Sharon drove the San Francisco market. In the 1860s the saying "as rich as Jay Cooke" had become popular. After making his fortune selling government bonds, Cooke directed the gold market and Wall Street's stock exchange. He prodded or curbed speculators, inflating or deflating stock prices as he deemed necessary.[16] In the 1870s Sharon controlled the San Francisco stock exchange in similar fashion. Speculators spied to see what Sharon bought or sold so they might follow suit. It was common knowledge that he issued cross orders, making an apparent sale of stock when he was buying. Brokers called one order he used a "settler." He would sell two thousand shares of several principal stocks, breaking the price of the entire list. With prices driven down, he bought, everyone else bought, prices rose, and stocks could be resold at a profit.[17]

In August 1874, using inside information, he bought between 20,000 and 30,000 shares of Ophir at $20. On October 25, 1874, the *Territorial Enterprise* reported that the Consolidated Virginia bonanza, with prospects beyond estimate, appeared to extend through the California mine into the Ophir.

By September a share of Ophir rose to $52. Sharon bought James R. Keene's block of stock and employed him to corner the market. Sharon hoped to secure over half the 100,800 shares before the stockholders' meeting on December 13; he was not only buying, but selling short—agreeing to sell at less than the purchasing price after his trustees were elected. Keene now bought shares at $75 or $80 when they were selling at $60 dollars. But Sharon's plan was stymied, because E. J. 'Lucky' Baldwin held the block of shares that controlled the mine. He forced Sharon to pay his price, $135 a share for 20,000 shares. At the same time, when it became known that Ralston was investing heavily, the price went to over $300 a share.[18]

With Sharon buying Baldwin's shares, the outcome was a foregone conclusion. The results of December's Ophir election were: President J. D. Fry; Directors A. K. P. Harmon, James Freeborn, Joseph Sharon, James H. Dobinson, Maurice Dore, and James A. Pritchard. Regarding the trustees, the San Francisco *Chronicle* observed: "The chief stockholder of the bank has a cousin by marriage; one it owns by right of appropriation, making use of him as St. Paul utilized his hired house at Athens; another is a brother; another is a private secretary [to D. O. Mills]; another is the land agent and confidential real estate operator of the bank; and the remainder are presumably friendly birds, as they are of the same plumage and roost in the same cage." These insiders were the Bank Ring's key Comstock managers. Fry was on the board of twelve of the major mines, Harmon on sixteen, and Dobinson on eleven.[19]

For a month after Sharon gained control of the Ophir, speculative mania caused stocks to soar. While continuing to encourage others to buy, Sharon surreptitiously sold his stocks. At the New Year, shares in the Consolidated Virginia climbed to $700 and those in the California mine reached nearly $800. Ophir stock rose to $315. Suddenly the public realized the mines were overvalued. Fear turned into panic. Stocks were thrown on the market. Shares fell to one-third their former value. (The Ophir had struck a vein that, although separate from the Consolidated Virginia's, yielded ore worth $4,351,492. But Sharon's directors declared no dividends.)[20]

One of those who lost heavily on Sharon's advice was Virginia City attorney Charles E. DeLong. He served as a member of Nevada's State Constitutional Convention and was the U.S. minister to Japan during the first years of that government's reform. A gifted orator, DeLong often spoke at Nevada rallies and public meetings.[21] After the crash Ralston responded to a note from DeLong's wife, expressing regret that DeLong held a large amount of Ophir stock but saying that others were confident of a future for the mine. On January 31, 1875, DeLong wrote to his wife:

> I am a little sorry you wrote to Ralston, and not specially pleased with his answer—Damn these monied aristocrats, they have no hearts no gallantry. . . .
>
>   I fear that this whole Ophir job was put up by Sharon and that he cruelly and wickedly advised his friends to buy and to keep buying and to hold when he himself was selling and that he then as wickedly as sin contributed all in his power to smash the market, thus getting his stock sold for 250 & 300 back at from 90 to 150. If this is true the man is a demon and deserves destruction.[22]

DeLong's anger at Ralston was misplaced. Ralston had lost so heavily in Ophir stock, it gave rise to a rumor that a conspiracy existed between Keene and Sharon to break him. The rumor was untrue. There was no conspiracy; all lost, except Sharon.[23]

Chapter Eight

FAILURE

IN 1875 SHARON'S FATHER, still a bank director in Smithfield, Ohio, died at age eighty-three. After Clara's wedding Sharon's wife Maria took to her bed. She was forty-two, suffering from stomach cancer. Living as an invalid for several years, she suffered her illness patiently and died on May 14, 1875. Sharon, continually at her bedside toward the end, was with her the afternoon she died. Besides her husband and Clara, sixteen-year-old Frederick and twelve-year-old Flora survived Maria. How the deaths affected Sharon is impossible to ascertain. No personal letters or papers have survived, and it is not reported that he exhibited any change in habits. Yet another tragedy—its effects on Sharon made apparent—loomed.

On February 20, 1875, a radical bill passed by an almost unanimous vote of both houses of the Nevada legislature. It replaced the Storey County bullion tax—25 cents on $100—with a tax identical to that levied on all other property—$1.50 on $100. Sharon did not oppose the new taxation; in fact, his manipulation was thought to be behind the proposal. Without new taxes, the Storey County fund that paid his railroad bonds might have been insufficient.[1]

Mackay, Fair, Flood, and O'Brien, working the great bonanza in the Consolidated Virginia and California mines, were infuriated. They would be forced to pay six times as much in taxes as Sharon's group had paid through the years, and their Consolidated Virginia and California mines would be funding the Bank Ring's railroad. The owners of the new bonanza declared war on Sharon. They attacked his income source by refusing to pay any tax. Several years passed before the courts forced payment.

They gave notice of striking further on May 19, filing a certificate of incorporation for the Nevada Bank of San Francisco, which would soon rival the Bank of California.[2]

Early in 1875, along with the market crash, California banks suffered a sudden cash drain. Depression had arrested finance in the East since the panic of '73, and the federal government, reestablishing gold backing for the dollar, now recalled old paper currency. Gold purchases in the East combined with the expense of shipping California's wheat crop to market to withdraw $20 million from circulation. In March H. R. Linderman, director of the U.S. Mint, informed Ralston that Mr. Morgan of Drexel, Morgan and Company (almost certainly Pierpont Morgan; the company later became J. P. Morgan & Company) expected the lockup of coin to continue until May 1.[3] As cash-flow problems continued past the projected date, Ralston and his bank were squeezed.

On May 20 the *San Francisco Chronicle* attacked the Bank Ring's management of the Ophir. Identifying Sharon as controlling the mine, it pointed out that assessments were levied even though 150 tons of ore were being taken out each day. The ore's reported value varied from forty dollars to seven hundred dollars per ton, said the paper, depending on whether management wished to raise or depress the stock. The article included salvos fired at the *Territorial Enterprise* and the *Gold Hill News*, noting that Sharon owned interests in both and their "highly wrought descriptive accounts" of strikes were part of a scheme inducing citizens to invest.[4]

Sharon's practices were coming under scrutiny, but his partner's were being more intently watched. In 1866, dying of cholera, William Ralston's brother James cautioned William to give up speculating in favor of more conservative banking practices. In 1875 another brother, Andrew, who had replaced Sharon as the bank's agent in Virginia City, came to San Francisco to similarly caution William. Andrew worried that some of those around his brother could not be trusted. William replied that people were ungrateful for what he did, and he was under a heavy load, but he thought he saw his way out.[5]

Bank Ring member Thomas Bell believed that the Bank of California's great success made William Ralston heedless. He commented that Ralston "seemed to have lost his head," attempting to control politics and other affairs as well as banking business. Sharon-run businesses, the Union Mill and Mining Company and the Virginia & Truckee Railroad, were garnering inordinate profits. Ralston was plunging from one speculation to another and losing heavily.[6]

A friend of Sharon's reported that Sharon warned William Ralston on more than one occasion "to pull in his sails." The friend said Sharon urged Ralston to rely on the railroad, mining low-grade ore and the milling company for his income. Asked by Sharon what he would do if no more bonanzas were found. Ralston reportedly replied: "Go to the cemetery."[7]

Attorney Joseph M. Nogues later charged that Sharon knew for many months that the bank might fail. Sharon had been William Ralston's partner for twelve years. He knew that Ralston used the bank's assets without supervision. He knew how the banker had financed their Comstock practices from the time he approved loans on mills that had little chance of success. Gambling that mines would strike ore, Ralston allowed large drafts for building the railroad and draws for the Union Mill and Mining Company in excess of what was deposited.[8] It was Sharon who reported that at one time the bank sank $3 million of its $5 million capital into the uncertain mining industry.

In 1874–75 William Ralston poured millions of dollars into the Palace Hotel, purchased large amounts of expensive stocks, continued developing New Montgomery Street, and lost millions in the Ophir crash. It would have been apparent to Sharon that Ralston had tapped bank funds, but after the fact, Sharon denied knowing anything was amiss.[9] His denial was necessary because, as Ralston's partner, he could be held liable for the banker's illegal business activities.

Ralston's extravagances reached their pinnacle in the construction of the Palace Hotel. But excesses in building his residence early in 1875 had caused Sharon to remark: "He never beat a retreat until he struck the ocean. In building the Pine Street house, it was to cost $25,000. The first

thing I knew it was up to $225,000."[10] Attorney Reuben Lloyd spoke
about the house to illustrate that at the end Ralston was not in his right
mind: "He spent three hundred and fifty thousand dollars, as we found
out. The way he would do a thing,—he would lay a plank and spike it
down,—then he would lay another plank on top of that and spike that
down, and then another and so on. . . . I think the man was worked out
mentally."[11]

Other perceptions challenge Sharon and Lloyd, saying that Ralston
had never spared expenses. When building Belmont, he spent $50,000
on stables. A friend related an anecdote about Ralston's visiting the studio
of the artist Thomas Hill. Hill's landscapes covered the walls; Ralston
glanced about, asked how much for everything, paid a generous price, and
hung the paintings throughout Belmont.[12]

Construction superintendent Henry L. King oversaw the building of
Ralston's Pine Street house while supervising construction of the Palace
Hotel. He said the house cost $140,000, an inordinate amount for the era
but substantially less than the others' estimates. King also illustrated why
costs ran so high. Ralston owned the West Coast Furniture Company.
In "fitting" the dining room at the house, the company charged $7,000 or
$8,000 for a job worth not more than $2,000. The company sent King a
new buggy so he would endorse the bill, and King informed Ralston. The
banker "laughed and said [the buggy] was the only return he ever got
for his expenditure and trouble in building up that concern." Ralston's extravagances in construction were nothing new. King undertook various
jobs for him through the years, including building a ballroom on the rear
of his house for a one-night event. Ralston was hosting a ball to appease
his wife, Lizzie, after a quarrel. King completed the work, leaving two men
to stay the night and tear it all down at sunrise.[13]

No matter his state of mind, and whether his excesses were now more
pronounced, in the spring of 1875 the banker suffered serious problems.
He had always provided money for others, but now he could not get it for
himself. In early May 1875, Ralston asked Sharon to buy his half of the Palace Hotel. Knowing how much the hotel meant to him, Sharon must have

understood the catastrophic straits in which Ralston found himself. Sharon agreed to pay $1,750,000 for the hotel. A short time later, saying he was unable to raise the cash, Sharon reneged and returned the deed.[14]

In July, when the Board of Directors' examining committee counted the bank's cash, they found over $2,000,000—the amount expected. It turned out that Ralston had borrowed the money for the accounting and returned it the next day, and that over the years he had left signed tags for cash he was appropriating from the bank vault. The actual amount of cash in the bank was $500,000, the rest accounted for by tags.[15]

There is no indication that Ralston speculated in self-interest; earning healthy returns for the bank (investors received 1 percent monthly) appears to have been his motive. Later he was struggling to find a way out of his ever more desperate predicament. The banker purchased three-fifths of the stocks of the Spring Valley Water Company at high prices, expecting to sell them to the city of San Francisco at a still higher price. Spring Valley through the years acquired watersheds, reservoir properties, and rights-of-way to transport water from hills south of the city through aqueducts to San Francisco, which lacked fresh water. In 1865 it provided 2,360,000 gallons of water a day to the city. In 1875 it provided over 11 million gallons, with stocks valued at $10 million. In early June the question of buying the concern came before city supervisors who, finally approving the deal, sent it to an appointed Board of Water Commissioners. The mayor opposed the purchase, and in late July the board rejected it.[16]

Bank secretary Stephen Franklin asserted that only $10 million remained in circulation in California by August 1, 1875, and the daily movements of money in and out of the bank ranged from $6 million to $9 million.[17] Ralston desperately needed to refill the bank's coffers. He sold a sixteen-thousand-acre tract of rich central California agricultural land to J. D. Fry for the bargain price of $90,000. After the fact, an audit discovered that he also issued a certificate of deposit for $500,000 that was not recorded on the bank's books; borrowed against Southern Pacific bonds worth $300,000, left with him by Leland Stanford; and, overissued $1,300,000 of bank stock—each activity transacted in secret.[18] The stocks were sold through Burling Brothers, a wealthy, trustworthy brokerage. They would find a savings bank or individual to act as a lender. The brokerage would present its note together with Ralston's certificate, stating that the stock would be delivered upon request. Whenever these loans fell due, Burling Brothers, by an interchange of their checks for Ralston's, paid the interest and renewed them.[19]

In early August the stock market was "feverish, active and higher." On the 5th, Ophir stock rose to $77, California to $75 and Consolidated Virginia to $360. Then they slipped during the next three weeks until, on the 24th, the Ophir was at $59, the California at $62, and the Consolidated Virginia at $305.[20] In mid-August Ralston's sales of property caused "quiet talking" among brokers and bankers. On the 21st muttering and rumors increased as people connected with the bank transferred property into other names. A few men of finance withdrew considerable sums.[21]

D. O. Mills testified that the first time he knew of the bank's trouble was three days before its failure.[22] Sharon approached him with the news that Ralston wanted to sell his railroad stock. If Mills would buy it at $700,000, Sharon would take half. Mills went to Ralston to make an offer for the railroad stock and $123,000 worth of bonds. Ralston asked for $900,000, to which Mills responded: "Mr. Ralston, we have already offered a larger price, as I think, for this railroad stock, and that amounts to $823,000; surely if you only need $900,000, that is not very far out of the way for the raising of that amount." Ralston accepted the offer.[23] In reporting the sale the *San Francisco Alta* remarked that Mills paid "fifty cents on the dollar of the railroad's cash valuation."[24]

Ralston's maneuvers to sell the Spring Valley Water Company now came under attack from the *San Francisco Call*. The *Call* was a one-bit paper (the cost of a weekly subscription being 12 ½ cents) in a town of two-bit dailies. Its readers were laboring men. The *Call* and sister evening publication the *San Francisco Bulletin* were not afraid to attack the rich and powerful.[25] In a secret interview with the *Call* and *Bulletin* editors, D. O. Mills discussed Ralston's financial difficulties and Spring Valley dealings.[26] The *Call* editorialized that the "ring of schemers . . . are seeking to pile up a debt of millions for working people to pay," and the *Call* and the *Bulletin* attacked candidates for supervisor "who are secretly pledged to vote and work in the interests of the Spring Valley Water Company."[27]

With Ralston under siege and without resources, James C. Flood of the Bonanza Kings notified him that they planned to close their substantial account. Ralston rushed to meet Flood, who agreed to leave the money in the bank several days more. Hearing of the interaction, the newspapers conjectured that Flood sought to create financial difficulty for Ralston. The principals gave interviews, speaking of their friendship, and denied the withdrawal.[28] In fact, Flood and Mackay were personal friends of Ralston's, "though not of William Sharon."[29]

On August 23 a quiet run began on the bank, and Ralston turned to London's Oriental Bank. The prestigious institution served as agent for the Bank of California in England (although years earlier it had rebuked Ralston for drawing twice the agreed limit of $1.25 million). He gave Oriental Bank agent and Bank Ring member Thomas Bell a stack of the bank's bills receivable, asking Bell to cable London, assure them securities were in hand, and ask for credit. A reply never came.[30]

Using the remnants of his previously incomparable influence, Ralston prevailed upon the president of a depository belonging to various companies to take all available bullion and mint it into coin. On August 25, hoping to quiet nervous depositors, Ralston piled the bank's counters high with new twenty-dollar gold pieces. A similar ploy had worked in 1869, and after depositor confidence was restored, Ralston had returned the money. This time the tactic failed.[31]

On several consecutive mornings in late August, B. F. Sherwood, Sharon's confidential broker, met with Sharon. Nothing was said of the bank's health, although Sherwood had heard talk of large transfers of real estate by Bank of California officers. On Thursday the 26th, after a 10 A.M. meeting, Sherwood called partner Joseph L. King into their private office, saying they needed to cash all their checks that morning. "The Bank of California will close this afternoon at 3 p.m.," he told him, "and not re-open tomorrow."[32]

The night before, on the 25th, millionaire broker James Keene had visited Ralston, offering to lend him $1 million, but Ralston declined.[33] At the same time the bank's Board of Directors met at Sharon's house. The bank cashier informed the directors that a considerable amount of cash that should be in the vault was not there. It also came to light that Ralston had appropriated $2,600,000 in bullion ($600,000 of which belonged to Flood and O'Brien) from refineries for his own account. Bank secretary Stephen Franklin put Ralston's debt to the bank at $4,000,000; Bell believed the figure was $4,500,000.[34]

On the 26th one large firm drew out $250,000, as did Lucky Baldwin, a loyal Ralston friend, who would not demand the balance of his reported $2 million until the bank might better be able to pay. E. P. Peckham instructed a number of friends to cash checks for him. Few others were aware of the bank's dire situation.[35]

Early that day the bank cashier came to Sharon and Mills. "That was the first time I knew the bank was in trouble," testified Mills, contradicting his testimony that he had known it was in trouble when he bought Ralston's railroad stock three days before. Later that morning, Ralston, Mills, and Sharon met at the bank with parties representing Flood and the Bonanza Firm. Sharon offered the bank $5 million of its capital stock and another $2 ½ million if Flood and his partners would assume the liabilities above that. On examining the bank's books, Flood's representatives declined the offer.[36]

There seemed to be no knowledge of the impending disaster among brokers when the San Francisco Stock and Exchange Board opened on August 26. Joseph L. King, later board chairman, commented: "Should any one have said to the average business man of San Francisco on Thursday, August 26, 1875, that the Bank of California would suspend that day; well, he would not have been believed. The bank was regarded in the same light as the United States Treasury."[37] At the 11 A.M. session, stock board members entered in usual fashion: "The members were laughing, jostling and settling into chairs." Then Sharon torpedoed the market. King noted: "Any order ever executed, in regular or informal session, was dwarfed by the great selling order sent by Sharon into the 11 O'clock session."[38]

Sharon used a broker named B. B. Rorke, who sold as long as there was a bid on the floor. Rorke did not even record the transactions, relying instead on the clerk and purchasers to record them. King and others quickly recognized that it was an unlimited selling order. Buyers became wary, "and only a part of the immense order could be executed on the call." The three principal stocks fell: California from 59 ½ to 48, Consolidated Virginia from 290 to 240 and Ophir from 54 to 36.[39]

No one at the Stock and Exchange Board mentioned the catastrophe they feared until the informal 2 P.M. session began. Then brokers began to talk of a run. Rumors flew that Sharon was seeking all available funds to shore up the Bank of California. Contrary to the rumors, Sharon deposited his earnings in Wells Fargo.

If the great institution could make it to closing time, perhaps it could regroup. At 2:15 P.M. the crowd at the bank was out the doors. By 2:30 it was to the street. King reported: "I looked into the bank over the heads of the crowd, say about 2:40 P.M., and Mr. Ralston was at the counter with Nicholson, the paying teller. Obviously, the order was given to pay out no more money. The porters closed the iron doors."[40]

An *Alta* reporter spoke with Ralston, asking what had caused the suspension. "Scarcity of coin in circulation—scarcity of coin obtainable," answered Ralston. He expected relief about October 1, when returns from wheat sales would be received. Asked if Flood and O'Brien had withdrawn $1.8 million the previous day, he said: "It is all nonsense, all balderdash." Relations with them, he insisted, were agreeable.[41]

When the bank closed its doors, a committee of four directors, including Bell and Mills, began to examine the books.[42] Though not a board member, Mills said he felt a moral responsibility for what occurred. "I walked the floor of my office, determining what course to take. I concluded that I would go down stairs and take off my coat and do all I could with those people to help them. . . . We were all full of trouble."[43]

Ralston called the staff together, saying the bank would not resume business. He complimented them on their fidelity, asking them to deport themselves as gentlemen in the trying circumstances. He promised each "a first class position." He was going to start a new life. Secretary Stephen

Franklin commented that the meeting was touching and characteristic of the "liberal and considerate" Ralston.[44] A dispatch was sent to Andrew Ralston in Virginia City, ordering him to publish an announcement that the bank's Virginia City and Gold Hill branches were compelled to suspend.[45]

That night, Ralston sent for A. A. Cohen, longtime associate. Cohen reports that Ralston said: "[I hope] to realize the assets of the Bank and to pay every dollar that is due to my depositors, and at least pay a large dividend out to the stockholders. . . . I do not expect to leave much to my children, but I do want to leave them a good name and that no man shall ever say that he lost a dollar by me."[46] But with his financial future convoluted by all that was happening and with pressure mounting, the next morning Ralston deeded all his property to his partner, William Sharon.

The same day, Sharon advised the bank directors to take action. Mills said: "I think Mr. Sharon made the first suggestion that it would be necessary that Mr. Ralston should resign." Mills conceded he might have agreed that "it was the proper thing to do."[47] Around noon on the 27th, the directors' committee reported that Ralston had taken large sums of cash. Bell said: "This statement of affairs was perfectly appalling; there seemed nothing possible but to throw the Bank into bankruptcy."[48]

A *Call* reporter dropped into the bank: "Senator Jones was talking in a rather excited manner to Mr. Ralston in one corner, the latter listening attentively, and evidently perplexed about the subject in debate." The reporter told Ralston that Flood doubted the bank could pay its depositors in full. Ralston insisted they would be paid to the last cent and commented that Flood's statement was rather unkind. When the reporter asked if assistance from friends could have staved off the difficulty, he called it "rather a sour subject" and dismissed him.[49]

Later Lucky Baldwin's attorney, Reuben Lloyd, met with Ralston, saying he seemed "completely collapsed." Cohen disagreed: "I saw [Ralston] two or three times in the morning. He seemed to be quite composed, meeting the situation with perfect self possession." Francis Newlands agreed with Cohen, reporting that while the directors were meeting, Ralston sat "apparently the most unconscious of all the rushing throng that surged around and through it."[50]

The *Call* reported that a meeting was called at 1 P.M. Ralston entered the room after the directors. "Mr. Mills, without further preliminaries, opened the meeting by informing Mr. Ralston that the Directors desired him to resign . . . after which Mr. Mills requested him to leave the apartment. All this took place within a few minutes."[51]

Flood's messenger, George Upshur, said that he was in attorney W. H. L. Barnes's outer office when Ralston, hatless, hurried in and met with Barnes in his private office. Upshur reported that after five minutes "we heard a door, leading from Barnes' office into the hall, slam. Ralston had gone."[52]

On the street Ralston bumped into Dr. John Pitman, telling him he was going to bathe in the ocean. Pitman warned him that he appeared overheated and should forego the swim. Ralston told him that resigning the bank presidency lifted the burden from him, and "[he] felt like a school boy off for his holidays."[53]

Ralston, who periodically bathed in the ocean, walked to Neptune Baths at North Beach. It was about half past three and stifling. Ralston, smiling, acknowledged the keeper, who told him, "You look pretty warm, Mr. Ralston." Ralston replied, "I will rub myself well and take a shower-bath." About twenty minutes later, two men reported something wrong with a swimmer. The keeper saw a man struggling far out in the water and exclaimed, 'MY GOD! IT'S RALSTON!'" By the time rescuers could get to him, he was floating face down. A physician arrived and kept up artificial respiration for an hour to no effect. As the news spread, men wept on the streets.[54] The occurrences of the last two days excited other emotions as well: "The very air seemed to inspire the feeling of panic. Not since the reign of the Vigilance Committee in '56, had there been such a spirit of uncontrolled and wild excitement manifest."[55]

On the Comstock, news of the bank's suspension and Ralston's death was met with incredulity and horror. The *Gold Hill News* reported: "No man, whose coin is not in his absolute possession, knows how much he is worth or how utterly bankrupted he may be."[56] Citizens hovered around the paper's bulletin board, waiting for releases. Rumors spread up and down the streets: that Andrew Ralston "blowed his brains out"; that Jim Keene shot and killed Sharon; and that a mob gutted the San Francisco offices of the *Call* and *Bulletin*.

The report of a mob attacking the *Call* and *Bulletin* offices was based in truth. A hastily called meeting had garnered a crowd of as many as ten thousand people. Leaders roused the listeners, who moved on the news offices before state militia turned them away.[57]

E. S. Tibbey told of a Sharon transgression at Ralston's death. Tibbey had copied Ralston and Sharon's articles of association when they were drawn up years earlier. Ralston kept his sealed transcript at the bank. Tibbey reported: "Upon Ralston's death Sharon called for that envelope and out the side of it took his paper out, replaced the envelope and said there was nothing in it."[58] With the immensity of Ralston's indebtedness surfacing, Sharon was denying the partnership.

Writer Gertrude Atherton, granddaughter of the venerable bank secretary, Stephen Franklin, related another offense on the evening of Ralston's death. All Ralston's closest associates were gathered at Colonel Fry's home, where the body lay in a temporary metallic casket: "That night Mr. Sharon said to my grandfather, 'Best thing he could have done.'"[59]

With Ralston's burial (up to half the city's population was estimated to have followed the hearse to Lone Mountain Cemetery), the public began to castigate those believed responsible. The Bonanza Kings were blamed for opening their bank, and many San Franciscans refused to do business at the new concern.[60] The *Call* and the *Bulletin* suffered directly as well, as five hundred subscriptions were canceled and two and a half columns of advertising were withdrawn from the *Bulletin*. Even subsequent to his death, the papers had criticized Ralston's policies in hopes of influencing the imminent election. Thousands revolted by voting for those Ralston had supported.[61]

Blame for Ralston's demise was also assigned to his associates. The *San Francisco Chronicle* said: "Mr. Ralston in the hour of his extremity, and at the moment when he most needed encouragement, was abandoned by those who should have felt their fortunes linked to his own." *Chronicle of the Builders* writer George H. Morrison, after interviewing many of the principals, wrote: "Many of his aides were incompetent; others thwarted him because of greed; still others betrayed him."[62] The *Alta* quoted Leland Stanford as saying that he could not understand why the directors did not help. He listed thirteen of them, estimating each one's worth; all were worth over $1 million, several over $5 million, and Mills and Sharon over $10 million each.[63]

D. O. Mills had asked Ralston for his resignation, initiating the action that led to his death. The *San Francisco Chronicle* editorialized that Ralston had transplanted Mills from country banker to the head of the state's greatest institution. Ralston, it pointed out, carried the burden while Mills traveled and "absorbed twelve millions of dollars." Of all others, it argued, Mills should not have deserted his friend.[64]

Joseph Nogues, attorney for Mrs. Lizzie Ralston, later accused Mills of complicity in breaking public confidence in the bank. When Mills said he had no recollection of exposing Ralston's financial position to the editors of the *Call* and the *Bulletin,* Noques asked if he had told them of Ralston's Spring Valley Water stock:

> *A.* I do not think I did.

> *Q.* Did you not inform them of the fact that he was trying to sell it for the purpose of realizing money to relieve himself from [financial] embarrassment?

> *A.* There might have been something of that said; I presume so—something of that sort. I do not remember anything that amounted to any particular meeting on the subject, or any particular talk.[65]

But for those assessing blame, the primary wrongdoer was Sharon. Charles Foreman, a Bank of California stockholder, believed the bank had failed in large part because Sharon refused to help. He commented: "Sharon owed everything he had to Ralston, as I have had it from his own lips and from Ralston's lips, and ought to have been willing to stand by his benefactor."[66] In a letter to Bertha Ralston Bright, Ralston's daughter, Ralston's friend Dr. John Pitman wrote: "[Ralston] had for some time been pursued by Senator Sharon, whose manipulations caused the suspension of the Bank of California, which was totally unnecessary, as the bank was solvent; but Sharon played his cards causing the suspension."[67]

Why did Sharon act as he did? To those who attributed malevolent motives to him, speculation centered on two possible scenarios: he was attempting to ruin the Bonanza Kings; or he wished to ruin Ralston.[68] In support of the first theory, it can be said that Sharon used the tactic of selling at any price to damage the fortunes of Jones and Hayward in 1872, and his action on August 26 did wound Flood, who was heavily involved in the market, and may have nicked O'Brien, who was a member of the stock board but rarely took part. It did not injure the other two; Mackay and Fair were practical miners, who took pains to insist they did not speculate.[69] The group's wealth emanated not from stocks but from the richest ore body in Comstock history. Sharon knew breaking the market would not break them.

The conjecture that Sharon was seeking to bring down his friend is easier to sustain, considering his "best thing he could have done" comment and the fact that he proposed Ralston resign the bank presidency. But Ralston maintained the utmost faith in their friendship, exemplified in the deeding of his property to Sharon. Although Sharon disparaged Ralston's manner of conducting business, nowhere did he intimate that Ralston was anything but a friend. Francis Newlands, Judge John Currey, and Alfred Bates, who interviewed Sharon's associates for the Bancroft biography of Sharon, all stated that fidelity to friends was part of Sharon's makeup. Treachery remains a possibility, but a third explanation is more consistent with Sharon's character.

After the bank's collapse and upon Ralston's death, friends and employees came forward in support of the deceased. D. O. Mills, William Sharon, and Thomas Bell did not. When they looked at how Ralston had managed the bank, culminating with the revelations of August 25, they simply decided not to rescue him. Contrary to reports that Ralston was composed at the end of his life, Bell remarked that the banker "seemed to have lost his head"; Sharon spoke of his never-ending "extravagances"; and Mills disassociated himself from his partner.

Twelve years earlier, a cheat had bankrupted Sharon. Now, in August 1875, his partner's creditors—thanks to his partner's behavior—threatened Sharon's fortune. His pastime was poker, an extension of economic competition wherein each individual succeeds or loses. In a crisis Sharon's instinct would have been to act in self-interest. Other financiers of the era, including Jay Gould and Andrew Carnegie, did so, to the ruin of their associates.[70] Sharon did so in selling his Ophir stock and in tearing up the contract of partnership. Facing the bank's imminent failure, he acted with disregard for his partner. Did he do it with the intent to cause Ralston's demise? The facts suggest only that he was protecting his own wealth. Nevertheless, to his discredit—whatever his motive—his actions precipitated the tragedy.

Chapter Nine

REBIRTH

BECAUSE BRANCH OFFICES on the Comstock closed their doors along with the mother bank, D. O. Mills sent word to H. M. Yerington to open a Virginia & Truckee Railroad account with Wells Fargo. A week later, the railroad announced: "The affairs of the Virginia and Truckee Railroad are in no way embarrassed by the suspension of the Bank of California and everything connected therewith is moving on as usual." Mills also informed Yerington that Sharon's business affairs appeared to be in order.[1] That Mills checked on Sharon was prudent. He was about to follow him into an unprecedented enterprise.

When the Bank of California directors began meeting again, Mills and attorney Samuel Wilson took the lead. The situation was dire; there seemed to be no way to resolve it but to declare bankruptcy. "There would be a dead halt in all operations of Pacific Coast finance." Half of California's circulating capital would be paralyzed, perhaps for many months.[2]

Ralston's attorney, W. H. L. Barnes, now took action. He advised the directors that if they attempted to file for bankruptcy, he would bring suit against each of them personally. They were guilty of neglecting their oversight duties—the bank had been insolvent for months. Moreover, it was a felony for corporation directors to collect unearned dividends. Their dividends, adding up to $6 million over ten years, continued after February 1873, when Ralston's $3.5 million debt virtually bankrupted the bank.[3] At the same time attorney Reuben Lloyd, representing Lucky Baldwin, the bank's largest creditor, told Sharon what Barnes told the others: "If something is not done, I shall have to attach every piece of property you have in the world, and hold you personally responsible."[4]

Other problems confronted Sharon. The money he had made rushing the stock market was needed. The Palace Hotel was nearing completion, and Sharon needed to pay the workers. He also directed the manager to continue hiring personnel, including the first staff of African Americans to serve as waiters, porters, and chambermaids in San Francisco.[5]

On Sunday, August 29th, the *San Francisco Alta,* attempting to assuage the public, announced: "The panic is over." The newspaper said confidence was being restored, pointing to diminished agitation in the streets. At the same time a *Bulletin* editorial predicted that the Bank of California would now disappear, creating financial trouble for many. That night, the *Bulletin*'s perception was closer to the truth. Bell reported: "Sunday intervening, gave the Board time to consider the dreadful effects of bankruptcy."[6]

Sharon was in the most precarious position. Although Sharon denied that a contract existed, the Ralston-Sharon partnership in mining and real estate was common knowledge. Mills later commented that either one or both of them told him they owned a lot of bank stock jointly as well.[7] By any measure, Sharon was Ralston's partner. He was also a bank stockholder and Ralston's assignee.

A writer for the *San Francisco Examiner* first used an oft-quoted metaphor: "[Sharon's] mind was like a battery, constantly radiating energy. . . . No scheme was too large for his wonderful mind to grasp, no detail too small for his memory to carry."[8] Now, amid the public frenzy and the directors' bewilderment, Sharon was formulating a plan. He listened to Lloyd argue that he and the others needed to "put [their] shoulders to the wheel, come in and put this thing on its feet again." Sharon balked, noting that he had contributed $4 million to his former partner's losing schemes.[9] But he had little choice. Liquidating the estate and letting the bank fail meant that Sharon's wealth would be attached.

The daunting task of reestablishing the bank would require three things: millions of dollars to pay creditors and restore its capital; the officers, directors, and stockholders remaining in their positions so the institution could maintain stability; and positive publicity to rebuild public faith. D. O. Mills would be crucial to fulfilling the first two requirements. To raise the required capital, Sharon thought to form a syndicate, calling on the city's prominent men to subscribe. Could Mills be talked into resuming the bank presidency and taking a lead role in forming the syndicate? He would lend credibility to the project and reintroduce a sense of security in the bank.

Sharon asked Mills to join him in subscribing $1 million each in order to convince others to join in the rebuilding. Mills turned him down, noting that he had given up his interest in the bank two and a half years earlier. Sharon demonstrated his hard edge, informing Mills that Ralston had never transferred his stock, so Mills still appeared as a stockholder. He pointed out further that while Mills was bank president, he had signed blank stock certificates that were part of the 13,180 overissued shares. Mills changed his mind. He would subscribe the million and accept the bank presidency, if Sharon would purchase the large Ralston debt from the bank.[10]

Sharon was beginning to realize the extent of Ralston's assets and consented to buy the debt for $2 million, as long as any profits above that amount would be his perquisites. Mills approved, but the next morning, after studying the books, Sharon balked at the price. He said, "I will take it at a million and a half, and if I get anything out of it, the bank shall have the credit of half a million more."[11] Mills agreed, and the directors, realizing this was their chance to get off the hook, acquiesced.[12]

Both Sharon's contemporaries and historians agree that his combination of business acumen and tenacity made the bank's resurrection possible. Historian and nineteenth-century banker Zoeth Skinner Eldredge observed that Ralston's liabilities to banks, firms, and individuals were so great and his ventures so complex and interwoven that "it was impossible to move on one part without moving on the whole."[13]

Lloyd commented that he never saw anyone display more energy than Sharon. Large, rough tables replaced the furniture in his parlors. Papers, pencils, and cigars filled the tables, and every morning at seven he came down to work. By nightfall, amid cigar smoke, the directors gathered in consultation. Night after night for six weeks, meetings continued.[14]

Sharon first sought to form the syndicate. In approaching prominent businessmen, he varied his ploys. Some were asked to help preserve Ralston's memory, while others were told how a reestablished bank would be stronger without the former president's extravagances. Francis Newlands said: "He appealed to the public spirit of some. He appealed to the pride of others. He encouraged the doubting. He threatened the cowardly."[15] James Keene originally subscribed $1 million. Thinking better of it, he told Sharon to take him off the list. Sharon talked with Mills and agreed to cut the subscription in half. Keene insisted on being released entirely. Knowing how critical it was to keep the powerful broker on the list, Sharon reduced the amount to $250,000 and guaranteed it in writing. Eldredge described other Sharon actions, saying he grabbed the pen from one subscriber who wanted to strike his name off the list. "He gave a verbal guaranty to Peter Donahue, who was a subscriber for a large amount. He told Michael Reese, a large creditor, that he would not be paid unless he subscribed."[16]

In one week Sharon collected pledges from sixty-three individuals and the Stock and Exchange Board, raising a total of $7,580,000, although this figure lists Keene's contribution at the original $1 million rather than $250,000. Most pledged $50,000 or more, including J. P. Jones, $200,000; A. A. Cohen, $200,000; Thomas Bell, $150,000; Henry Yerington, $100,000; J. D. Fry, $50,000; and Lucky Baldwin, with $1,700,000 still tied up in the bank, subscribing an additional $1 million.[17] I. Glazier and Company pledged $250,000, although it was known to "all the financial world" as a broker for the Bonanza Firm. Coll Deane was president of the Stock and Exchange Board. It made sense for the board to subscribe, but it may have been personally distasteful for Deane to work with Sharon and Mills. He later commented that Ralston's business mistakes "can be fairly traced to the disloyalty and treachery of those on whose fidelity and friendship he implicitly trusted."[18]

The *Alta,* the *Chronicle,* and other newspapers now began a steady rallying drumbeat, saying the bank was soon to reopen. In the *Territorial Enterprise* of September 3, editor Daggett used his uniquely florid prose to extol Sharon's efforts: "After all that has been said by a vindictive press about Mr. Sharon, his words . . . will give the people of the East a new idea of the man: 'I am worth fifteen millions in solid wealth and permanent real estate. Mr. Ralston was my friend; through him I made it, and I will devote the full half of it before there shall come a stain upon his honor.'"

At the same time Sharon was seeking subscribers, he was settling debts with Ralston's creditors. Questioning the contention that he knew nothing of Ralston's financial straits before the fact, Ralston biographer Cecil Tilton comments that Sharon's knowledge of claimants "strangely resembled" Ralston's. Sharon, Mills, and Bell quickly ensured that the bank's overseas transactions would continue by personally guaranteeing $1,250,000 to London's Oriental Bank.[19]

Another matter of immediate concern was the overissued stock. At the collapse of the bank, Sharon had taken his stocks and what he could borrow from other stockholders, canceling those certificates so the stock would not appear overissued.[20] He advised Odd Fellows Bank officials to "come in with the rest," although he had not yet closed with anyone. He told them that liquidating Ralston's estate would return only 25 percent of its real value and that with the entire load on his shoulders, a 50 percent payment was the best he could do. He promised to raise the amount in the future if possible, and they accepted the 50 percent. With other creditors who threatened legal action, he settled at close to full value.[21]

Sharon used the same approach with bank depositors. Joseph King told of an acquaintance whose entire savings was in the bank. Sharon offered the man sixty cents on the dollar. King told him to wait, that the bank would reopen, and "he surely would receive dollar for dollar. He did so and was made happy."[22]

Sharon needed a show of faith to reassure the public. His tip regarding the bank's closure had allowed brokers Joseph King and B. F. Sherwood to cash checks in order to accumulate gold coin. They now reciprocated by settling a $25,000 stock dispute and depositing the checks in the closed bank.[23] Yet the action did not stop "the clamor and harm" of certain newspapers; the *Bulletin,* using D. O. Mills as a source, reported Ralston's issue of fraudulent stock and his use of from $3 million to $4 million of the bank's money for himself.

Sharon and others met at Mills's house, and Mills sent letters by special dispatch to the *New York Herald* and Doten's *Gold Hill News* in Nevada. Mills denied *signing* any statement regarding fraudulent stock. The *New York Herald* publicized how Ralston's estate would pay his debt to the bank and how bank assets now exceeded liabilities.[24] Doten commented that Ralston had acted honestly in his predicament by signing his property to a friend to liquidate his debts and continued, "Moreover, it is now announced by that friend, William Sharon, that the property thus turned over will pay every debt of Mr. Ralston to the Bank of California and other corporations and individuals, and leave a surplus."[25]

The drumbeat continued, with interviews of Sharon, General George S. Dodge, and James Keene appearing in the *San Francisco Chronicle:* "The statement of the *Bulletin,* that there had been an over issue of stock, Mr. Sharon declared to be absolutely false. The records of the bank afforded no evidence of such over issue, and the thorough work of the Investigating Committee had not brought to view any such questionable transaction. Neither had the accounts been falsified." Dodge and Keene echoed Sharon and asserted that the Ralston-caused shortage would be easily repaid by his assets.[26]

Mills's letter to the New York newspaper, the Comstock editorial, and the interviews in San Francisco included the same points, at least two of which—no overissue of stock and no falsification of accounts—were lies. Sharon later steadfastly denied that Ralston's assets repaid his debts.

Shortly before the reopening, the directors announced that the bank would file a certificate of continued existence and assess capital stock at 10 percent to pay debts and replace funds. Two brothers, stockholders in New York, filed suit saying that the certificate of continued existence and assessment changed the fundamental nature of the institution. U.S.

Circuit Court judge Lorenzo Sawyer disagreed, finding for the bank. The *San Francisco Alta*'s support of the bank was fervent, commenting: "The ghouls have been again defeated."[27]

While the suit was being contested, Sharon was dealing with other ramifications of the Ralston debt. The Spring Valley Water Company liabilities were about $4,250,000, and three-fifths of the firm belonged to Ralston. Of his overissued stock, $600,000 was for loans from San Francisco savings banks from which Spring Valley also borrowed heavily. At the bank's collapse, the savings concerns were badly shaken. Sharon infused money into them. He called in 20 percent of the syndicate funds and visited each bank. He ascertained how much they needed and added 50 percent.[28]

Concealing business affairs had long been a Sharon characteristic. Never was it more important than during this period. To restore public confidence, it had been necessary to hide the extent of Ralston's practices and the bank directors' negligence. Each creditor was dealt with in private, settlements depending on how far Sharon's pokerlike bluffs carried. Moreover, speculation held that he was using the deceased banker's estate for his own gain. Asbury Harpending came to San Francisco to gather firsthand information about his friend Ralston's assets. He stated: "No one seemed anxious to know the facts. Quite the contrary was the case. When I proceeded to gather information of a most important character, J. D. Fry, uncle of Mrs. Ralston, commanded me in the name of the family to cease." Harpending believed that Ralston's resources would have more than repaid his indebtedness. He listed Ralston's large estate—including the Union Mill and Mining Company, the Palace Hotel, all properties on the street front along two blocks of New Montgomery Street, the Spring Valley Water Company, and mining stocks—and commented: "I should say that a conservative estimate of these properties alone was not less than $15,000,000. Besides, he had numberless industrial investments, residences and immense acreages of real estate in various parts of California." James Keene's accounting supported Harpending's. He wrote that Ralston's assets were sufficient to pay all debts and leave a balance of $3 million.[29] Sharon disagreed. He maintained that not only did he not make anything from estate transactions; he paid substantial amounts to make up deficits.

In 1884 the Odd Fellows Bank suit against Sharon prompted a court-ordered audit of the Ralston estate books. Years afterward the lawyer who did the accounting compiled a statement that read in part: "It was demonstrated that the assets received by Mr. Sharon, under and by virtue of the blanket Deed, executed to him by Mr. Ralston, were amply sufficient to have paid every creditor of Mr. Ralston in full and would have left a very large surplus running into the millions."[30]

The day before his death, Ralston deeded his business enterprises and his vast real-estate holdings to Sharon. For $1.5 million, Sharon rid himself of any claim to them owned by the bank. Creditors dealt with him; he reported to no one. The $500,000 owed the bank was never paid, although it appeared as a payment when outsiders finally viewed Sharon's balance. Tilton noted, "The first inventory of Ralston's possessions was not made public until all legal means [to avoid doing so] were blocked." He listed discrepancies and omissions in Sharon's accounting and commented that a question remains: "Where did Ralston's vast estate go?"[31]

Chapter Ten

SETTLING UP

Twenty percent of the syndicate subscription to save the Bank of California was $1.5 million, and by September 29, 1875, nearly the entire amount had been collected. Capital assessments were also being paid.[1] The bank's reopening was imminent.

Saturday, October 2, 1875, was to be the grand opening of the seven-story, eight-hundred-room Palace Hotel. Sharon ensured that it would be memorable by scheduling the bank's reopening for the same day. (The Bonanza Kings were to open their rival Nevada Bank of San Francisco that day as well.) At nine that morning, people from all stations of life began assembling in the street in front of the Bank of California. The question was, Would the populace merely withdraw their money, kept from them for five weeks? An hour later, as city clocks chimed, a hundred flags were run up their poles at sites near the bank. An animated crowd blocked California Street to through traffic. Atop Telegraph Hill, guns were fired in the air and the bank's great front doors opened inward. Tellers and clerks stood ready, piles of gold stacked on the counters.

Ralston's office was filled with onlookers, including Sharon, Bell, Lloyd, Keene, Fry, Barnes, Stanford, and Baldwin. They watched anxiously to see what the public reaction would be. From the first customer, they saw that community spirit imbued the city. The *Chronicle* reported: "Not a man drew coin from the bank during the day who had not immediate necessary use for it." At closing time $1,130,000 was deposited, only $254,000 withdrawn.[2]

On the Comstock, the Bank of California branch offices opened with equal fanfare and similar results: "From the top of Mt. Davidson to the Sutro Tunnel flags waved, cannon thundered and the people cheered."[3] Congratulatory speeches rang out, ironically including the keynote address by Charles DeLong, who, when the Ophir crashed at the beginning of the year, had wished the "demon" Sharon destroyed.

Sharon's feat was remarkable. Serving a short term as branch manager hardly qualified him to reestablish the once omnipotent bank, which would be a power far into the twentieth century. Fifty years later, economic historian Ira Cross commented: "Its reestablishment as a sound financial institution amazed not only the Californians but financiers throughout the world. The impossible had been accomplished by relatively untrained men, living and working in a young frontier community."[4]

That evening, the city's attention moved to the Palace Hotel. A vaulted glass roof, seven stories above, crowned the wide circular driveway of its grand court. Great doors allowed four in hand carriages to tour the flagged marble yard. Pillars, archways, and young palm trees lined the arcade surrounding the court.[5] The area was heated by large brass braziers of burning charcoal and lit by 516 gaslights. People filled the yard, the adjacent dining rooms and storefronts of the ground floor, and the balconies that lined each floor above. After a band's serenade that included "Hail to the Chief," George S. Dodge, on a temporary platform at the south end of the court, introduced Sharon: "Ladies and Gentlemen: I take great pleasure in introducing to you Hon. William Sharon (applause), first and foremost in sustaining the credit of the city of San Francisco and the great State of California."

After praising the people for their forbearance, Sharon graciously directed attention to Ralston:

> Yet, in the crowning hour of victory, in the presence of this grand
> witness of your skill in mechanic arts, in this glorious temple of
> hospitality, amid all the flood of light and music, I experience a
> sense of almost overpowering sadness. I miss, as you do, the proud
> and manly spirit of him who devised this magnificent structure,

and under whose direction and tireless energy it has been mainly reared. I mourn, as you do, that he is not with us to enjoy this sense of beauty, and I offer here, with you, the incense of regret and affection to his memory. Peace be to his ashes. . . .

But one especial cause of our rejoicing tonight is that the Bank of California, of which William C. Ralston was the founder, has again opened its doors. . . . My only wish is to thank the people, as I do with all my heart, for what they have done for themselves and for the honor of San Francisco.

Prolonged cheering answered the speech. "The Beautiful Danube" and "Home Sweet Home" were played, and a time later the crowd dispersed.[6]

On October 26, three and a half weeks after the Bank of California reopened, much of Virginia City (all north of Taylor Street) burned down. The fire started typically enough when a coal-oil lamp shattered during a drunken row at "Crazy Kate" Shay's lodging house (a euphemism for brothel) on South A Street.[7] It quickly spread out of control. Calling the fire a "Fearful Conflagration!" the *Gold Hill News* reported that the north end was "a seething sea of flames." The *Territorial Enterprise* said: "A breath of hell melted the main portion of the town to ruins." With the fire approaching, miners covered the hoisting-works floors with up to three feet of sand and filled shafts "to a depth of thirty feet to where the cages had been lowered."[8] With reports that the Consolidated Virginia and Ophir works were ablaze, the market fell to new lows.

The recovery began three days later, when Mackay reported that the fire did not ignite the works underground, reassuring the market. Within months a new Comstock boom began. Rebuilding started, with more men employed than ever before and the Consolidated Virginia and the California each milling one thousand tons of rich ore a day. Each paid monthly dividends of more than $1 million. The high-water mark in Comstock history would be 1876.[9]

Virginia City's rejuvenation, along with that of the bank, and the opening of the Palace Hotel were boons to the growing Sharon fortune. But there were personal claims against the Ralston estate that continued for years. The most publicized was that of Ralston's widow.

Lizzie Ralston was said to be eccentric, and her husband had been consumed with business; interaction between them had been inconsistent. On the occasion of a son's birthday each parent, without the other's knowledge, invited a large group of friends to his party. The house was not big enough for the number of guests, half of whom were dressed for dinner, half informally. Husband and wife fought bitterly over the mix-up, and ill feelings persisted until Ralston arranged a grand ball for Lizzie that occasioned the erection of the temporary parlor that was removed the next morning.[10]

As Ralston became the most important man in California, entertaining guests from around the world, Lizzie studied with a tutor to acquire the abilities expected of someone with her status. She also began to spend long periods away from home. In 1867 she spent ten months with the children and two maids in Europe, and she visited Europe for several months more in 1869. In his newspaper column Ambrose Bierce reported that Ralston took a mistress during Lizzie's first stay in Europe, and rumors spread of a romance between Lizzie and an artist named Inman during her second trip. But it was generally acknowledged that for all the failings in their marriage, Lizzie loved her husband.[11] Ralston's Last Will and Testament, filed for probate on September 29, 1875, stated: "After the payment of all my just debts, I do give and bequeath to my beloved wife, Lizzie Fry Ralston, in fee simple and full ownership, without any conditions or restrictions whatever, all my property, real, personal and mixed."[12] The day before his death Ralston signed the deed of trust transferring all property to Sharon, an instrument that nullified the will.

On January 11, 1876, four and a half months after her husband's death, Lizzie gave W. H. L. Barnes general power of attorney to act with A. J. Ralston to settle her accounts with Sharon. Nine months later she signed over any claim to her deceased husband's estate for cash and property amounting to approximately $85,000. When Lizzie signed the conveyance, Sharon was through dealing with Ralston's claimants, declaring he had paid several hundred thousand dollars of Ralston's overages. Because there was no estate left, he said, nothing remained for Ralston's heirs.[13]

The settlement consisted of the following:

1. $50,000, evidenced by two notes of $25,000 each at current rates of interest.
2. A homestead account of $15,000.
3. "Little Belmont," the former residence of Ralston's Belmont Superintendent, on thirty acres worth $17,256.72, into which Mrs. Ralston was obliged to go.
4. A cash payment on July 3, 1877 of $3,000.[14]

When individuals representing Sharon's interests wrote of the settling of accounts, two other figures were included: life-insurance policies that paid $68,000 and a dividends payment from the Virginia & Truckee Railroad of $18,111.50. D. O. Mills was the source of the dividend. A time later he stated: "[Sharon] asked me to join him in making her a present of the dividends in the Virginia & Truckee Road, which was just about being paid. . . . It was made out purely in a good will to do some service to Mrs. Ralston."[15]

The Belmont estate, at which Ralston had hosted all individuals of importance who visited California, was a "wonder of the West Coast." It was identified, along with Jay Cooke's Chelton Hills mansion and Charles Crocker's residence on Nob Hill, as being among the three "most magnificently hospitable mansions in the United States."[16] Sharon, when first contemplating Ralston's affairs, announced that Belmont would be opened to the clientele of the Palace Hotel as a country hostelry. A short time later he changed his mind, and by the end of 1876 he had moved his family there. Maintaining a suite of rooms at the Palace Hotel, he split his time between the two. (Colonel Fry moved into the Ralston house on Pine Street.)[17]

The Palace Hotel recovered from a shaky financial start in part because Sharon used the device he exploited with the Virginia & Truckee Railroad. Less than a year after the hotel opened, he appeared before the board of equalization, asking that its $2 million assessment be cut in half. He argued for the reduction because the hotel was a public improvement and "an ornament to the city." Noting that it cost over $5 million to build, he declared its value at not more than $1 million. On a seven to two vote, against the assessor's judgment, the amount was reduced to $1.5 million.[18]

By December 1876 the Palace Hotel was being called "the pride of California." Guests and locals alike took their meals there, and in the courtyard on Monday evenings band concerts were presented for the fashionable set. Five months after the assessment reduction, according to Sharon, the hotel was "considerably more than paying expenses."[19]

Sharon's growing fortune made him vulnerable to the charge that it was at the expense of the bank, creditors, and Mrs. Ralston. Even Mills charged Sharon with not allowing dividends for him at the same rate as for the Ralston estate.[20] One of Sharon's friends described the Sharon-Mills relationship as less than congenial: "Sharon says that Mills is the most cold-blooded, fish-like, ungrateful and altogether repulsive specimen of a man that he ever came in contact with, but their business interests are too closely identified to make them enemies. Their contempt for each other, though, is probably mutual."[21]

In the suit brought against Sharon by Lizzie Ralston, Mills was asked why Sharon had never paid the Montgomery Real Estate Company debt to the bank. "There was no money to ask after, or anything in the matter that required my inquiry," said Mills. When attorney Joseph Nogues asked if the improved real estate had depreciated to the extent that $2 million in indebtedness was negated, Mills responded: "I do not know." Nogues commented that if Mills could give no information about Ralston's Bank of California dealings, "I don't know anybody about the bank that can."[22] Although an expression of frustration and a rebuff of Mills, Noques's statement was essentially correct. Ralston's accounting was so convoluted as to be indecipherable. When Sharon acquired all the records and devoted himself to interpreting them, he kept his findings secret.

Many sources, including Ralston's former friend Asbury Harpending, broker James Keene, A. J. Ralston, and bank secretary Stephen Franklin, believed the Ralston estate included large surplus. Emilita Ralston Page later suggested that Sharon took advantage of her father and recovered between $6 million and $10 million from Ralston's properties.[23] Nogues charged Sharon with keeping $150,000 worth of property that Ralston had declared in writing belonged to his wife and children. Sharon maintained that the property was his, since he was "a creditor of Mr. Ralston in his lifetime."[24] Biographer Cecil Tilton alluded to Sharon's insistence that the estate left nothing for Ralston's wife and compared Sharon to the tiger beetle and its "heinous" larva, setting living traps for innocents.[25]

In November 1877 Lizzie Ralston, complaining that Sharon had defrauded her, asked that the estate be reopened. Sharon refused. It was not until October 8, 1880, that her suit came before California's Superior Court.[26] The document was 265 pages long, "one of the most voluminous complaints" ever filed in California. It claimed the Ralston estate, at the time of his death, was worth perhaps $30 million but that Sharon, with custody of the books, never filed an inventory. It demanded that Sharon provide "a schedule of all books, papers, writings or secret ciphers, with key thereto." And it asked for an account of the "frauds perpetrated by him in obtaining an assignment from plaintiff."[27] On December 26 the executors of Ralston's estate filed a reply, saying that Sharon had paid far more on Ralston's liabilities than the value of the estate covered.[28] Lloyd and Newlands, acting for Sharon, put in a demurrer because the complaint did not state sufficient cause of action. The plea was overruled.

Charges were also brought against J. D. Fry and A. J. Ralston for advising Mrs. Ralston that the estate was insolvent. They admitted that they had never taken inventory and had acted "entirely under the direction, control and authority of Sharon." Represented by W. H. L. Barnes, they sought a stay in the proceedings until another court determined whether the instrument signed by Mrs. Ralston, conveying rights to Sharon, was valid. They also used a scheme that was to be repeated a time later, arguing that the case could not be heard in Superior Court because Sharon was still a Nevada citizen, although he had not resided or owned a residence there for a number of years. Since Lizzie Ralston lived in California, they contended the case needed to be heard in federal court. Month after month, legal maneuverings kept the case from being heard.[29]

Nearly two years passed before Sharon agreed to settle Lizzie's suit out of court on October 12, 1882. The newspapers speculated that the defense compromised either to avoid scandal or because of Sharon's feeble health. The parties agreed to keep the settlement secret, but information was leaked: "One intimate friend of Mrs. Ralston states that $160,000 in cash and a large ranch in the northern part of the State was handed over by Mr. Sharon, as well as $25,000 in cash and a lot of land on California street as a fee for her lawyer."[30]

Sharon fought other legal battles over the estate as well. On November 3, 1879, the Odd Fellows trustees, from whom Sharon had purchased Ralston's overissued stock, brought suit against him. In one of his first deals after the bank's collapse Sharon had paid fifty cents on the dollar to Odd Fellows but had promised to do better if possible in the future. The trustees now asked the courts to determine whether his obligation was legal and what it might entail. This case also lingered in the courts for years. It was a contentious affair. At one point Judge T. H. Rearden needed to advise the participants that although all were unduly eager for success, all were also "men of standing in the community, and it was not proper to fling distrust upon one another."[31]

Five years later, in December 1884, Judge Rearden issued a *Statement of Facts*. Sharon, in producing his evidence, admitted that the Odd Fellows trustees might have some claim upon his honor or good faith but had none in a court of law. Judge Rearden found otherwise, saying he could enforce the claim "having once ascertained its nature and extent."[32]

Sharon's attorneys argued that the inadequacy of Ralston's assets was glaringly apparent, and an accounting would be futile. The court decided that it could not assume an inadequacy, instead finding that the relief to be given at that stage of the litigation was to order an accounting.[33] The court order authorized Charles Lee Tilden to inspect the Ralston estate books. After six weeks of study, the examiner found against Sharon: the assets were sufficient to have paid all creditors in full, leaving a surplus into the millions.[34]

Sharon claimed to have paid hundreds of thousands of dollars above what Ralston left. Yet it is notable how much Ralston property he retained, including the Belmont mansion and estate, the Palace Hotel, the Grand Hotel, all the property on both sides of New Montgomery Street for two blocks from Market to Howard, the as yet undeveloped eight-hundred-acre Burlingame Residential Park, ranches and timberland (twenty thousand acres in Fresno alone), Bank of California stocks, Spring Valley Water Company stocks, mills and mines, assorted companies, and numerous properties in the city.

Years later, the *San Francisco Examiner* estimated Sharon's worth at "upward of $20,000,000." The *San Francisco Call* interviewed his attorney, W. H. L. Barnes, in 1885: "[Sharon has] been for years the largest taxpayer in the State, and has, for the last six or seven years, paid about one-fiftieth of the entire taxes of the State and of this city and county."[35]

Chapter Eleven

AN ILL-FITTING
TOGA

ON DECEMBER 6, 1875, the First Session of the Forty-fourth United States Congress was gaveled to order. The new senator from Nevada, William Sharon, immersed in bank and Ralston estate business, was not in attendance. Two months later, on February 12, the *Territorial Enterprise* announced Sharon's imminent arrival in Virginia City from San Francisco. It attacked other papers that railed at him for missing so much of the session but added: "The masses have not blamed him, for they knew he was detained simply because he had voluntarily taken the burdens of others upon his shoulders to carry."[1]

In the Senate on February 28, 1876, after several bills from the House were referred to appropriate committees, Senator John P. Jones of Nevada presented Sharon. Twelve weeks of the session were recorded before the *Journal of the Senate* stated: "The credentials were read; and the oaths prescribed by law were administered to Mr. Sharon, and he took his seat."[2] The session ran into August, but Sharon returned home at the end of April. The journal is a substantial tome, 1,376 pages long. Senators are cited throughout: presenting, referring, making motions, remonstrating against, praying for, and generally performing the tasks of the people. Except after votes where members are listed as voting yea or nay, Sharon is not mentioned.

On May 12, 1876, the *San Francisco Chronicle* interviewed the novice senator at his Palace Hotel suite. (His Nevada constituents were left to read his comments two days later, when the *Enterprise* reprinted the article.) Ignoring the fact that Sharon was at that moment absent from his seat, the reporter questioned him on issues of the day. On the silver question, he said his colleague Jones gave a "very able" speech advancing the cause of those who would raise its value. Because of scandals, Republican prospects in the 1876 presidential election appeared dismal. Sharon asserted that although Roscoe Conkling of New York was a possibility, to be successful the candidate should come from a border state. The top candidates, he said, were Oliver Morton of Indiana and Rutherford B. Hayes of Ohio (who would receive the nomination and win a contested election).

The "Chinese problem" was also discussed. Sharon never mentioned that Chinese labor had built the Virginia & Truckee Railroad nor that his trusted servant was the immigrant Ah Ki. He condemned those who would use violence to remove them but reintroduced the ideas he had proposed to the Comstock miners. He said he believed the Chinese created a "pernicious effect." "Their manners and customs, their dress, their very diet are different from ours."[3] But he concluded, given that it attracted little attention outside California, that it was not a national issue. When the reporter was ushered out, Sharon turned to bank and estate business, leaving matters of state to others for eight months.

Seven months later, the selection of the president of the United States came before Congress. The public railed against financial malfeasance by Republicans, giving them little chance of victory. In dire straits, they turned to a proven stratagem: "waving the bloody shirt," blaming Democrats for the casualties of the Civil War. The tactic still resonated. Although Democrat Samuel Tilden won the popular election by 250,000 votes, he won only 184 electoral votes, needing 185, with four disputed states yet to be counted: South Carolina, Louisiana, and Florida, under carpetbag governments and suffering from ultraconservative backlash, and Oregon. Late night subterfuge, the brokering of a Senate seat, and the trading of electoral votes for an agreement not to enforce civil rights in the South played integral parts in the Republican victory.[4]

The House and Senate officially began their sessions on December 4.

On December 6 the *Territorial Enterprise* displayed a sparkling example of irony, featuring juxtaposed columns from other newspapers. From the *San Francisco Chronicle* of Monday the 4th was an article entitled "Sharon Interviewed." It described the hospitality of the Belmont manor's lord and his bucolic estate: "The lawns are trim, the flowers and shrubbery rich and splendid in variety." Sharon commented that he had concluded his personal business—the Bank of California, the Palace Hotel, and Ralston estate dealings—the previous year. "As far as that matter is concerned I could leave the coast to-morrow without inconvenience."[5] Nowhere is it explained why he remained.

Columns next to the interview were filled with news of the election crisis. South Carolina was called a "tinder-box," with nothing but troops preventing the "wholesale massacre of Republicans." Democrats were said to have tampered with Florida's election board. And on the floor of the House a resolution was brought asking for the investigation of frauds in New York, Jersey City, and Brooklyn. After commenting that doubtless there was fraud on both sides, Sharon predicted that "the better sense of the good men of both parties" would prevail. He was then asked when he would leave for Washington. His nonchalant response was startling against the backdrop of the nation's maelstrom: "About the 22d of this month—just before the holidays. That time suits my purposes better than any other."[6]

On December 25 Sharon left in his special railroad car. He stopped for a day or two in Virginia City before continuing east. On January 1, 1877, in Chicago, his car was attached to the afternoon train from Omaha on the Rock Island Road. The *Chicago Times* reported that his "house on wheels" provided all the conveniences and most of the luxuries of a mansion. Calling it a "portable palace," the paper noted that the senator traveled with "his family, his valet (Ki, described as 'diminutive and chunky'), his cooks, chambermaid, etc."

Sharon told the *Chicago Times* reporter his mind was not made up on the constitutional points of the electoral vote but that the law would govern him. "It is vastly more important to the nation that peace should be

preserved than that either Tilden or Hayes should be declared President."
"You anticipate no outbreak then?" asked the reporter. "Most certainly
not. I attach no importance to any warlike rumors."[7]

On January 11, 1877, five and a half weeks after the Second Session began, the *Journal of the Senate* announced: "Mr. William Sharon, from the
State of Nevada, attended." This time Sharon stayed through the session,
but he submitted no resolutions, nor called for or issued any reports.
Sharon remained in Washington for a special session that began March 3
and lasted two weeks. During that time, he was appointed chairman of the
Committee on Mines and Mining.[8]

Asked about life in Washington, D.C., in an interview, Sharon responded: "Outside of political circles it is dull. It never was intended for a
city—only as the seat of Government, and excepting when Congress is in
session there is very little done."[9] Because he was attending to personal
finances, or perhaps because of the dullness of the environs, when Sharon
left Washington, he did not return for nearly two years.

The Spring Valley Water Company was one of the businesses that occupied Sharon's attention during that time. In the last third of the nineteenth century, beginning with Mark Twain's use of it to give impetus to
his "Massacre at Dutch Nick's" tale in 1863, the company's name was constantly before the public.[10] Discussed in boardrooms and government
offices, it was the topic of editorials and was railed against at sandlot rallies. People complained that its costs were too high, the margin of profits
was too large. Ranchers and developers protested that in acquiring watersheds, the company usurped the rightful resource of surrounding counties. City officials worried that Spring Valley's capacity was too low for future provision.

In 1875, the year Sharon acquired the majority of its stock, the company
purchased extensive water rights, "including two important keys to the
water situation on the Alameda Creek," greatly expanding its service capabilities.[11] Hermann Schussler, who in 1873 engineered the remarkable
water pipeline that brought Sierra Nevada water seven miles out of the
mountains to Virginia City, was Spring Valley's chief engineer. One of the

business traits that enabled Sharon's success was a policy of paying managers superior wages. Schussler continued his service with Spring Valley for fifty years.[12]

As San Francisco grew, Spring Valley burgeoned. A California law passed in 1858 provided for a fair return on private capital and arbitration regarding price. As volume rose, prices dropped, from 406/10 cents per one thousand gallons between 1865 and 1870 to 286/10 cents between 1875 and 1880. Still, customers and critics saw prices as exorbitant, and the new state constitution of 1879 abolished arbitration, placing the establishment of rates into the hands of city authorities. Francis Newlands managed negotiations for Sharon. To ensure profits, the company sold stocks and bonds when necessary to increase capital.[13]

In a newspaper interview in December 1876, Sharon tried to alleviate taxpayer concerns about Spring Valley Water Company's being foisted on the city while promoting the company's record. Spring Valley was adding one hundred houses to its list monthly. It was ready to build the Calaveras reservoir, ensuring the city plentiful water for a hundred years. Sharon was in no hurry for the city to purchase the works: "It will not press their sale, but should it conclude to part with them, will be ready to negotiate on what it considers a reasonable basis. Meanwhile it will continue to increase its facilities and wait patiently for the public appreciation."[14]

A year later, Sharon was ready to sell. He offered the company to the city for $13,500,000. But between August and October 1877, Denis Kearney was organizing the Workingmen's Party, exhorting crowds to support labor at the expense of corporate owners. Because they would gather on empty lots and street corners, the campaign became known as the "sandlot" movement. Kearney preached against various "outrages": the corruption of politicians, the length of the workday, and especially the importation of Chinese workers. He urged every workingman to get a musket. This stirred power brokers to hurriedly pass a gag law that prohibited "suggesting" violence in meetings.

Sharon's proposal to sell Spring Valley Water Company to the city prompted Kearney to call the company Sharon's "rotten water works."

The crowd responded by chanting, "hemp, hemp, hemp," insinuating that Sharon should be hanged. Nothing came of the threat.[15]

The *Call* and *Bulletin* fought the purchase of the water company just as they had when Ralston owned it in 1875. The city made a counteroffer of $11 million. Ever patient and calculating, Sharon turned the offer down.[16] The family kept the franchise until 1908, when it sold to William Bourn.[17]

By the end of November 1877, Sharon's absence from the Senate had become a heated topic. In a special dispatch from Virginia City, the *San Francisco Chronicle* reported: "Great indignation is expressed by Republicans here on account of Senator Sharon's absence from Washington. They say that Nevada is entitled to her full representation." The Democrats were demanding that Sharon resign so that Lewis "Old Broadhorns" Bradley, the governor, could succeed him.[18]

Sharon did not wish to abdicate his seat, yet he was not ready to go to "Washington City." The *New York Tribune* reported that owing to business, Sharon would not take his seat before December 20. But he was under pressure. A dispatch received in Washington, D.C., stated: "If he is importuned by many Senators as he has been by the one to whom he telegraphed he will resign."[19]

On November 21, 1877, the *Territorial Enterprise* responded to charges of Sharon's neglect by "waving the bloody shirt": "Nothing could more rejoice [the Democratic press] than Mr. Sharon's inability to attend . . . [except] his resignation and the filling of his place by Governor Bradley with some one of the numerous ex-Confederate officers with whom our state is blessed." The article then recapped events of 1875 and Sharon's effort to "bring back prosperity from seemingly irretrievable ruin." The *Enterprise* noted further that Sharon understood that no important issues would be addressed in this special session, assuring readers that he intended to attend the December session and would leave for Washington shortly. The assurance was misplaced: Sharon missed the entire seven-month Second Session as well.

The issue commanding Sharon's attention—besides his estate—was state business. A convention to write a new California Constitution convened in September 1878. The primary issues of import to Sharon included the regulation of corporations (especially banks), the regulation of Spring Valley Water, and a system of taxing the immense tracts of land owned by single entities. Of special concern was the fact that of the 152 elected delegates, 51 came from the Workingmen's Party. David S. Terry, a nonpartisan from Stockton, California, later Sharon's bitter adversary, wielded considerable power in the convention, notably with the Workingmen's Party. Introducing an amendment to protect bank depositors, he "denounced the opposition as enemies of the people and tools of the monopolists."

The capitalists were also well represented at the convention. Their contingent included W. H. L. Barnes, Samuel Wilson, John S. Hager, J. P. Hoge, and Eugene Casserly, all San Francisco attorneys associated with Sharon or the Bank of California. But Terry and the Workingmen's delegates outgunned them. A number of provisions increased the accountability of bankers and corporation directors, and a state Board of Equalization was created. The California Constitution, denounced by conservatives as "communistic and malicious," eventually passed by a majority of less than 11,000 out of 450,000 votes.[20]

Shortly after the constitutional convention produced unhappy results for Sharon, the Third Session of the Forty-fifth United States Congress began. Five weeks after it started, on January 7, 1879, Sharon attended. On January 24, for the first time in the four years since his election, he made a presentation. He delivered a memorial of the Nevada legislature in favor of a law "prohibiting discriminations, exactions, and extortions by the Central Pacific Railroad Company."[21]

Sharon's presentation was disingenuous. Unquestionably, the Central Pacific cheated Nevadans with "back-haul" rates. Rates for goods carried from the East to the road's terminus at San Francisco were substantially lower than those for towns it passed through. In 1877 a car of coal oil brought from New York cost $300 if delivered in San Francisco; that same freight unloaded in Reno, 306 miles closer to New York, cost $536. If the coal oil was left in Elko, Nevada, 619 miles closer than San Francisco, the company charged $800.²² But the "Big Four," the Central Pacific's owners, were Sharon's friends and business allies. They were consistently on the guest list for fetes at Belmont. Leland Stanford and Charles Crocker each lived for periods at the Palace Hotel; Mark Hopkins and Collis Huntington maintained suites there, using it as their West Coast headquarters. When in San Francisco, Crocker met his cronies daily at the Palace bar. Sharon had sought Hopkins's help in reducing railroad assessments before the Virginia & Truckee construction was completed. And Sharon's lieutenant, Yerington, worked closely with Central Pacific agents to control Nevada politicians for the good of all railroads.²³

Sharon made no attempt to influence senators against the Central Pacific. The memorial was referred to committee. Rates went unchanged until 1910, when the Interstate Commerce Commission gained enough power to intervene.

Sharon cast some votes during the session but missed more. After voting on a procedural matter on February 25, he cast no further votes. The session adjourned March 3, but appropriations for the next fiscal year were needed, so the First Session of the Forty-sixth United States Congress commenced on March 18, lasting until July 1. Sharon did not attend.

One West Coast business item that kept Sharon from senatorial duties was the *Virginia Evening Chronicle*'s frontal attack on the Virginia & Truckee Railroad. Assigned to cover the state legislature, reporter Arthur McEwen, later a renowned San Francisco newsman, did so with a vengeance. He named names and called names, referring to legislators as "male Magdalens" and "slaves of the sack."²⁴ But even when he harried politicians into quitting, others stepped forward to look after Sharon's railroad interests.

Legislator F. E. Fisk told of attempting to stand up to Sharon's Bank Ring. He campaigned for the legislature by pledging to pass laws regarding "extortionate" freight charges. The week after his election Yerington sought him out, advising him of the expectation that he would vote with the railroads. Fisk declared that he would live up to his promises. Yerington first intimated that Fisk could make money by going along then threatened to injure him in business. While Fisk stood fast, others caved in. He commented, "Those who were loudest in their denunciation of the thieving corporations . . . were the first to yield."

Sharon's forces were unyielding. D. O. Mills's brother, Edgar Mills, was president of Nevada's Eureka & Palisade Railroad (a Bank of California–funded project of which Sharon was a stockholder). When the legislature adjourned, Edgar Mills pressured Fisk's employer until R. P. Dayton, a senator who always voted for the railroads, was named to replace Fisk. Fisk went to work on a newspaper in which he owned an interest. According to Fisk, "[the railroad men] commenced to injure my paper, and continued to do so until I was compelled to sell out and leave the State, or be ruined. . . . I concluded to try the shotgun plan on a few of them, but was dissuaded." Fisk charged: "I know that members of the Ninth Legislature were bought, body and soul, and money was paid almost openly."[25]

There is no doubt of Sharon's part in plundering by the Virginia & Truckee Railroad and its confederate lines in Nevada. While his relationship with managers of other railroads is less well documented, Sharon's association with the Virginia & Truckee's Yerington is recorded. In numerous letters, Sharon directed or advised him.[26] Sharon's involvement in specific cases of spoliation is undocumented, but he set policy, and the companies' gluttonous behavior would not have proceeded without his approval.

In San Francisco Sharon had assumed Ralston's role as preeminent host. On September 20, 1879, Ulysses S. Grant, maintaining his hero status after the scandals of his presidency, steamed into San Francisco Bay from his tour of the world. He was taken directly to the Palace Hotel. Flags and garlands hung from the seven tiers above the regal courtyard. From the galleries, five hundred choristers sang his welcome: "Their voices filled the court to its high roof."[27] He and his wife were feted at many venues, but foremost were days spent at the Belmont mansion. Two thousand invitations were sent for the reception. Railroad cars carried guests from the city to Belmont's station, where one hundred carriages transported them to the gala. "House and grounds were day-bright with 'illuminations' and flowers were everywhere. Mr. Sharon and his daughter Flora . . . received with General and Mrs. Grant."[28]

Beginning in 1875 with Flora's debut, in which one thousand guests took part, and a spectacular ball for General William Sherman and the Earl and Countess of Dufferin, Sharon hosted many parties at Belmont. A dowager commented on the mirrored oval ballroom and its great crystal chandelier that cast sparkle throughout: "I have never seen a more effective setting for a ball." But, she continued, "something was missing; some flourish or touch of romance which in Ralston's day had lent character. . . . Belmont had become conventionally plutocratic." In 1889 the *San Francisco Examiner* offered a similar view: "His entertainments were regarded by many as designed to advertise the fact that Sharon could set as big a spread as any."[29]

On December 1, 1879, the Second Session of the Senate commenced—as each regular session had since his election—without Sharon. On December 12 the *Carson Valley News* accused Sharon of allowing the suspension of operations at the Carson City Mint by remaining in San Francisco and ignoring the issue. When the *Reno Journal* discussed the opposing views of Senators Jones and Sharon on greenbacks (Sharon favored them), the *Carson Valley News* emphasized that neither man was in the Senate: "It is not at all surprising that Senators, so widely separated as is Leadville from San Francisco, would entertain entirely different views upon national questions."[30]

On January 7, 1880, Sharon finally arrived in Washington. A special dispatch was sent to Nevada: "Sharon arrived today; whether on a visit or to occupy his seat is not known. The Secretary of the Senate says that if Sharon asks for back pay, he shall decline paying him until legally advised so to do, as no case of this kind has been presented of late years."[31] Sharon voted on several minor issues, being absent for others. On March 11 he presented a petition for the reduction of the duty on certain paper and chemicals used in the printing of a journal in Eureka, Nevada. He observed that the duty, with labor and capital, raised the price of paper beyond a fair profit. It was not, he proposed, war between capital and labor

(labor needed capital, and capital was "very certain to fly from danger"), but that capital and labor were at war with production to inflate prices that fleece the masses.

After the Senate agreed to refer the petition to the Committee on Finance, Sharon continued:

> Mr. President, before I take my seat I wish to allude to another matter. . . . Just after my election, I found that an associate and friend had involved myself to the extent of millions of dollars. It was a question with me whether I should then continue in the Senate or resign. I confidently expected to arrange my affairs immediately and be continually present. That pleasure and duty were denied me. . . . I know my duty to my State and my country, and nothing but these great difficulties could keep me from performing that duty. I wish to say one word more. These complications may again call me away for three or four weeks, and I ask the kind indulgence of the Senate on account of my absence. I have said all the time that should my constituents demand my resignation it is in their hands.

Senator Henry Dawes then called for information on soldiers who had killed Big Snake, a Ponca chief, and Senator Lew Wallace introduced a joint resolution for the enforcement of the eight-hour law.[32] Senate business went on without Sharon for another three months, until its adjournment on June 16, 1880.

In Nevada the campaign for the November 2, 1880, election of state legislators (who would either reelect or replace Sharon as U.S. senator) began in August. It would solidify Nevada's reputation as the "rotten borough" of politics. In 1913 Sam Davis commented: "In the entire history of Nevada politics there had never been such a saturnalia of corruption as in this campaign."[33] Davis said the buying of votes was done in the open and instead of the usual five to ten dollars per vote, votes sold for as high as eighty dollars.

The campaign went as it did because the Democrats nominated James

Fair to battle Sharon. Fair, one of the Bonanza Kings, had won admiration for his mining accomplishments. But he was notoriously unlikable, and at his death in 1894 no one mourned. Arthur McEwen said: "Since James G. Fair died last week, his name has been on everyone's lips. I have yet to hear a good word spoken of him." After interviewing Fair, biographer George Morrison called him "a very cool man . . . no conscience to trouble him, no sentiment."[34]

During the campaign Fair visited mines and mills during the day, bars at night. He dressed in a miner's flannel shirt, boots, and slouch hat, giving up his luxurious carriage for a one-horse buckboard, providing an obvious contrast to Sharon.

On August 7 Republicans rallied in Virginia City to support their national standard bearers, James Garfield and Chester Arthur. Sharon's speech alternated between an apologia and attacks on Democrats who would "bow down to [the] golden calf." Needing to justify visiting the state so few days during his term, he used an interesting stratagem: "I am a resident of the State of Nevada by virtue of my office." That he spent most of his senatorial career in San Francisco required further explanation: "I have not been much in the Senate because your interests, involving twenty millions of dollars, demanded my attention. I did not shrink, but put in my money and sustained the banks." Displaying the politician's knack for disingenuous blather, he continued: "You have never heard the wail of the orphan or the cry of the widow caused by any act of mine. My efforts have always been to win your smiles and your esteem." He sandwiched his defense with diatribes against attempts to buy the election: "Cursed be the hand that dares to buy or sell votes of freemen. I understand this to be a nation of people sworn to freedom and the protection of human rights, and when a man says 'unless you vote for me you shall not work for me,' he is a traitor to the nation and to liberty."[35]

On August 19 word was received of big Republican victories in Indiana and Ohio that portended success in November. Reno and Carson City celebrated with torchlight parades and rallies. Sharon spoke to a large crowd in Carson. Ironically, he attacked Fair with charges identical to those made against him: "[Fair] says he is an actual resident of Nevada. These words were penned at his place on [San Francisco's] Nob Hill. . . . They think he possesses the means to purchase or oppress the voters of Nevada. . . . It makes the blood curdle in my veins that a man should perpetrate such a crime."[36]

On August 27 the *Enterprise* published what was certainly an apocryphal anonymous letter from a widow whose florid style bore a striking resemblance to editor Daggett's. The melodramatic (at times laughable) account told how after the collapse of the bank, Sharon saved her and her six children from ruin: "In one blow all was changed. . . . [Self-destruction] would have been my fate if little children's hands had not kept me from it." With tremulous steps she approached Sharon, and though "dumb and pain stricken," managed to present her story. Sharon responded: "Those babies shall not starve." He then loaned her money and invested it, reaping great dividends. She had never met Sharon before. Now, she believed him a prince. "This story will suggest why he was so absent [from the Senate]. . . . His days and nights were taken up in working for the public good." The narrative concluded fittingly—echoing Sharon's campaign theme: "His millions are made useful in railroads, houses, factories, mills and hotels, which give work and comfort to thousands of laboring men and women."[37] On August 30, after giving a speech whose crux was "I am for the Union as long as I have life," Sharon left for San Francisco.[38]

Sharon maintained that business prevented him from spending more time on the Comstock, but in 1880 there was another reason: Sarah Althea Hill. They met in the spring by chance at the entrance to the bank.[39] Hill, in her late twenties and unmarried, was by all accounts precocious and exceptionally attractive. One admirer called her "my angel with the corn-flower-blue eyes and hair like the sunrise."[40] Sarah Althea Hill had grown up in Cape Girardeau, Missouri. Her father served as a state legislator. Her mother's line could be traced back to the Revolution. Both died in her youth. Her uncle, also deceased, was a state auditor and governor. Her cousin was a senator, and her guardian was a gentleman of great wealth. Hill said Sharon, hearing she was doing well in the market, teased her about being a stock sharp and told her about stock he was putting on the market. He invited her to stop by his office if she was interested. When they bumped into one another a week later, he chided her on not coming to see him. She invited him to her rooms to discuss the stock.[41]

Sharon returned to Virginia City on September 29 to speak at another rally, hammering the familiar theme of planting hundreds of homes "where those who sneer at me as a non-resident are planting one." Sharon's opponents were also spreading a story that Senator Jones would support Fair against him. Jones's denial was read to the crowd, listing reasons the Republican Party should be kept in power. It was a lengthy note that nowhere mentioned Sharon's name.[42]

About the first of October, Sarah Hill moved into rooms at the Sharon-owned Grand Hotel, directly across the street from the Palace. An enclosed bridge above Montgomery Street connected the two, leaving people on the street or in the Palace Hotel's inner galleries unaware of traffic between the hotels. Hill furnished the rooms with purchases at Sharon's (formerly Ralston's) West Coast Furniture Company. When there was a problem repainting the parlor, she wrote enlisting Sharon's help. He directed the manager to assist her.[43]

Election day, November 2, 1880, was relatively quiet on the Comstock. By evening telegrams told of Republican victories sweeping the East, but in Nevada James G. Fair bucked the trend. Sam Davis reported that his "'sack bearers' were in every county and precinct on election-day, and the State elected a Democratic legislature for the first time in years." Fair would replace Sharon as senator from Nevada.[44]

When the Third Session of the Forty-sixth United States Congress began on December 6, 1880, Sharon was hosting his daughter Flora's wedding at Belmont. Flora was described as beautiful, with a gentle spirit and clear mind.[45] Sir Thomas Fermor-Hesketh, seventh baronet, had courted Flora when he visited the city in his steam yacht, the $800,000 *Lancashire Witch*. Although older than Flora and unremarkable in appearance, Hesketh was described as affable and "a thoroughbred."[46]

Sharon was impressed when he investigated the titled man's character.

He told cronies: "Hesketh is a good one. I doubted him at first, and sent three men to Liverpool and London—it cost me $10,000—to hunt up his record. It was a good one. But I say (to Senator Jones) it would have been a jolly idea if Hesketh had concluded at the same time to hunt up mine, eh?" Won over, Sharon gave more than his blessing to the union; according to the papers, only D. O. Mills and William K. Vanderbilt ever provided dowries equal to that Sharon bestowed.[47]

The reception was as spectacular as the one for Clara and Newlands. The Metropolitan Orchestra from New York was brought west for the affair. Newspapers gloried in its extravagances, while Ambrose Bierce's *Wasp* depicted it in cartoon form, featuring hogs in a drunken revel. Among the guests, "in fine fettle and fine satin," was Sarah Hill, who had previously visited Belmont on several occasions and had been seen frequently in public with the senator.[48] To observers Flora's match was a fairy tale: "The bridegroom came sailing through the Golden Gate on his yacht, *Lancashire Witch,* bound around the world from Liverpool, and they sailed away on her for the honeymoon, and back to England."[49]

On January 17, the wedding behind him, Senator Sharon attended the Senate session that had begun six weeks earlier. He stayed in Washington for several weeks, appearing in the Senate on occasion. On February 4 he missed two votes, then he voted with the minority against rewording a resolution regarding counting presidential votes. Thus ended his senatorial career. The session continued until May 20, but there is no further record of Sharon's presence.[50] Russell Elliott has summarized: "Sharon's record in the United States Senate is one of the worst in the history of that legislative body. His record of inaction is unbelievable. He was seated at only five sessions and was recorded on less than 1 percent of all roll calls."[51]

Senator William Sharon. Courtesy of The Bancroft Library, University of California, Berkeley

Sharon's bitter enemy, Adolph Sutro, pictured in an advertisement for his tunnel.
Courtesy Special Collections, University of Nevada—Reno Library.

San Francisco, ca. 1850. Courtesy of The Bancroft Library, University of California, Berkeley.

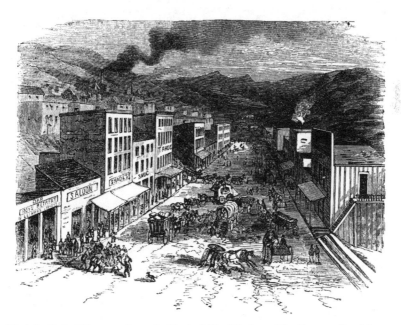

Virginia City's C Street, as shown in *Harper's Monthly,* June 1865. Courtesy Special Collections, University of Nevada—Reno Library.

The Bank of California building on C Street in Virginia City. Sharon's lodgings overlooked the town from the second-floor windows. Courtesy Nevada Historical Society.

V.& T. R.R. Bridge over Crown Point Ravine, Gold Hill (Comstock Lode).
Storey County, Nevada, 1 Mile south of Virginia City, Photo 1893.

The Virginia & Truckee trestle rose to a height of ninety feet behind the Crown Point
mine. Courtesy Special Collections, University of Nevada—Reno Library.

"Lyon" was the first engine to run on Virginia & Truckee track. It was built in San
Francisco for $16,500 and named after the Nevada county. Courtesy Nevada Historical
Society.

John Mackay, "The Honest Miner," began battling Sharon and the Bank Ring in 1868.
Courtesy Nevada Historical Society.

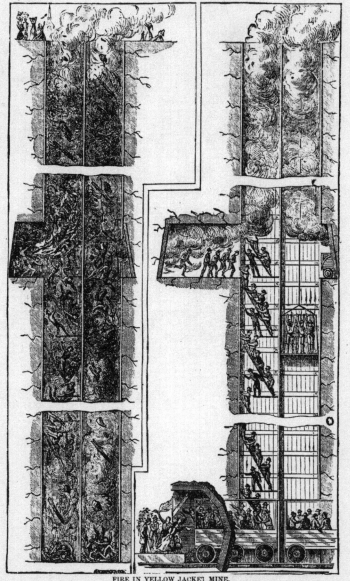

FIRE IN YELLOW JACKET MINE.

At this fire forty-two miners lost their lives; had the Sutro Tunnel been completed and connected with this shaft he men would have escaped unharmed, as illustrated in the right-hand cut.

Adolph Sutro's Yellow Jacket fire illustration. Courtesy Special Collections, University of Nevada—Reno Library.

Sharon's Belcher mine, its total production touted. Courtesy Nevada Historical Society.

John P. Jones, "The Commoner,"
seized ownership of the Crown
Point mine from Sharon then ran
against him for the Senate. Courtesy
Special Collections, University of
Nevada—Reno Library.

Alf Doten, publisher and editor of
the *Gold Hill News,* fought for
Sharon. Courtesy Special Collections, University of Nevada—Reno
Library.

Territorial Enterprise editor Joseph Goodman. Courtesy Nevada Historical Society.

The *Territorial Enterprise*'s new editor, Rollin Daggett, championed the Sharon cause. Courtesy Nevada Historical Society.

Virginia City, with mine tailings in the foreground. To the far right are the tailings of the Consolidated Virginia, the California, and the Ophir mines. Courtesy Special Collections, University of Nevada—Reno Library.

Sharon's patron, William Ralston, who financed the building of much of early San Francisco, in 1875 found himself unable to raise money to save the Bank of California. Courtesy Special Collections, University of Nevada—Reno Library.

Rough tables replaced the furniture in Belmont's parlor, where Sharon met with bank directors day after day. Courtesy of The Bancroft Library, University of California, Berkeley.

The Ralston-built Belmont estate became Sharon's part-time residence. Courtesy of The Bancroft Library, University of California, Berkeley.

The Palace Hotel courtyard. Courtesy of The Bancroft Library, University of California, Berkeley.

James G. Fair, who openly bought votes in a "saturnalia of corruption." Courtesy Special Collections, University of Nevada—Reno Library.

Sharon, and daughter Flora's wedding, lampooned by *The Wasp*'s suggestion of a monument in Golden Gate Park. Courtesy of The Bancroft Library, University of California, Berkeley.

Distinguished Californians "At the Play." Sharon's prominence is emphasized by his placement: front row, third to the right from the middle aisle. John Mackay is two places farther to the right. Sharon's partner, D. O. Mills, is front row, second to the left from the aisle. Courtesy Special Collections, University of Nevada—Reno Library.

Sarah Althea Hill. Courtesy of The Bancroft Library, University of California, Berkeley.

David S. Terry. Courtesy of The Bancroft Library, University of California, Berkeley.

SAN FRANCISCO, SATURDAY, MARCH 22, 1884.

A NECESSARY PRECAUTION.

The cover of *The Wasp,* illustrating trial testimony. Courtesy of The Bancroft Library, University of California, Berkeley.

Sharon, nearing the end. Courtesy of The Bancroft Library, University of California, Berkeley.

Sharon's heir, Francis G. Newlands. Courtesy of The Bancroft Library, University of California, Berkeley.

Supreme Court Justice Stephen S. Field. Courtesy of The Bancroft Library, University of California, Berkeley.

Chapter Twelve

THE ROSE

WILLIAM SHARON'S San Francisco had changed dramatically by the 1880s. Tumultuous at the time of his arrival in 1850, it now was a unique cosmopolitan milieu, equal parts pomp, decorum, and bustle. The town's disordered plank buildings and brick two-stories had given way to business blocks of three- and four-story ornate structures. Theaters, restaurants, and saloons were tucked between the offices. Hotels rose over smart shops of every variety. Residential areas included Italianate-style houses with wide eaves and thin pillars; workers' cottages; old manors converted into boarding houses; and, on the hills, the imposing mansions of millionaires. Horses pulling wagons made their way among horse-car lines and cable cars. Masts of ships from around the world bobbed in rows above the bay.

Residents found plenty to do. In the 1880s "restaurant living"—frequenting the abundant eateries—was a way of life retained from the days when only men had resided in the city. At least one pundit blamed the resultant loss of time at home for the demise of domesticity and the preference of the city's youth for the street rather than home.[1] After matinees on Saturdays, theatergoers promenaded on Market Street. Evenings Kearny Street hosted congested promenades, strollers admiring each other as well as the handsome wares in store windows. The proportion of wealthy inhabitants in the city was large, many owing their rise to the luck of the market. The sole requirement of the elite being wealth, it was a matter of comment that many led lives of "excitement and dissipation."[2]

Sharon lived in his rooms in the southwest corner on the fourth floor of the Palace Hotel. He hosted a weekly poker game; tallying his good plays rather than his winnings.[3] Newlands spoke of Sharon's skill in social discourse, calling his conversation witty, humorous, and instructive: "He delighted in philosophical subjects, in social questions, in the relation of man to his fellow-man and to his God, and in the scientific relation of the universe to its great cause."[4]

In 1881 Sharon, now sixty years old, suffered an "attack of heart disease," and his health became more fragile. He was susceptible to changes in atmospheric pressure and periodically took to his bed. Even before the attack he did not avail himself fully of the hotel kitchen, the largest in the country. (It employed a renowned chef, five assistants to carry out his orders, and three special cooks: a chief confectioner from Milan, a chief baker from Vienna, and Muffin Tom, who specialized in corn bread and hot egg muffins.) One chef noted: "With the entire resources of the hotel's larder and wine cellar at his command, [Sharon] habitually dined frugally, washing down his simple fare with weak tea."[5]

On February 18, 1882, a day after the birth and death of her son, named Sharon, Clara Sharon Newlands died. Having inherited her father's constitution, she was described as "highly wrought" and sensitive, "very happy when she is happy, very miserable when she is miserable, but quite unselfish." Newlands was considerate of her frailness, and they enjoyed a happy marriage. One of their three daughters said, "My father bore great burdens gallantly." One spoke of her Grandfather Sharon as well: "A rather small man with very piercing eyes and a quiet, dignified manner. We were great friends. We were never reproved by him. A glance was probably enough. I always felt he saw my misdeed as if written in a book."[6]

The small, quiet, dignified man accumulated wealth in large part because of his genius for knowing when to buy or sell. In 1875, when Sharon threw his mining stocks on the market, the Consolidated Virginia was producing the richest returns in Comstock history. Nevertheless, Sharon did not resume mining speculation, and that strike turned out to be the last. While millions were lost searching for the next bonanza, Sharon expanded his fortune by purchasing real estate. He accumulated as many as four hundred properties in San Francisco, many houses on corner lots, "for which Mr. Sharon had a special liking," as well as numerous buildings and lots.[7] He was followed into property investments by two of the Bonanza Kings, Flood and Fair, as well as by his nemesis, Sutro. Each of the four became a San Francisco land baron.

Sharon visited his office at the bank daily, settling affairs with a single word. He was also caught up in litigation over the Ralston estate. As for the Bank of California, once it was reestablished Sharon paid it little mind. Former mayor William Alvord succeeded Mills as president, capably managing it into the twentieth century.

In the 1880s water was a rancorous issue, involving costs to consumers and riparian rights. After two years of fighting regulatory powers, Francis Newlands, representing the Spring Valley Water Company for Sharon, developed a new, sophisticated approach. He insisted on negotiating deals on a predictable basis and introduced the concept that once assured a reasonable profit, corporations needed to be fair in dealing with their clients and the government. While others fought court battles, William Sharon's interests were managed in a less contentious and more profitable fashion.[8] Sharon once remarked to a socialite: "If I had been at all greedy like some men I would have been, without doubt, the wealthiest man in this state."[9] In his early sixties, he was not far from it.

Then on Saturday, September 8, 1883, as he was about to catch a train to the East, Sharon was arrested. He was accused of adultery. The story quickly spread across the country. Headlines spoke of Sharon's "Trouble," his "Predicament," his "Tribulations," and his "Torment." The charge of spousal infidelity was surprising, since he was generally thought to be an unmarried widower.[10]

Sharon had participated in extramarital affairs since living on the Comstock. The *St. Louis Globe Democrat* noted the "notoriously bad character of the senator." The *Chicago Daily News* called him the "amorous statesman" whose morals provide "a sad commentary." In the trial to follow, Sharon was forced to concede that for many years he had paid monthly amounts to a large number of mistresses.[11] The judge in the case later described him as "a libertine ... possessed of strong animal passions."[12]

Sharon had been reportedly attentive to his wife when they were together, especially toward the end of her life. The Palace Hotel manager mentioned that they were "much attached to each other." Still, there is anecdotal evidence regarding Sharon's open infidelity when they lived mostly apart. He reputedly gave Belle Warner, "his Nevada mistress at the time," a tip regarding the Chollar mine that earned her $150,000. This, like the incident of his registering at the Glenbrook Hotel as "William Sharon and lady," occurred in the early 1870s, several years before Maria Sharon's death.[13]

The charge, in September 1883, included references to Sharon's relations over the previous three years with "nine women, including Gertie Dietz." The intimacy with Dietz was complicated by the birth of a child apparently fathered by Sharon. Neither Dietz nor any of the other eight women brought the charge of adultery. It was the work of Sarah Althea Hill, whose company he had kept in 1880 and 1881.[14]

In the Gilded Age the home, where wives and mothers "carry society to its loftiest planes," was perceived as the strength of the nation. The commercial mart was outside the "realm of the fairer sex."[15] In San Francisco in the 1880s, some women—such as Hill—refused to follow convention, choosing adventuresome lives instead. The problem for most was economic: jobs for women paying any but the lowest wages were unavailable. The exceptions were those blessed by fortune in the stock market or, as was the case for Hill, an inheritance.

The day after his arrest, Sharon gave a $5,000 bond to appear and left for the East. When curious reporters sought information, his friends in San Francisco were "conspicuously absent." This included his son-in-law Newlands, whose house was locked. From the East, Sharon proclaimed the suit a blackmailing scheme. This prompted Hill to allow the *San Francisco Chronicle* to publish the text of a document dated August 25, 1880, signed by herself and Sharon, in which they took one another as husband and wife. She also produced a letter from Sharon, written in the Senate Chambers in January 1881, addressed to "My Dear Wife."

Sharon struck back. The next day, when questioned in Arlington, Virginia, Sharon responded: "I never wrote that nor anything like it in my life.

If there is any such paper in existence it is a forgery. . . . No, sir; the whole story is a malicious and unmitigated falsehood. It is a penitentiary offense."[16] He immediately hired investigators to examine Hill's background. I. W. Lees, the former chief of San Francisco Detectives who had investigated John P. Jones years earlier, was given responsibility for the case. He and his associates also began looking into the history of W. M. Neilson, who had assisted Hill in filing the suit.

Three weeks later, Sharon returned to San Francisco and filed a suit of his own in the U.S. Circuit Court. He called all claims maliciously false and the document fraudulent. The *Chicago Tribune* reported: "Sharon is greatly worked up by what he terms a conspiracy by Neilson and a crazy woman for the purpose of blackmailing."[17]

Sharon's filing suit in federal court was of crucial importance. Divorce proceedings are the venue of the states, except when the litigants reside in different states. Only because Sharon, living in San Francisco for well over ten years, was again using the ploy of Nevada residency could a federal court assert jurisdiction. Whatever his original purpose in traveling to the East, Sharon's business after the arrest was meeting with longtime friend, Supreme Court Justice Stephen J. Field. Field, who presided over the Ninth Circuit—the Pacific Coast states—lived at the Palace Hotel when he was in San Francisco, reportedly without charge, and received a $25,000 loan from Sharon that was never repaid.[18] It was Field who, in 1872, had ruled for Sharon when he was accused of stealing the V-flume design to move timber.

Field was a judicial reactionary and the author of "Ninth Circuit Law," which protected corporate interests. To Field, in cases regarding economic rights, the burden of proof was incumbent on the state. The due process and equal protection clauses of the Fourteenth Amendment, intended to extend the Bill of Rights to former slaves, were corrupted to define corporations as "persons," establishing the pursuit of business goals as largely above the purview of public authority. His arguments asserted that property is an inalienable right. Field believed that creating an elite of businessmen strengthened the nation by allowing conglomerates to spread prosperity. His brother Cyrus Field was a close associate of Jay Gould; his brother David Dudley Field was connected with Tammany Hall, Boss Tweed, and Jim Fisk. For his part, Justice Field always took the side of his friends Stanford, Huntington, Hopkins, and Crocker and their railroad trust.[19]

When Sharon consulted with Field, the justice suggested he talk to the leading advocate of the era, Joseph H. Choate, in New York. Choate recommended that for his defense, Sharon look no further than Choate's former student and Ralston's former personal attorney, W. H. L. Barnes. More important, either Choate or Field counseled Sharon to file his countersuit in federal court, where Field would be the ultimate adjudicator.[20]

While Sharon's detectives were investigating and he was filing his motion, Hill was playing to the public in San Francisco. The press identified her as "well known in society circles of this city" and commented that rumors had circulated for a month or more identifying her as married to the senator.[21] She told the papers that Sharon had asked her to keep the marriage secret because it took place while he was running for reelection. At the time he had sent a woman to Philadelphia to deliver a child she claimed was his, and word of his marriage would "raise a row."[22] As to why Neilson, a recent arrival from Australia, assisted her instead of an attorney's doing so, Hill explained, "I had been trained by Mr. Sharon to believe that he could buy all the lawyers in this city, and I sorely needed an advisor."[23]

Hill was noted both for her beauty and for her volatile temperament. She was something of an intriguer, reportedly engaged to three boys at one time, yet untouched by scandal. Late in 1870, she had claimed a modest inheritance and traveled to San Francisco to live with her grandaunt. Her younger brother, Morgan, settled in the Bay Area as well, marrying into the Murphy family. Using his wife's land, he created a 4,700-acre estate, Villa Mira Monte (later the South Bay city named after him, Morgan Hill).[24]

Hill's family was "scandalized and shocked beyond measure" that she even contemplated marrying Sharon. A judge, in whose house she once lived, stated: "I was surprised to hear of her engagement with Senator Sharon. His millions would hardly compensate a handsome and accomplished young woman for his age and reputation, and certainly no one can have a higher family connection than she has."[25]

It took six months for the Sharon divorce case to come before the court. Preliminary pleadings, skirmishes, and posturing ensured that public interest was maintained. On October 20, appearing in Police Court were Neilson; attorney G. W. Tyler, representing Hill; and Sharon and his representative, Barnes. George Washington Tyler—unkempt, with a beard to his chest—was a courtroom brawler who walked with a slight limp, proudly it was said, because it was caused by a bullet wound he had suffered while speaking out for the Union among Confederate sympathizers.[26] W. H. L. Barnes lacked Tyler's trial experience but was a civic leader. He was dapper and clean shaven except for an enormous moustache and was called "General," although no one knew how he came by the appellation.[27]

A crowd filled the room to capacity. Neilson said that witnesses for Hill were intimidated, the police did not serve requested subpoenas, he was threatened, Gertie Dietz disappeared, and the father of Nellie Brackett—Hill's confidant—suddenly acquired wealth. Defense witnesses rebutted Neilson's statements, and the hearing turned into a shouting match between Barnes and Neilson. Barnes asked the judge to let him lash Neilson if he would not quiet down. " 'The way he talks,' said Barnes, 'would make one think that the alleged adultery had been committed on him.' "[28]

Tyler stated that the court had repealed the statute under which he filed the complaint, and the case as written could not be pursued. The judge agreed and ordered the case dismissed over Barnes's objection. He wanted to force the accusers to present the alleged marriage document. The press reported that the fact the certificate was not produced confirmed suspicions it was forged.[29]

Amid rumors identifying Neilson as an adventurer, convicted of forgery in Australia, he took his case to the streets, addressing a crowd in a sandlot near city hall. Sharon supporters pelted him with eggs. Neilson, finding it strange that an unpopular ex-senator would have such ardent supporters with eggs on hand, shouted that the eggs were thrown at Sharon's direction, and he would make use of the fact. Another day, Neilson appeared with bruises on his face. He swore an attempted murder complaint against unknown assailants who had attacked him as he left his home.[30] Although no evidence indicated Sharon's involvement, the incident was reminiscent of the attack on Conrad Wiegand the day he distributed the anti-Sharon *People's Tribune* on the Comstock.

The divorce case was redrawn and, at a procedural hearing on November 8, Hill produced her contract. She appeared with Tyler, Neilson, and her friend Nellie Brackett. The courtroom was again packed. When Sharon, his attorneys, and his investigators arrived, it was reported that they took their seats at the counsels' table "with an air that said plainly, 'Everybody must give way for us. This is a millionaire's case.'" Hill fished the contract from the "depth of her bosom" saying it protected her honor, and she wished for neither Barnes nor Sharon to touch it. Barnes said they needed to handle it to inspect it. Hill responded that Sharon knew the contract as well as she did. Sharon shouted that it was a damnable lie, "the damnedest ever uttered on earth." When the paper was finally turned over, Barnes glanced at it and handed it to Sharon. "It's a forgery," he cried. Tyler leaped to his feet, bellowing that Sharon was not under oath. He and Sharon traded insults. Sharon continued to mutter and glare at Tyler until the exasperated judge ordered him from the courtroom.[31]

The display reveals the stress Sharon was under. Although he was consistently described as implacable and cool under fire, able to make snap decisions worth hundreds of thousands of dollars, Sharon's temper sometimes flared. There were instances when he had confronted powerful (and physically imposing) Comstockers—John Winters, Joseph Goodman, John Mackay—and anecdotes of his directing assistants to throw extortionists from his office.[32] But this outburst differed from others, because it was done before the community. His public mien as the dignified, poker-faced speculator was shattered.

As for the contract, it was written on two sides of a sheet of notepaper in Hill's hand. It was worn, with some words appearing darker, as if they had been written over as the paper aged. It read:

In the City and County of San Francisco, State of California, on the 25th day of August, A.D. 1880, I Sarah Althea Hill, of the City and County of San Francisco, State of California, age 27 years, do here, in the presence of Almighty God, take Senator William Sharon, of the State of Nevada, to be my lawful and wedded husband, and do here acknowledge and declare myself to be the wife of Senator William Sharon of the State of Nevada.

Sarah Althea Hill
August 25th, 1880, San Francisco, Cal.

I agree not to make known the contents of this paper or its existence for two years unless Mr. Sharon himself sees fit to make it known.

S. A. Hill

In the City and County of San Francisco, State of California, on the 25th day of August, A.D. 1880, I, Senator William Sharon, of the State of Nevada, age 60 years, do here, in

On the reverse side, at the very top of the page, four more lines were written above Sharon's signature. They were a bit smaller than the lines on the front and read:

the presence of Almighty God, take Sarah Althea Hill, of the City of San Francisco, Cal., to be my lawful and wedded wife & do here acknowledge myself to be the husband of Sarah Althea Hill.

/s/ Wm. Sharon, Nevada
Aug. 25, 1880

Late in November, Tyler requested that the San Francisco grand jury be discharged. It was planning to indict Hill for filing a false charge, and he accused Sharon of claiming to control nine jury members. He wrote a letter to the grand jury asserting that Sharon, whom he called a "financial and erotic giant but an intellectual and moral pygmy," was paying some of them. Tyler was promptly cited for contempt.[33] On November 24 it was announced that the grand jury "has indicted Miss Hill, who claims to be the wife of Senator Sharon, and Wm. M. Nelson, her attorney, for forgery, perjury and conspiracy."[34] Barnes invited the press to his depositions, apparently intending to illustrate that Hill owned a "frail character" outside the norms of decent society.

The testimony of a star witness blew up in Barnes's face. Sharon's detectives had turned up Fredrick Buchard, soon dubbed by the press "Poor Freddie." Buchard said that he had been engaged to Hill when her document showed her as married to Sharon. He reported that he had even traveled with her, without Sharon, to the Belmont estate for a weekend with another couple. Newspapers were quick to print the revelation. Then Tyler took charge of the questioning.[35]

The attorney's ferocious manner caused the witness to forget his date of birth. When he came to the question of what caused the end of the engagement, Buchard regained his composure: he had found she was after his money. Tyler then read a long letter from the witness to Hill that contained a salient point: "I have written this immediately after leaving your room, a gentleman that would lay down his life for you. God knows, if I did not love you as I do, I never could have stood such harsh, cruel words as I have stood from you." When asked about the cruel words, he was forced to admit that they were about two hundred dollars she loaned him. The missive was signed: "Always your friend and slave. Fred C. Burchard." Buchard fell apart. After admitting for the record that a pronounced limp was the result of a venereal disease, he left the state.[36]

Barnes took his turn bullying a witness, Sharon's elderly ex–business manager, C. D. Cushman. The former Methodist preacher testified that signatures on the marriage contract and letters were the senator's. Barnes then spent two days forcing him to repeatedly deny "misdeeds with various chambermaids." The *St. Louis Globe Democrat* reported: "His cloth did not save him from very unceremonious handling by the attorneys."[37]

And it became worse for Cushman: he was thrown out of his apartment at the Palace Hotel. The watchman at the Palace would later be prosecuted for battery pursuant to his actions against the elderly witness.[38]

An audience across the country was engaged. One paper described the "racy character" of the case: "Not a day has passed but has witnessed some exciting manoeuvre of counsel or some startling denouement," concluding, "[it] promises to be one of the *causes celebres* in the history of California jurisprudence." The papers dubbed the pair "Juliet Hill and Romeo Sharon" and called her "the Rose of Sharon."[39]

Chapter Thirteen

IN SUPERIOR COURT

THE COURTROOM WAS CROWDED every day of what would be a very lengthy trial. Thirty-three-year-old Jeremiah F. Sullivan presided. The attorneys would call 111 witnesses, many of whom were either rumormongers or perjurers. The plaintiff and four lawyers sat at the center table. Sharon, when his health did not keep him away, occupied a seat at a side table between Barnes and his associate, Oliver P. Evans.

The first witness was Martha Wilson, a middle-aged African American dressmaker for Hill. Her testimony progressed in fits and starts because of objections and theatrics on each side. She said she had seen the marriage contract after Hill asked that she accompany her to the West Coast Furniture Company in October 1880. Hill was furnishing rooms at the Grand Hotel and showed the certificate to prove she was not about to become a kept woman.

Wilson was illiterate, which, Barnes pointed out, made her identification of the document highly suspect. Fortuitously for Hill, while she was showing the contract to Wilson, Mrs. Vesta Snow had visited, and she had read the document outloud to Wilson. Snow testified that not only did she read the document to Wilson; she saw it again the following year, when Hill hid it behind a picture in Wilson's house because she feared Sharon wished to destroy it. Snow was an impressive witness with no stake in the case. She did not work for Hill, barely knew her, and—when asked if she had expressed surprise at hearing of the secret marriage—said she had laughed at the idea.[1]

When it was Hill's turn to testify, the *Chronicle* said she looked as "demure, innocent and sweet as the arts of the toilet could make her." But it also described her in terms often applied to Sharon. Her face "betrays intense nervousness," and "quickness of perception." The *Chronicle* went on to record her statement regarding going to his office in the spring of 1880: "I gave him $7,500 to invest. He said he wanted me to love him, and that if I would let him love me he would give me $1,000 a month and a house. I told him he mistook the woman, and that millions could not buy me. He said he was only teasing me; that he loved me better than any one since his wife died. He proposed a secret marriage, but I resented the proposition."[2]

She related Sharon's story of Gertie Dietz's going to Philadelphia to deliver a baby Dietz claimed was his. When Hill expressed doubts about the story, Sharon produced a letter and tore off and gave Hill half to prove Dietz's existence. The fragment said that the birth had left Dietz in pain, unable to exert herself, concluding: "I was dreadfully lacerated, but can now enjoy your sweet society to its greatest degree. Ain't I naughty?"[3]

Hill testified that the possibility of a secret marriage was discussed for weeks. Then on August 25, 1880, Sharon demanded an answer. He read from law books to convince her that a secret marriage was legal. Finally, she acquiesced. He paced and dictated, and she wrote. She took little care, thinking it would be recopied later, but it never was.[4]

Once married, Hill said, Sharon provided her with five hundred dollars a month and the use of his carriage. After he lost the election, they went to dinner at various restaurants and were often about town together. She frequented Belmont on weekends, describing one instance of playing hostess: "After his return he told me he wanted me to go down to Belmont to entertain some friends of his, and to invite my grandmother, uncle and brother. They objected to going on my invitation, and said they should be invited by him, and he invited them. Cornelius Vanderbilt, Colonel and Mrs. Stagg, Governor and Mrs. Reighart, Mr. Luxton and Mr. Burril were among those who went down."[5]

Five missives from Sharon to Hill, dubbed the "Dear Wife" letters, caused as much contention as the marriage contract. The first of these was sent in October 1880, while Sharon was campaigning in Virginia City. Hill was moving into Sharon's Grand Hotel and wrote complaining of problems with the hotel manager and with decorating the parlor of her suite. Sharon's reply read:

> My dear Wife:
>
> In reply to your kind letter I have written Mr. Thorn and enclose same, which you may read and then send it on to him in an envelope, and he will not know that you have seen it. Sorry that anything should occur to annoy you and think my letter will command the kind courtesy you deserve. Am having a very lively and hard fight. But think I shall be victorious in the end. With kindest consideration believe me as ever.
>
> Very Truly
> Wm. Sharon.[6]

Four other letters with the "Dear Wife" salutation were introduced as exhibits. Each was a short note dealing primarily with the five-hundred-dollar monthly stipend. A typical one, written in the spring of 1881, read: "My Dear Wife: Inclosed send you by Ki the balance, two hundred and fifty, which I hope will make you happy. Will call this evening for the joke." The last of the "Dear Wife" letters introduced was undated. It was of particular interest, written while he was ill ("Am much better to-day. Hope to be up in three or four days."), and said that they would talk about her eastern trip when he recovered.

Other notes were presented addressed "My dear Allie." They revealed a playful side to Sharon: "Come over and join me in a nice bottle of champagne, and let us be gay before Christmas." Beneath his initials it read: "If you don't come over and take part in the bottle, I may hurt myself."[7]

The relationship fell apart in the fall of 1881. A series of unseemly incidents accompanied the breakup. On one occasion Hill hid behind the bureau in Sharon's bedroom as Sharon retired with a strange woman, reportedly the wife of a prominent San Franciscan.[8] Hill said that another time, because she would not hand over the marriage certificate, Sharon choked her until she fainted. Finally, Sharon instructed the manager of the Grand Hotel to evict her. She went to her grandmother's and, upon returning, "I found every door of my rooms taken off, the bells out and the carpets ripped up. I had only my furniture and the bare floor. My maid had fled in fright and I was left alone."[9]

Hill wrote several letters to "My dear Mr. Sharon." She explained her actions and pleaded for him to do the same. "You once said to me, 'There was no woman that could look you in the face & say, William Sharon, you have wronged me,'" wrote Hill. "Don't let me be the first to utter the cry."[10] Her initial appeals fell on deaf ears. Then came two short reconciliations, the second involving a night when her friend Nellie Brackett hid behind the bureau to hear talk of the marriage. Sharon's arrival led to an amorous encounter involving more than talk, and Brackett was forced to wait out the course of events in her hiding place.[11]

Barnes's associate, O. P. Evans, conducted the cross-examination. Evans was "gentlemanly and quiet," maintaining decorum when the other barristers battled. The *Alta* believed that he would come through the case "with less of its filth clinging to his skirts" than anyone else.[12] Evans pressed Hill concerning the $7,500 she said she gave Sharon to invest. Were they greenbacks or gold? What denominations? How long did it take Sharon to count it? Hill repeatedly answered that she could not tell. "Were they $5, $10, $20, or $100 notes?" Exasperated, Hill said: "I tell you I cannot tell you and you cannot put words into my mouth." He asked if she had ever received investment advice from Sharon. She said yes but could not remember what it was, adding that it was bad advice though, since she lost money.

On the second day of his questioning, Evans turned to her ardor for the occult. Hill answered no when asked whether she had ever given Sharon any powders or potions or had ever worn his clothes. Tyler objected. He admitted that Hill wore the senator's shirts and socks in order to exercise powers over Sharon but claimed that it was "an idle superstition which women of all ages and countries had entertained."[13] Later testimony revealed that Hill had put potions in Sharon's drink and used his clothing for spells to win his affections. The exchange revealed the plaintiff's tendency to lie if backed into a corner. Evans now asked about the relationship between her and her family. She responded that it was not good. When he asked why, she turned the query to her advantage: "My brother did not consider Mr. Sharon my equal by any means, but thinks he is of very low birth. We are somebody by birth, and Mr. Sharon is like a thistle in a field by birth. . . . We had many a fight about Mr. Sharon and many a heartache."[14] Hill was proving herself a dangerous adversary—not always truthful, but wary and smart.

On three occasions the next day, Evans, following a line of questioning, suddenly changed the subject. In the first instance he asked, "In the month of October, 1880, did you in company with two gentlemen and Mrs. Bornemann go to the Fourteen Mile House?" Hill stammered and first said that she had never eaten at a public house. Then she said that she did not know it was the Fourteen Mile House.[15]

There was reason for her discomfiture. The Fourteen Mile House, outside the city, and the Poodle Dog, on Bush and Dupont, were the area's two establishments known more for the trysts that occurred under their roofs than for their meals.[16] Private dining rooms featured "a couch and a door which locked on the inside." The elevator man at the Poodle Dog was a closemouthed individual said to wear diamonds.[17]

Minutes later, Evans asked whether she remembered on May 10, 1880, only a few months before her alleged marriage, taking poison at a gentleman's office because she was disappointed in love. She denied the charge, claiming that she had fainted after a disagreement with the gentleman and, in attempting to take laudanum for relief, accidentally took too much.[18]

Evans was careful not to mention the gentleman's name; he was referring to Sharon's associate, attorney Reuben Lloyd. A later witness testified that even after her association with Sharon, Hill regarded Lloyd as "her only man." The incident Evans was questioning Hill about was either attempted suicide or a melodramatic scene meant to represent it. She had needed her stomach pumped and had spent the night at the doctor's office. Tyler conceded that the incident had occurred. In fact, he contended, it accounted for why she so quickly became enamored of Sharon: she was rebounding from heartbreak.[19]

The third time Evans changed the subject, he caused an unanticipated reaction. Evans asked if Hill had ever threatened the senator's life. She responded that she had told Barnes if she was wrongfully convicted, she would take Sharon's life and her own. Barnes rose, denying she had said any such thing to him. David Terry, seated quietly at the counsel's table since the second day of the trial, now rose to his feet. Staring at Barnes, he said that if it was a question of veracity between witness and lawyer, he believed the witness. Barnes chose not to contest the point.[20]

David S. Terry was one of California's ablest and most feared men. In his sixties and physically imposing at six foot three and over two hundred and twenty pounds, he had fought in the Mexican-American War, practiced law from the age of eighteen, and was elected California Supreme Court chief justice when the Know Nothing Party swept into office in 1855.

In 1856 Terry had confronted the vigilance committee that took control of unruly San Francisco. When a group of vigilantes attempted to arrest a witness who sought Terry's protection, a brawl erupted. Terry, known to carry a bowie knife under his coat, stabbed a vigilante in the neck, severing his carotid artery. Later, Terry surrendered to the vigilantes. Somehow the wounded man survived, allowing the vigilantes to save face by releasing him. In 1859 Terry resigned from the court after David C. Broderick accepted his challenge to a duel. Broderick, an ex–New York fireman, was one of California's U.S. senators. Terry killed Broderick and was charged with murder. Freed on a technicality, he made his way to the Comstock.

At the outbreak of the Civil War, rumors had spread that Terry, and Southerners who would follow him, might forcibly take control of the mines for the Confederacy. Instead, Terry abandoned the territory to fight as a Confederate brigadier general. Returning to California and his law practice, he regained the spotlight by leading the contingent representing workers at the state constitutional convention in 1878 and 1879.[21] Now, in 1884, he was an advocate for Sarah Althea Hill and soon to become more than that.

With or without Terry's advocacy, additional witnesses buoyed up the plaintiff's case. Hill's friend Brackett said that to prove she was acting morally, Hill had showed her the marriage certificate and some of the "Dear Wife" letters early in 1882. She also described the "well-known" hiding-behind-the-bureau incident: "At one point [Sharon] said, 'Who is my own little wife and nobody knows about it?' After some time, when she heard the senator breathing heavily, Nellie tiptoed out.

> Barnes looked overwhelmed, . . . "You didn't!"
> "I did," said Nellie.
> "You did?" asked Barnes despairingly. Nellie nodded.[22]

Another legendary figure, Mary E. Pleasant, nearly seventy years old and known familiarly as "Mammy," sat directly behind the plaintiff in the courtroom, occasionally holding counsel with her. Pleasant, delivered from slavery at nine years old, had worked for years as an indentured servant in Nantucket. Then moving to Boston, where she met and married James W. Smith, a wealthy mixed-race merchant, she joined his work with the Underground Railroad. When he died (rumor said by poison) sometime between 1844 and 1848, she inherited his fortune. Pleasant continued working to free slaves until she was forced to flee to San Francisco. There, she helped former slaves fight extradition and obtain housing and work. She returned to the East to help finance John Brown's war, escaping a second time after Harpers Ferry. In San Francisco she ran men's boardinghouses, some reputed to offer more than room and board. She also managed laundries and catered meals for men like the Bank Ring members. In the 1860s Pleasant invested in the Comstock, becoming a millionaire. She was known to assist those who were down and out, especially young women.

Calm and subdued in court, she identified herself as Thomas Bell's housekeeper. While it was true that she oversaw Bell's household for many years, she was his business partner and her wealth was as great as his. An author later wrote two sensationalized books contending that Pleasant was the brains behind Bell's success and was also his murderer.[23] A contemporary described her as a picturesque, solitary figure who walked like a duchess.[24] On the witness stand, Pleasant said that she saw the marriage certificate when Sharon evicted Hill from the Grand Hotel. She confronted Sharon, whom she knew through Bell, about the woman's circumstances, asking him to provide a house for her. Sharon first agreed, then he changed his mind.[25]

What role Pleasant played behind the scenes in the trial was widely conjectured. Hill described her as a "great and true friend." One of Sharon's attorneys charged her with being the sole financier of Hill's case, involved for a percentage of possible winnings. Among those believing the contract and letters were forgeries, speculation centered on Pleasant's masterminding the plot.[26]

Tyler ended the plaintiff's case on the ninth day. It was time to learn what Sharon's money had uncovered. Sharon's defense team was intent on discrediting Hill. One witness claimed that the plaintiff had told her she cared only for Sharon's money. Another testified that Hill had said she had rejected a Sharon marriage proposal. Other witnesses corroborated these stories. On cross-examination, each witness faced brutal questioning from Tyler.[27]

Mrs. Julia Bornemann, reportedly a "stunning beauty," had arranged the ride to the Fourteen Mile House with Hill and two gentlemen. She testified in a voice "soft as a lute" that Hill had indicated to her that she was not married to Sharon. On cross-examination Tyler, exhibiting newfound gallantry, led her to say that nothing untoward had occurred on the ride with Hill and the gentlemen. She explained that it could not have, since she never engaged in questionable conduct. As she left the stand, Mrs. Bornemann smiled at Tyler, telling Barnes, "He isn't so bad at all, is he now?"[28]

One paper, noting "especially spiteful" replies by female witnesses, concluded that dislike for Hill was the impetus for their testimony rather than Sharon's money. But it found no public sympathy for the unpopular Sharon either. The correspondent for the *Chicago Daily News* noted strange occurrences: "Witnesses on the plaintiff's side have gone over to the defense, and several have mysteriously disappeared. . . . It is strongly intimated that Sharon's agents are using money and could tell where the absent ones are."[29]

Testimony on Sharon's behalf by two women, Mrs. Fanny M. Samson and Mrs. Mary Shawhan, was discredited. Both were attractive and well dressed. Samson charged that the plaintiff had offered to buy her testimony. "She wanted me to help her, and would give me $100,000, and I could travel the world over with the money." Shawhan testified that as late as 1882 or 1883, Hill told her she was going to bring a breach-of-promise suit against Sharon because he had broken their engagement. During cross-examination, it came out that both women had worked to find witnesses for Sharon "in the murkier strata" of the community. Later, two witnesses said Samson owed considerable sums of money that, she assured them, would be repaid at the case's conclusion. Another witness said that when she told Samson she knew nothing of the case, she was asked whether she would testify if something were "suggested" to her.[30]

With each of these women, Tyler's cross-examination was merciless. When he proposed to show that Shawhan "dined at disreputable places and visited an assignation house with strange men," a commotion erupted. Shawhan reached in her pocket as if to pull out a gun but was grabbed by one of the lawyers for the defense. Her son, in his early twenties, rushed toward Tyler. Tyler's son, an attorney assisting his father, stopped the young man, threatening to shoot him if he drew a pistol. Judge Sullivan ordered the mother and son removed and called for a recess. Stating that he was "tired of sitting here in the midst of an arsenal," the judge directed that thereafter everyone who entered the courtroom be searched.[31]

The day of the gunplay, Sharon's son, Fred, sat next to Shawhan's son. It was the last mention of his attendance. Soon afterward, he married Louise Tevis, daughter of the president of Wells Fargo, in a hastily organized affair. Louise Tevis was recovering from a marriage to the disinherited son of Vice President John Breckinridge, a match that had produced three sons and a $500,000 debt run up by the handsome ne'er-do-well. The night of the Sharon-Tevis ceremony, the couple left for Europe. Fred did not return to San Francisco until his father was on his deathbed. His sister Flora, her social position in England injured by the trial, was reportedly so disgusted that she cut off all communication with her father. One paper noted: "The old man was always weak physically, but the mortification and chagrins, the reproaches of his friends and the coldness of his children, all growing out of his relations with the pestiferous Sarah Althea, are more than human nature can stoically bear."[32]

The defense now called a host of occultists. All testified that they had assisted Hill, whose intent was to win Sharon back. Attempts included various "love draughts," at least one of which "seemed to make him sick at his stomach"; Hill's wearing two of Sharon's socks, dipped in whiskey and tied around her left knee; a fetish using three drops of her blood drawn at midnight of the full moon; a pigeon's heart stuck with nine pins and nine needles; and a spell that, the *Alta* said, required: "One single hair from the scanty locks which straggle over the Senatorial brow like railroad routes across a new country." This last was to be cut into equal lengths and consumed in an omelet shared by the couple.

There was also what one paper described as a "hoo-doo scene." A grave digger had seen the plaintiff and Nellie Brackett place a package at the bottom of a new grave. The *Chicago Daily News* reported that, when produced, the package emitted a stench that "drove everybody from the temple of justice." The paper commented: "Strange as it may seem, the charm failed to work, and Sarah found on investigation that her aged lover was not true to her—that other women shared her 'Sen's' affections."[33]

Barnes's efforts revealed Hill's superstitious nature but nothing regarding her marital status. Moreover, newspaper descriptions of the courtroom antics—using adjectives such as "curious," "remarkable," "sensational," and "scandalous"—denigrated the ex-senator as well as the plaintiff.[34]

Then came the testimony from Ah Ki, who had served Sharon since 1863. The *Territorial Enterprise* called the valet renowned although "unostentatious of manner."[35] When he testified, it was reported that "Ki, the Chinese body servant of the ex-Senator, has been on the stand, and, although he is very far removed from a fool, he has made as much fun as any clown ever did." Most of the humor can be attributed to Ki's impish manner, though some of it was a result of racism. When Ki was called, an attorney suggested that he be sworn in Chinese style, by cutting off a rooster's head. The papers reporting Ki's comments emphasized his pronunciation by substituting the letter *l* for *r*, *s* for *t*, and *ah* for *er*.[36]

Ki provided one piece of relevant information: before their breakup, Hill had stayed with Sharon several nights a week, often taking breakfast with him. His testimony also revealed the plaintiff's dark side. Ki had visited her rooms many times, including once when Sharon instructed him to show Hill Gertie Deitz's baby. Another visitor and Ah Ki agreed that the baby looked like a little "Sen." Angered, Hill took Ki aside and told him that she would pay to have him steal the baby and kill it so that it would receive no part of the estate.

After Sharon drove Hill out of the hotel, she constantly coaxed Ki to let her see him, give him a message, or sneak into his rooms to apply magic: black powder sprinkled on furniture, white in bottles of alcohol, clove spice under Sharon's pillow. Finally, Ki stood firm against Hill's gaining entrance, saying that if he let her back the senator would cut his throat. Later she fooled Ki, claiming to have been invited to dinner. Finding her, Sharon shouted at her for rifling through his papers and stealing money. This was the occasion on which, Hill claimed, Sharon became so angry that he choked her.[37] Tyler's attempts at cross-examination caused only confusion. When Ki was excused, he left the stand "bowing ingratiatingly" to the room.[38]

Another witness of interest was William Neilson, the man who had initiated the case for Hill. When the attorney asked why Neilson felt competent to advise Hill, he replied that a prominent attorney had advised him. "Who?" asked Barnes. "General Barnes," Neilson answered. As the flummoxed Barnes looked on, Neilson described meeting the interrogator on three occasions. Neilson quoted Barnes encouraging him to file suit:

"If you can give me a dead sure thing there is nothing would please me better than to go after the damned old rascal." But, Neilson reported, at the third meeting Barnes said that Sharon denied the whole business, so he looked elsewhere for an attorney. Barnes could take the stand, but that would disqualify him from representing the defendant. So he merely slumped "in impotent despair."[39]

But Sharon's defense was hardly impotent. It hired a number of experts to examine the marriage certificate and "Dear Wife" letters. Because of the plaintiff's apprehensions regarding care of the documents, Judge Sullivan ordered all examinations conducted in open court. A microscope was brought in, and the experts worked at a table at the front of the room. Once their examinations were complete, they were called on to testify. The man whose testimony carried the most weight was a "microscopist" named Hyde.

Mr. Hyde's testimony was laborious. Every time he made a point, he would locate the document and the judge and key players would march single file to the microscope and "shuffle past like school children at a drinking fountain." Hyde found erasures and believed someone other than Sharon had written the salutations of the letters. He testified further that the signature on the contract was written before the body of the document. When folded, the dried ink caused a breaking of the paper fibers that differed from the text and Hill's signature and ran and blotted at the folds.

As was his wont, Tyler vigorously challenged the findings. He forced Hyde to admit that the salutations could be the senator's, "particularly if done when he was ill, nervous, or under the influence of alcohol." As to the folds in the marriage certificate, Hyde admitted moisture—for example that which collected in a woman's bosom—might cause inks to blot in unusual ways. Tyler then put him through blotting experiments that extended his testimony to four weeks.[40]

In mid-May Martha Wilson, who had testified that she saw the marriage document in 1880, took the stand to recant. But on being redirected, she decided that her original testimony was true, except that Snow did not read the contract to her. It then came out that Shawhan had visited Wilson, spending three days threatening, cajoling, and offering her a $1,000 bribe to change her testimony.[41]

On May 28 Sharon, absent for several days, appeared in court, and, without fanfare, Barnes called him to the stand. Barnes asked Sharon to address the $7,500 that, Hill claimed, she had given him to invest. He denied ever taking money from her: "She made some little inquiry about stocks, evidently wanting to go into a deal of some kind, but as my experience with women is that when they win they never divide and when they lose they never pay, I changed the subject." He said he did indeed pay her $7,500, but for an entirely different reason. By November 1881 he wanted to break off their relationship. He offered her $5,000, she wanted $10,000, and they settled on $7,500. "Her stories about giving me money are all false. The money was paid to her in order to purchase my peace of mind."[42]

Sharon's testimony challenged Hill's claims. In his version, after their initial meeting he saw her once more before going to Nevada to campaign. Upon his return, she again visited him at the bank and invited him to visit her at her room at the Baldwin Hotel. He did, making a social call. A few weeks later she came to his office, "sheepishly" asking for money. He gave her $150.

As Sharon told of first dining with her in his rooms at the Palace Hotel, the plaintiff, "face aflame," held a fan before her, never taking her eyes from the witness. He told of passing merry hours until midnight or one P.M.:

> She seemed to be so agreeable that I offered her a salary of $250 a month to be my mistress. She refused, and in an instant I had offered her $500 a month. She said she wanted the money badly, but she did not care to be my mistress. I said, "All right, Miss Hill; it is too late for you to return to the Baldwin. You take that room and I will take my own, and you will be perfectly safe." I then walked into my room and retired, and about half an hour later she came in. I considered her coming to my room an acceptance of my proposal, and after that I paid her $500 a month, besides giving her presents.[43]

Many observers saw Sharon's frank testimony as credible. It explained the notes sent her with checks. Barnes stressed that the letters were not at all what a loving new husband might write. Sharon insisted that he had never addressed Hill as "wife," and the inflection in the notes was altered substantially with the word omitted.

Still, some of Sharon's admissions were more difficult to attribute to a man and his mistress: accompanying Hill to meet her aunt and grandmother; the invitation to his daughter's wedding and numerous other invitations to Belmont; dates to the theater and to Oakland to visit friends.[44] As to the choking incident, Sharon said that it occurred after he "had some trouble with [Ms. Hill]." He agreed to help her go to New York to study for the stage to get rid of her. But before arrangements were made, at a time when he was sick, she dropped through the transom into his room. She walked about, disturbing him, until he finally pushed her into another room. "Here she threw herself on the floor, mule like, and I poured a pitcher of cold water over her. Then she came to her senses and I said: 'Miss Hill, if you act like this I shall call the watchman. Get up and go to bed.' I never took her by the throat in my life."[45]

Sharon went on to say that Hill was invited to his daughter's wedding only to keep her from becoming a marked woman at the Grand Hotel when everyone else was invited. A couple of days after he received her receipt for the $7,500, she begged to stay with him. Various things, including the receipt, disappeared. He accused her of theft and ordered her out of the hotel.[46]

One news account described Tyler's cross-examination as "very sharp and interesting." But while displaying aspects of Sharon's character and skill at repartee, it did nothing to determine which of the parties was telling the truth. The *Chicago Daily News* described Hill as "an old man's darling" while calling him "her ancient lover" and "a decrepit old moneybag."[47] Tyler called attention to the elderly man's style of wooing a young woman. He asked if Sharon sang "Auld Lang Syne" or quoted verse that first night with Hill. Sharon said he might have recited something regarding friendship or the Divine Power: "Just an airy mess, you know such as any gentleman would give a lady in a social call. In the presence of ladies, if they are sprightly and good looking, a little sentiment is always inspired in a gentleman." Tyler soon moved to a more telling question. He pointed out that, despite all he now said about their relationship, Sharon had introduced Hill to socialites at the Belmont estate as a respectable woman. Sharon responded, "I spoke of her simply as Miss Hill. I never said anything about her respectability."[48] At another point Sharon said: "I always feel kindly to any human being or animal, or anything that lives and moves, unless they try to destroy me. I certainly never was attached to the woman in any sense of the word. . . . She never aroused my affections in any way. It was merely friendly intercourse."[49]

When the topic turned to the plaintiff's alleged use of voodoo charms, Tyler took up the clothing from the grave. He thrust a sock in Sharon's face, demanding to know if it was his. Sharon would not touch the item and said he could not tell. When Tyler picked up a piece of shirt and shouted, "Do your shirts ordinarily resemble this?" Sharon replied, "I would like to compare my shirt with yours."[50]

As the cross-examination was coming to a close, Sharon pronounced nearly all the documents entered as evidence to be forgeries. Tyler asked what degree of certainty he possessed. Sharon said that he would almost stake his life on it. Tyler asked if he would stake his life on anything: "Yes, on my honor." Tyler looked incredulous, causing Sharon to say, "You need not appear so doubtful, sir. I said my honor. I did not say your honor. I would not stake my life on that."[51]

When Tyler was asked if he rattled Sharon during his examination, "'Rattle him,' exclaimed [Tyler], 'do you suppose I can rattle a man who can bet a fortune on a busted flush and look as if he were going to sleep at the same time?'"[52] But Hill's counsel did wish to address one last topic: Sharon's paid relationships with women. David Terry said they wished to show that Sharon used money to gain access to women, supporting Hill's claim that when Sharon's wealth failed to win her, he resorted to the marriage contract. Tyler pointed out that of all Sharon's mistresses, Hill was the only one he introduced to family. Sharon was "a great deal agitated."

The defense held a consultation. Attorney Evans then issued a statement that they would "admit that the defendant was a man who was habitually free with women; that he had other mistresses besides the plaintiff; that he had never appeared in public with them; that he had never introduced any of them except her to his friends or acquaintances or any member of his family; that he had invited none of them except her to Belmont on the occasion of the marriage of his daughter; that he had allowed none of them except her to entertain his guests at Belmont or be of any party visiting him there." With this remarkable admission the case was continued for one term, to be called again six weeks later on July 14.[53]

Chapter Fourteen

PRESSING ON

ON JUNE 6, during the trial's continuation, the Republican Party met in Chicago to nominate its presidential candidate. Sharon traveled there, arriving on the morning of Saturday the 7th. On June 10 the *Chicago Herald* reported on a party the ex-senator hosted at the Palmer House. Sharon sat swinging his legs on the side of a bed, dressed in shirtsleeves, smoking a cigar. In attendance were several friends, including J. P. Jones. Sharon believed Jones had stolen the Crown Point mine from him, and during their bitter battle for the Senate Sharon brought forward accusations that Jones had started the Yellow Jacket fire. Sharon had also caused a market crash in an attempt to break Jones. For a short time Jones had supported Sutro's tunnel against Sharon's wishes, and he later threatened to build a railroad to rival the Virginia & Truckee. But eventually, Jones withdrew support from those projects and assisted Sharon in his successful bid for the Senate. They served together for four years, maintaining a collegial relationship the rest of their lives.[1]

At the Palmer, the men drank from a decanter on an ebony end table and joked. Sharon quoted poets, talking of his "bad scrape" and saying how thankful he was to be getting out of it. He wondered what any of them would have done under similar circumstances. "It was pretty tough to go on the stand and admit that I had been such a fool," he said, "but what are you going to do—be blackmailed? Not much." One of his friends asked how he could get into such a predicament. Sharon reached for the ebony stand. "What is it the poet Thompson says?

'He saw her charming, but he saw not half
The charms her downcast modesty concealed.'

"Who could resist it? I read the 'Maid of Athens' to her. She melted; then 'the kiss snatched hasty from the sidelong maid,' did the business. Whatever might have been lacking, $500 a month supplied."

Somebody suggested that perhaps a couple of thousand dollars would fix the thing up. Sharon assured the men they did not know the crowd he was up against. "I treated her honorably, as the world would call it. I gave her a splendid income. But she wanted more." Knowing that she wanted him to marry her, he offered her $7,500. "That was right, wasn't it Jones?" Jones agreed. "I could have settled it at any time for $20,000—$10,000 to her and $10,000 to Neilson. But not one cent! Millions for defense—not a cent for tribute." He went on to say he believed he had paid perhaps $40,000 to date. "But I will not be blackmailed out of a cent. . . . I mean now not only to beat her blackmail suit, but I will land her in the penitentiary." A few moments later, he softened the sentiment: "I don't care to crush the woman any more than necessary, but if it were necessary we would show her to have been an adventuress from her twentieth year."[2]

Sharon's monologue was revealing. He illustrated his remarks with scraps of verse, demonstrating uncommon erudition. The dialogue also reveals a sense of humor. ("Whatever might have been lacking [in his love-making], $500 a month supplied.") His resolve in choosing to look the fool rather than succumb to paying tribute illustrates that his pugnacious nature superseded any regard for community standing. His contention that he treated her "honorably" apparently refers to the "splendid income" he bestowed. Owing to the mores of the group and the era, the sophism—if enough money is involved, an illicit relationship might be worthy of esteem—went unchallenged.

Back on the West Coast on June 10, the California Democrats convened what proved to be a controversial state convention in Stockton. Sharon's friend, Justice Stephen Field, was seeking the Democratic nomination for president. In a state divided over its railroad plutocracy, Field's court decisions made him the acknowledged leader of the pro-railroad forces. David Terry, Hill's champion, was one of the leaders of the anti-railroad group. Asked to endorse Field, who believed that Terry could win over the convention, Terry replied, "If I could I would not, as his judicial record would absolutely prevent my giving him my support; . . . no place in the records of his decisions could it be found that he had ever given a judgment for a poor man against a rich one, no matter what the evidence."[3]

Field's supporters included Sharon's attorney, O. P. Evans, and Francis Newlands. Unfortunately for Field, they were part of a tiny contingent. An overwhelming majority passed twenty-four resolutions. The first declared the party antimonopoly; the last repudiated Field as a candidate.[4]

Bancroft's *Chronicle of the Builders* includes a dramatic account of Newlands taking the platform to support Field before six hundred "turbulent" men. Newlands asked to be heard, and they shouted him down. When order was restored, he began, "I am a friend of Mr. Justice Field." Derisive shouts again rose. He held his ground, speaking between interruptions until some in the crowd helped silence others and he was allowed to finish. The theme of the speech was that if the conventioneers wished to strike down the greatest expounder of the Constitution since John Marshall, strike down Stephen J. Field. His speech was hailed as "brave and eloquent" but changed no votes. The twenty-four resolutions passed, 466 to 13.[5]

A week later, on June 23, 1884, a newspaper announced that Sharon had received William Neilson's record from Australia. Calling him a "precocious scoundrel," the article said that Neilson had served a term in the penitentiary for forgery.[6] Three weeks later Neilson dropped out of the case. Papers published a history of his involvement, quoting him: "I treated indictments with disdain, and even made light of an attempt to assassinate me, from the effects of which I suffer to this day." But he claimed to have discovered facts that weakened his belief in the plaintiff's case. He also felt threatened from each side: "The lady's ingratitude and the unbridled temper on the one hand and the defendant's unparalleled persecutions on the other have been too much for me. . . . I am broken down in health."[7]

Soon, newspapers carried a Neilson claim that the "Dear Wife" letters were forgeries, and the newspapers speculated that Neilson's evidence might turn the case in favor of Sharon. But he was never called. Asked why he did not want Neilson as a witness, Barnes replied, "He would have been so thoroughly impeached that the time passed in taking his testimony would have been fruitless."[8]

Despite the sensationalism and polemics, the "greatest divorce case the Pacific Coast has ever known" hinged on only one issue: Were the terms of the Civil Code of Marriage fulfilled; that is, was there an assumption of marital rights, duties, and obligations? If those criteria were met, the marriage was legal and a divorce could be granted.

Nonetheless, when the trial resumed on July 15, 1884, the process of taking more, mostly irrelevant, testimony recommenced. Hill again testified, remembering that on the day of the purported cemetery incident, she was on a visit to Mrs. Pleasant at the house of Thomas Bell. Thomas Bell and others in the household corroborated this testimony.[9] Nellie Brackett was recalled and refuted Hill's refutation. She said that they did indeed bury Sharon's clothes. On cross-examination, she revealed that her father was paying her bills. He was not working, and she did not know where he was getting money.[10]

Hill also denied telling anyone that she loved Reuben Lloyd after meeting Sharon, or, after August 25, 1880, telling anyone anything inconsistent with being married. Sharon returned to the stand as well. He denied asking Mrs. Samson to secure fraudulent testimony and said that he paid no more than fifty dollars in expenses when she sought witnesses. One other witness of importance was called. Max Gumpel was a handwriting expert. The court required a bench warrant to secure his appearance. He explained that Barnes had hired him to testify for the defense, but his findings made him reluctant to appear. When asked about his training, Barnes interrupted to say that Gumpel was eminently qualified. The wit-

188 THE INFAMOUS KING

ness then testified that the marriage-contract signature was Sharon's and that no part of any "Dear Wife" letter was erased.[11]

The trial now neared its end. Costs were exorbitant. Observers speculated that Hill's money came from a stock company formed by Tyler. One newspaper reported that a wealthy widow (certainly M. E. Pleasant) was heavily involved. Regarding Sharon, it said: "[He] has three attorneys, several short-hand reporters and half a dozen spies and detectives. His expenses cannot have been less than $1,000 a day."[12]

It took twenty and a half days for the attorneys' final statements. One argument involved Pleasant's testimony. Barnes accused her of producing "martyrs in the cause of Miss Hill." Tyler pointed to her testimony, saying that if believed, it proved the marriage contract's validity. Judge Sullivan, in an age of extreme racial prejudice, was being forced to decide who was truthful, a power broker of surpassing wealth or an African American female.[13]

Terry later concluded that because Hill told the truth and Sharon lied, a respectable woman's reputation, never before questioned, was threatened. Barnes agreed that the two litigants' stories were irreconcilable: "If [Hill] is right, I do not hesitate to say, with Judge Terry, that a more deeply wronged woman never lived; if [Sharon] is right, a more unfortunate and guilty woman has rarely existed."[14]

Chapter Fifteen

BITTER END

In October 1884, Judge Lorenzo Sawyer of the U.S. Circuit Court ruled on a plea for dismissal of the Sharon-initiated federal case. Sawyer was a protégé of Stephen Field, called in at least one instance his "toady."[1] Months earlier, Sawyer had decided that the case came under federal jurisdiction. The new argument involved two points: the suit in state court was the same as that in federal court; and Sharon was a citizen of California, as was Hill, so the federal court lacked jurisdiction. Sawyer ruled that the state suit was for divorce, while the federal suit sought cancellation of the marriage contract. Hence the suits "call and pray for entirely different and inconsistent relief." As to Sharon's residency, the filing was too late. Three months were allowed for testimony, and over five months had elapsed.[2] The federal case would proceed.

As for the case in Judge Sullivan's court, reports leaked that the decision would be announced at 9 a.m. on December 24. The courtroom was filled to capacity. Hill was dressed in striking fashion: a blue velvet coat over a black silk dress. Sharon, reportedly in the building, did not come to the courtroom. At ten minutes after the hour, the judge entered, looking pale. He read the decision in a low voice, rarely raising his eyes. The press account read: "After reviewing the testimony [Judge Sullivan] concludes by declaring that under the laws of California the plaintiff is the legal wife of Sharon, and as such, on the ground of willful desertion, is entitled to a divorce and a division of the common property."[3]

Judge Sullivan's decision included answers to the questions of whether the contract was legal and the marriage consummated. He considered

Max Gumpel the most reliable handwriting analyst, since the defense had recruited him but he did not find for them, and his competence was unquestioned. The judge found Sharon's argument that Hill was nothing but a mistress without force when his actions were considered. Would an ex-senator desecrate the marriage feast of his daughter with the presence of a "lascivious wanton"? Hill's family was invited to Belmont. Sharon accompanied her to be introduced to and visit with her grandmother and uncles. The jurist asked: "Would the defendant have had the effrontery and shamelessness, combined with the heartless cruelty which would characterize such conduct, if his statement were true?" The distinction Sharon made between the manner in which he treated Hill and his "uniform manner of treating his mistresses" could not be overlooked. From August 25, 1880, their relations were as intimate as those of husband and wife.[4]

Reactions to the ruling were predictably mixed. Barnes addressed the press for the defense: "It is an entire surprise to the profession, both as to law and facts." Tyler commented that with the state court's decision, the federal suit became a nullity, commenting, "There is nothing left to decide."[5] That evening a reporter located the defendant with Senator Jones at the Palace Hotel. Sharon looked "a trifle out of sorts" and persisted in asking the reporter what he thought of the case. The reporter asked him what he proposed to do. "Fight it to the bitter end," he said, "in all the courts and on all sides. . . . The contracts and letters are forgeries, and that knowledge keeps me in the ring."[6]

Flushed with joy, Hill spent the afternoon doing her Christmas shopping, charging gifts under the name Mrs. William Sharon. Reporters caught up with her in her rooms. "I'm so happy," she said, "I feel just like a young kitten that has just been brought into the house and set before the fire. The poor, dear old 'Sen!' I'm sorry I beat the old man, for I love him still. . . . Only for the principle of the thing I would have compromised long ago, but I was after his name, not his money. I married that man fully believing he would act fairly."[7]

On February 13, 1885, Judge Sullivan made his judgment regarding alimony. It was set at the considerable monthly sum of $2,500. The judgment further stipulated $55,000 in fees to be paid Hill's counselors. Sharon called the award "an infamous conspiracy" and commented flippantly that: "Judge Sullivan evidently rated Althea's value a great deal higher than she did herself. 'When she and I had to fix her value, she rated it as $500 a month.'"[8]

The defense immediately filed to stay proceedings pending appeal. To do so, Sharon had to post $305,000, double the amount of the alimony and lawyer fees, and double the monthly payment for three years—the estimated time of settlement of the appeal.[9]

As both sides prepared for the next stage of the ordeal, the lead attorneys gave way to a pair of western courtroom legends: Senator William M. Stewart for Sharon and David S. Terry for Hill. Stewart told Sharon that they should try the federal case as if there had been no state trial. If Sharon won the U.S. Circuit Court judgment, the state court's decision would be of little value. Stewart blamed Barnes for making the state trial "notorious" and lacking the necessary courage in confronting Tyler and Terry: "Barnes blustered and spent a great amount of money in all sorts of proceedings, but when Terry and Tyler remonstrated he lowered his flag in the dust."[10] During a later hearing, when Tyler objected to something Stewart said, Stewart, a large physical presence who had trained in mining-camp courts, illustrated how he believed the opposition should be handled—he reached for a gun. Tyler protested that he only wished to dispute with words, but Stewart continued advancing on him until others restrained him.[11]

On the other side, in early spring 1885, a breach developed between Tyler and Hill. The cause was threefold. After Judge Sullivan announced his decision, Tyler—against Hill's wishes—announced the terms of his contract with her: he was to receive half of the settlement. Also, she wanted him to file suit against the *Alta* for printing Neilson's accusation regarding the forging of the letters, but Tyler refused.[12] And most objectionable, Tyler's failure to file a timely objection to Sharon's claim of residency necessitated retrying the case in federal court. Terry stepped forward.

Two cases of perjury that evolved from the *Sharon* v. *Sharon* trial and one case of battery against the watchman who evicted former business manager Cushman from Sharon's hotel were tried in 1885. Sharon testified at Martha Wilson's perjury trial. He told the court that he wanted to relate the facts of Hill's forgeries, but the judge silenced him, ruling that they were not pertinent to the case before him. Wilson, who recanted her testimony and then disavowed her retraction, was eventually acquitted.[13]

In the federal case a commissioner took depositions, with Stewart, his associates, and Terry conducting the questioning. Hill attended each deposition. Her propensity for erratic behavior was becoming pronounced. At one point she reportedly accosted the state supreme court justices in their chambers. She later claimed that the incident was greatly exaggerated and that she had simply visited to ask when alimony might be given her.[14] On another occasion, during a deposition, she pulled a gun from her purse. O. P. Evans, Sharon's attorney, refused to proceed. It was not the first time she had threatened Sharon's representatives. Justice Field, receiving the complaint, ordered Hill disarmed prior to any session. The press attributed her stress to circumstances. Sharon had paid no alimony, "and to all appearance the plaintiff is as far away from her goal as she was in November, 1883, when the suit began."[15]

In its mid-March number, Ambrose Bierce's *Wasp* used its double-edged sword, sarcasm and criticism. As was his wont, the curmudgeonly pundit waded in against all parties. He spoke first of Tyler, Hill, and Neilson having been "shot apart by the mere inherent energy of their mutual repulsiveness." Calling Hill "vicious, ignorant, headstrong, and whimsical past all example," Bierce argued that she betrayed or was betrayed by everyone close to her except Judge Terry, and he was next. Sharon, portrayed as dupe to a team of pettifogging attorneys, was included: "Honest William Sharon doubtless coddles the bright and beautiful dream of coming by his own, or what is left of it. The hope is fallacious; there has been no falling out among the attorneys, nor will there be while anything remains to the good old man but his stainless character and honored name."

Bierce concluded: "We think we could mention three persons, of three sexes, of whom two will soon be in the penitentiary and one in a lunatic asylum. When Time shall have paid us the usual compliment of fulfilling our prediction, we shall have the pleasure in recommending the worthy Mr. Sharon for appointment as Moral Instructor at the prison or Chaplain at the madhouse. He will need the salary."[16]

The newspapers were making their own predictions. The *Chicago Herald* announced: "The scandals which have beset his name, the dreadful cost of the Hill litigation, the possibility that he may yet be mulcted in half his fortune, and the terrible annoyances of the past year promise to land the badgered millionaire under the sod in a very short time."[17]

On March 27, 1885, Hill was ordered to produce the letters and contract in federal court for new Sharon handwriting expert R. U. Piper. Piper wanted to make scrapings of the ink to test it. Stating that she would not allow the papers to be mutilated, Hill stayed away from court. When she failed to show a second time, Judge Sawyer ordered her jailed for twenty-four hours. Upon her release, Sawyer again demanded that she produce the documents. She again disappeared, and after a time the effort was abandoned.[18]

In a lengthy editorial, the *Fresno Democrat* charged that Sharon was buying a ruling from the unscrupulous Judge Sawyer. It said that early in the proceedings, Sawyer had agreed that the state and federal cases involved the same issue. Only when Sharon's "employee" William Stewart brought his influence to bear did Sawyer decide that the state would not determine the authenticity of the marriage contract.

The *Democrat* reported that Sawyer had known Sharon as a resident of California for ten years. It was only after Sawyer met with Justice Field that he determined a man might live in one state and establish citizenship in another. It presented a variation of the account that Field advised Sharon to file suit in federal court. This version described a man of standing from San Francisco overhearing Sharon and Field discuss the idea at the train station in Reno. "Don't forget what I have told you; bring your suit in our court and you will be all right." The article concluded that because Hill would not turn over the marriage document, Sawyer would content himself with Sharon's presumption regarding its illegality.[19]

In the courts Sharon's forces were winning. Twice the California Supreme Court upheld an order to hold in abeyance payment of alimony and counsel fees.[20] In pleading against the granting of alimony in California Superior Court, Stewart offered an argument later echoed by justices in the federal trial: Even if the contract was genuine, the plaintiff and defendant were not married unless there was also a mutual assumption of marital rights, duties, or obligations. The mutual assumption, Stewart argued, involved the wife's taking the husband's name or taking charge of household duties, the husband's becoming the wife's protector or becoming the head of the family, each assuming the character of wife or husband. "Dodging about the corridors of the Grand and Palace Hotels to secure clandestine meetings," Stewart said, "was no assumption that such meetings were lawful or proper; on the contrary, it was conduct tending to show that the marriage relation did not exist."[21]

The only new witness whose testimony created an impact was the handwriting expert, Piper. He had come west at the behest and expense of the *Alta*. The paper then referred him to the Sharon team for employment. Piper's experience included two hundred cases across the country. His exhibits were enlarged reproductions of microscopic images transmitted by a glass prism. He proclaimed that at least three of the "Dear Wife" letters were tracings. He believed that the signature on the contract predated its body, but unlike the seven other experts, he was certain it was forged. Shockingly, he identified the forger as fellow expert Max Gumpel.[22]

As summer turned to fall, testimony came to an end. As in the earlier case, closing arguments took six weeks, paralleling the previous statements. Sharon had appeared in court less and less frequently. He rarely went to his office now or met with cronies. He even gave up the weekly poker games in his rooms. As weeks passed, fewer guests were admitted to see him. Ki was there but not many others.[23] In October he suffered another attack of angina pectoris, acute pain caused by restricted oxygenation of the heart muscles. He never again rose from bed.

By November 3 his heartbeat had become so feeble that a clot formed in his right leg, shutting off circulation. Pain in his chest drained his strength. His breathing was constricted, and he was propped up in bed with the window wide open. Bellboys guarded the hallways to prevent access and ensure quiet.

A reporter informed Hill of Sharon's condition. "I'm so sorry, so sorry!" she exclaimed, continuing, "In spite of all that has passed I can still say this: That during all the time we were together no one could have been treated more kindly or with greater tenderness than he showed me. . . . had Newlands and the rest only left him alone, we would be living together now."[24] Was Hill being disingenuous, playing to the public, or was she deluded in blaming Newlands and others?

Whatever her feelings, Sharon shared neither them nor her professed wish for reconciliation. On November 5 he moved to protect his estate by filing a twenty-page deed of trust, leaving his son, Fred, and son-in-law Newlands as trustees. The deed instructed them to hold his divided property "for the following persons: One-third of all the property for Fred. W. Sharon; one-third of said property for Lady Fermor-Hesketh; three-twelfths (one-twelfth each) to the three children of Frank G. Newlands, to be held in trust by him for them, and the remaining one-twelfth for Frank G. Newlands." Attached to the deed was a declaration stating that Hill was never his wife, that the marriage contract and letters were forgeries, "and that the testimony of the said Sarah Althea Hill as to the marriage relation between herself and the party of the first part given in said case is false."[25] The deed of trust meant he would die with no estate, leaving only $775.55 worth of clothing and jewelry for probate.

Sharon also called for Fred and Newlands on the 5th and "extracted from them a solemn promise that they would never abandon the contest with Sarah Althea upon any terms."[26] Afterward he lost consciousness, and was revived with a strong dose of morphine. When he opened his eyes, he said to General Barnes, who was spending much of each day there: "Barnes, my friend, I've navigated my ship to the close." But for the first time in many days, he was able to retain a small quantity of port wine and slept after "subcutaneous injections of morphine." His entire family, except Flora, was now in attendance. Friends, including J. D. Fry, visited. "All who saw him expressed their surprise at the clearness of his mind while his body was so enfeebled."[27]

Sharon now regularly called for his son and Newlands. He spoke of the management of his business, the weather, and ordinary affairs. Short periods of sleep were interrupted by leg cramps needing hypodermic injections to relieve them.[28] He did not quail at his approaching death, saying he was ready: "I'd like to live for my children's sake, but it can't be, and I cheerfully give up the battle of life. I face death without fear and can look back on my life as a busy one, full of work and ambition and not devoid of pleasure and satisfaction."

Asked if he was sorry to leave his fortune, he replied that he only gathered it "to save my children from the hard fight I had to fight" and that he would die happy knowing his family would be provided for.[29] But the *San Francisco Chronicle* for November 7 reported that his mind was not at ease. "Several times yesterday he referred to [the divorce suit] . . . 'Oh, how I wish this dagger were out of my heart.'"[30]

On the afternoon of Friday, November 13, Barnes, Fry, Ah Ki, and the family gathered in Sharon's room. At 3 P.M. he opened his eyes. Ah Ki asked what he needed. Sharon whispered, "Well, Ki," twice, closed his eyes, and died.[31]

Chapter Sixteen

RESOLUTIONS

OBITUARIES FOR William Sharon in the San Francisco newspapers were long and detailed, outlining his life and achievements. They also described his last day, commenting on his stoic endurance, and mentioned the torment of the divorce trial. The *Chronicle* reviewed the protracted litigation, reporting Judge Sullivan's finding of the validity of the marriage and the various appeals not yet decided.[1]

An earlier edition of the *Call* had published a list of Sharon's vast holdings, including real estate in the Central Valley, Burlingame, and Washington, D.C.; bank stock; railroad, mill, and mining interests; the Belmont estate; the Palace Hotel, "which alone represents many millions"; and "most of the stock of the Spring Valley Water Company." It took more than a full column to list his real-estate holdings in the city, "nearly all of which pay good rent."[2]

The funeral was held at Grace Church on November 16. The pallbearers included: J. D. Fry; Judge John Currey; ex-senator John Hager; Fred's father-in-law, Wells Fargo president Lloyd Tevis; Sharon's railroad partner, H. M. Yerington; Nevada senator John P. Jones; and several Bank Ring members. Mr. and Mrs. Fred Sharon, Francis Newlands and Sharon's three granddaughters, other members of the family, and Ah Ki followed the casket. The church was filled before the 1 P.M. service, and outside a crowd blocked the sidewalk for some distance. The Episcopal service was completed at the church, because rain threatened to continue through the afternoon. Chopin's funeral march played as the crowd watched the cortege depart for the cemetery.[3]

It was not until four years after Sharon's death that Andrew Carnegie espoused his "Gospel of Wealth." Carnegie argued that wealth brought with it an obligation: after providing moderately for the wants of those dependent upon him, the wealthy man should administer his riches to benefit the community.[4] It was observed at the time Sharon executed his will that he had made no benevolent bequests. On November 21, 1885, the trustees announced fifty-six thousand dollars in charitable contributions, allotted to San Francisco orphan asylums, infants' homes, shelters, and aid societies in amounts from five hundred to five thousand dollars. Virginia City charities received four thousand dollars. Fred Sharon and Newlands also notified the San Francisco park commissioners that, pursuant to instructions, fifty thousand dollars would be donated for some substantial improvement to Golden Gate Park. One proposal was to use the money to build a marble arch at an entrance that would read "Golden Gate Park, Sharon 1884," but public outcry suggested that such an arch would just be a monument to Sharon. Instead, officials settled on a children's playground and a William Hammond Hall–built lodge, completed in 1887.[5]

On December 26, 1885, six weeks after Sharon's death and almost a year to the day after Judge Sullivan's verdict, the federal decision in the case of *Sharon* v. *Hill* was delivered. Matthew P. Deady, district judge of Oregon, joined Sawyer to render the decision. In the late 1860s Deady had been a friend of William Ralston, who acted as his agent in at least two financial transactions.[6] To twenty-first-century readers, some of Deady's findings are remarkable. Others are egregious.

Deady began by addressing the question of Sharon's domicile. He conceded that the federal court could not rule on the case if both parties resided in the same state. Fortunately for the Sharon side, Deady believed that physical presence played no part in residency. If Sharon wanted to be a citizen of Nevada, then it was of no consequence that he had resided in San Francisco the ten previous years.[7]

Deady also believed that men and women who engaged in a sexual relationship outside marriage must be judged differently. He entirely ignored the question at issue: Hill's contention that she had married Sharon be-

fore engaging in sexual relations. Instead of giving equal weight to the testimony of the two principals, he found that the male was more apt to be
truthful: "The sin of incontinence in a man is compatible with the virtue
of veracity [and] does not usually imply the moral degradation and insen-
sibility that it does in a woman." He also concluded that wealth suggested
the ability to tell the truth. Hill, "comparatively obscure and unimpor-
tant," was more likely to make false statements in legal proceedings:
"Other things being equal, property and position are in themselves some
certain guaranty of truth in their possessor."[8]

Deady found that R. U. Piper, the senator's new handwriting analyst,
contributed significant testimony. That Piper's fee was contingent on the
case being found for Sharon, Deady held, was no reason for his testimony
to be influenced. As for Gumpel, the handwriting expert whom Judge Sullivan thought convincing, Deady found him "suspicious and unsatisfactory." Since the forgery of Sharon's signature required "a remarkable pen-
man," the judge agreed with Piper that Gumpel had probably written
it. As to why the text of the contract was written after a forged signature,
Deady theorized that perhaps Hill had stolen an "innocent forgery."[9]

Deady found Sharon's paying Hill $7,500 to be rid of her more likely
than that she had invested money with him. Nellie Brackett repudiated
her earlier testimony in making her declaration for the federal case.
Among other things, she described helping Hill artificially age the "Dear
Wife" letters. A servant substantiated the claim, so Deady discounted affi-
davits saying that Sharon was supporting Brackett's family and accepted
her revised testimony. At the same time he dismissed the statements of
Snow and Pleasant, both of whom consistently reported seeing the marriage document many months before the suit. He also bought all of the
Sharon team's contentions regarding Pleasant: "In my judgment this case,
and the forgeries and perjuries committed in its support, have their origin
in the brain of this scheming, trafficking, crafty old woman."[10]

These circumstances, together with the couple's living conditions
(separate rooms in separate hotels), led Deady to conclude that Hill was
not Sharon's wife. Judge Sawyer spent two hours delivering an opinion

that mirrored Deady's.[11] On January 15 the two judges filed a decree directing the marriage contract's delivery within twenty days to the court clerk. They also issued a perpetual injunction against using the contract to support any claim against Sharon or any interest in his property.[12]

The federal court's ruling was the opposite of the state court's finding, but the ultimate resolution of events could not have been guessed. Since his wife's sudden death the year before, Terry's attentions to Hill had become the subject of increasing comment. "Charmed by her audacity" and "natural brilliancy," on January 7, 1886, less than two months after Sharon's death, Terry and Hill married. He was sixty-two. She was thirty-two.[13]

On February 3, 1886, Fred Sharon, planning to resume life in Europe, filed a renunciation of his powers as executor of the Sharon estate.[14] Newlands was left as sole defender of the family's legal interests. In his late thirties, Newlands was said to move "with a hurried step, 'as though trying to crowd five minutes into one.'"[15] For some time Newlands had harbored political aspirations, but he needed to fight to overcome the public perception of his Sharon connection. He struggled to remain out of Sharon's divorce litigation, which he called the "wretched case."[16] But with Sharon's death and Fred's abdication of responsibility, he was forced to become involved.

The California Supreme Court continued to affirm Judge Sullivan's finding of a valid marriage and divorce, although it held the payment of the awards in abeyance. On February 3, 1887, Newlands wrote to Fred Sharon in Paris to tell him that it might be necessary for him to take up residency in New York. The strategy, urged by William Stewart, was to ensure that the case remained in federal court by keeping their residences in states other than California, where Sarah Hill resided.[17]

At the end of 1886, in a controversial ruling, the California Supreme Court disbarred attorney Tyler. There was much speculation about the timing, in light of the Sharon case's highly public nature. Tyler's misdeed had occurred six years earlier and was generally believed to be "venial, if not trivial." The court disagreed, and Tyler never practiced law again.[18]

A case was also brought against W. H. L. Barnes. Charges of conspiring to steal and attempting to suborn perjury resulted from his actions against Sarah Hill. The theft was a setup. Barnes's detective had burglarized Tyler's office, removing a document created specifically to prove that he and other operatives were involved in illegal undertakings. Although Barnes acknowledged paying twenty-five thousand dollars of the defendant's money to buy the document, the court found that the detective had acted without encouragement from Barnes.[19] The other charge was also casually dismissed. When handwriting analyst Gumpel had determined Sarah's documents were genuine, Barnes offered him a substantial increase in fee to testify that they were not. The same court that had disbarred Tyler found Barnes not guilty. The judge for the majority wrote: "I do not believe that Barnes thought that the money would cause the witness to change his opinion. He regarded, as he well might, the arguments of the witness as mere intimations that he wanted more money. . . . it would have been more in accordance with exalted ideas of propriety for Barnes to have denounced the witness and dismissed him, but I doubt whether many practitioners would have acted differently."[20]

On January 31, 1888, the California Supreme Court handed down its decision on the Sharon team's appeal of the divorce order. The justices voted four to three that a valid marriage need not be public; therefore, "the marriage contract and their subsequent cohabitation supported Judge Sullivan's conclusion that Sarah and the Senator had been legally married." Although setting aside fees to be reconsidered, the court confirmed that Sarah Hill was entitled to the divorce decree.[21]

The papers announced it as the case's final chapter. Barnes conceded defeat, telling a reporter: "There is nothing left to say. The child is dead and that's the end of it. I have worried and worried, and there is no use of worrying any more." Since the federal case was restricted to determining the validity of the marriage contract and the marriage had been declared legal, its validity seemed immaterial. Judge Sullivan ordered the back payment of alimony, a total of $6,600. But as a matter of course, it was stayed under appeal.[22]

On March 12, 1888, a reviver petition was filed in federal court in the name of Frederick Sharon. This petition sought once and for all to force Hill to surrender the marriage contract. The case was argued before Judge Sawyer and Stephen J. Field.[23] The volatile personalities of Hill and Terry would now be pitted against the opinionated Supreme Court justice.

Clearly, the justice should have disqualified himself. Years earlier, when the charge of adultery had first been brought, Field had advised William Sharon on how to proceed. Field stayed at the Palace Hotel when he was in San Francisco and never repaid a $25,000 loan from Sharon. He sent a letter to the American ambassador in London describing Newlands as a "warm personal friend," and he owed a political debt to Newlands for defending him at the hostile Stockton convention.[24] The antagonistic history between Field and Terry spanned thirty years. Field credited Senator David Broderick, whom Terry had killed in the infamous duel, with once saving his life. Even before that Field and Terry were adversaries, dating to when Field served under Terry on the state supreme court in California's earliest days. Field steadfastly supported the cause of big business; Terry was a leading proponent of farmers' and workers' rights. Among other things, Terry said that Field was "corrupt and dishonest in all his decisions."[25] Yet the proceeding was surprisingly uneventful, and the case was held under advisement.

While they waited, Terry continued his extensive practice from his offices in San Francisco, Fresno, and Stockton. The enmity between the Terrys and the justices was kept before the public. Terry charged that Sawyer "was a bribe-taking judge who had taken his orders from Field" and that Sawyer was bought in cases regarding Chinese immigrants and habeas corpus.[26] On August 14, 1888, two weeks before the decision was to be handed down, Judge Sawyer was riding the train. The Terrys came down the aisle behind him. Upon passing him, Sarah pulled his hair, saying: "I will give him a taste of what he will get by and by. Let him render this decision if he dares." The couple sat across from Sawyer, and Terry declared that there were too many witnesses, but "the best thing to do with him would be to take him out into the bay and drown him."[27] Sawyer bided his time.

On September 3, 1888, before another courtroom filled to capacity, Field announced that the earlier federal judgment would stand. He ordered Sarah Hill Terry to turn over the marriage contract for cancellation and never again propound its authenticity. When she stood, questioning him in a loud voice, Field ordered her to sit down. She continued to object, and he again ordered that she be seated. The court record reported: "She then said, in a very excited and violent manner, that Justice Field had been bought, and wanted to know the price he had sold himself for; that he had got Newlands' money for it. . . . Mr. Justice Field then directed the marshal to remove her from the court-room."[28]

When Marshal J. D. Franks moved toward his wife, Terry warned him not to touch her. When Franks tried to push past, Terry knocked him to the floor. A crowd pulled down Terry and pinned him.[29] Sarah, too, had been knocked down. She was drawn to her feet and removed. Terry regained his feet and, following his wife, drew his bowie knife. Deputies grabbed him, and Marshal David Neagle wrenched the weapon from his grip.

After further struggle, unarmed, Terry was admitted into a heavily guarded anteroom to see his wife. Both were placed under arrest. Field and his associates had remained seated during the violent confrontation. With the defendants now out of the room, he finished reading the decision.[30] Besides ruling against them as regarded the marriage contract, for the violent disturbance the court sentenced Sarah to thirty days in the Alameda County jail, Terry to six months.

While he was in jail, Terry was talked into informally appealing the sentence and sent a letter with a friend to Justice Field. Field responded by filing a widely publicized order that labeled Terry's behavior an "insult to the emblem of the nation's majesty." The law credited prisoners five days a month for good behavior, but—commenting that the full six months would give Terry time to "cool down"—Field returned to Washington, and Terry served to the last hour.[31]

In court on May 3, 1889, Sarah was ordered to produce the contract as demanded by Judge Sawyer. Terry rose and announced: "Since the night of Aug. 11 last the marriage contract is no longer in existence. On that night my office in Fresno was burned with all contents, and among the valuable documents destroyed was the marriage contract." The announcement, which completely surprised Sawyer and the Sharon attorneys, effectively resolved the matter since, as one attorney remarked, "[Now] she will have to fight without it."[32]

In 1888, when the California Supreme Court denied the Sharon team a new trial, the decision was appealed. By June 1889 three of the justices who had found for Sarah were replaced, and the appeal was granted. Newlands wrote Fred Sharon predicting that the next opinion would controvert earlier findings and be nearly unanimous in their favor. On July 17 the court took unprecedented action in confirming Newlands's prognostication. It reversed itself and found in favor of the Sharon forces.[33]

The new members joined with those who had dissented in the original judgment. They found that the document's secrecy clause did not alleviate the necessity of displaying a mutual assumption of marital rights. Sharon and Sarah had not lived together "in the way usual with married people." The court explained that although Sharon had received her and introduced her to friends in a wifelike manner, "This man had sinned so long and so openly in this respect that he did not care to conceal his wrong-doing even from his own family."[34]

Ironically, the justices found that the hotly contested "Dear Wife" letters and marriage contract were largely irrelevant, since even a verbal consent to marriage might be upheld. The strongest evidence against Sarah were the letters *she had written* when turned out of the Grand Hotel, all addressed to "Mr. Sharon." Justice J. D. Works wrote for the majority: "She appeals to his *friendship,* but not to his love or to his duties and obligations as a husband. She pleads her service to him as a friend and as a nurse, but not a wife. No claim of her right to his protection; no assertion of her rights as a wife."[35]

Terry ran into a friend as he left the courthouse after the decision was rendered. "The Supreme Court has reversed its own decision in the Sharon case, and made my wife out a strumpet," he said. When asked how he would respond, Terry said, "What can a person do in the face of

Sharon's millions? It is infamous! What is the world coming to, anyway? The corporations and capitalists are centralizing their power in all departments of the government, both Federal and State. Justice has a dark outlook."[36] Terry then filed a petition for a rehearing, arguing a court could not controvert its own decision. But a month later the drama played out in a venue other than the courtroom.

The animosity the Terrys felt toward Field and Sawyer intensified after their arrest. Even while being transported to the Alameda jail, Sarah repeated a number of times that she would kill them both. Terry later called in a newspaper editor and told him that Field "put a lie in the record about him, and when he met Field . . . if he did not take it back, and apologize for having lied about him, he would slap his face or pull his nose." The editor pointed out that Field would take umbrage, likely resorting to the use of a weapon. Terry responded: "Well, that's as good a thing as I want to get."[37] In April the U.S. marshal in northern California wrote to the U.S. attorney general requesting protection for Field, and the attorney general authorized hiring deputies at five dollars a day. David Neagle, the marshal who had wrested the bowie knife from Terry in court, was appointed Field's bodyguard.

On the morning of August 14, 1889, Field and Neagle sat together in the railroad-station dining room at Lathrop, near Stockton, California. They had been traveling on a train that also carried the Terrys. The next morning the Terrys were to answer criminal charges arising from the September court incident. Suspecting that the couple would breakfast at the station, Neagle recommended that Field eat on the train. But Field insisted on the dining room.

Neagle proved to be correct. When the couple entered, Sarah noticed Field and immediately turned and left the room. Terry passed Field, being led by the host to a corner table. The host, who knew Terry, asked if his wife was going to do anything desperate. Terry told him that he should watch her. When the restaurateur returned to the door, he saw Terry walk behind Field and "lightly" slap the judge on the cheek twice.[38]

Neagle later gave unsubstantiated testimony that Terry drew his arm back with doubled-up fist to strike a third blow. The court record stated: "Neagle, who had been observing him all this time, arose from his seat with his revolver in his hand, and in a very loud voice shouted out: 'Stop! Stop! I am an officer!' Upon this Terry turned his attention to Neagle, and as Neagle testifies, seemed to recognize him, and immediately turned his hand to thrust it in his bosom, as Neagle felt sure, with the purpose of drawing a bowie knife. At this instant Neagle fired two shots from his revolver into the body of Terry, who immediately sank down, and died in a few minutes." At least one witness contradicted Neagle, saying that there was no "perceptible lapse of time" between the slap and the shooting.[39] A search showed that Terry was unarmed. Sarah returned, collapsing over her husband and crying for help.

Neagle was arrested at the scene. He was later brought before Judge Sawyer, who determined that the state had no power over federal employees acting in pursuance of their duties. His final statement was that Neagle's killing of Terry was not only justifiable but also commendable. And Neagle was freed.[40]

The divorce case went through several more phases, but Sarah, without a champion, lost at every turn. She deteriorated mentally and physically. Mary Ellen Pleasant took care of her, disproving contentions that she had earlier helped her only for financial recompense, until in the spring of 1892 she signed a petition for Sarah's commitment to the state asylum for the insane in Stockton.

Sharon's army of lawyers and connections had saved the wealth he bequeathed his children. Almost certainly, the courts' final decisions were correct. The "Dear Wife" letters, without salutations, were little more than notes accompanying monthly stipends. Sarah's letters after her eviction were not those of a wife to her husband. Late in the litigation, Barnes used Sarah's records from the Bank of California to lend credence to Sharon's version of their relationship. The records showed that at their initial meetings, she desperately needed money: "She had in 1879 an aggregate cash capital of somewhere between seventeen and eighteen thousand dollars, which seems to have gradually disappeared until its last bank balance in the month of February, 1880, when, so far as her account shows, her entire cash capital was precisely $11."[41]

The other participants met various fates. George Washington Tyler never regained the right to practice law and died in 1895. W. H. L. Barnes, maintaining his role in San Francisco society and at the bar, died in 1902. William Stewart returned to the U.S. Senate, serving from 1887 to 1905, then retired to private practice in Nevada, where he worked until his death in 1909. Stephen J. Field, his interpretation of the Constitution having bulwarked the Gilded Age, died two years after retiring from the bench in 1897. Although practically useless in his last years, he refused to resign until he broke John Marshall's record (since surpassed by Justice William O. Douglas) for longest tenure on the United States Supreme Court. Mary Ellen Pleasant was involved in several scandals near the close of the century, including one stemming from the questionable death of Thomas Bell, damaging her name. She died, at age eighty-nine, in 1904.

Sarah Althea Hill Terry remained in the asylum forty-five years. Liked by patients and staff, she was given free use of the grounds. She seemed normal at times but at others claimed she was married to Abraham Lincoln and General Grant.[42] In 1936 writers Oscar Lewis and Carroll Hall visited her. She sat in a rocking chair, white haired and stooped. When asked about persons and episodes of the trial, a few she seemed not to recall, others she remarked about. She remembered Mary Ellen Pleasant: "Took charge of my trial. She was *smart*." She knew of no marriage contract and recalled Terry as "one of my husbands. He was a big man." She recalled that "Judge Sullivan tried the case. I won." And that Ah Ki "used to sit outside Mr. Sharon's door." Sharon "was a rich man. He owned the Bank of California. Is he dead? Do you know my brother, Morgan Hill? Do you know Fred Sharon, my stepson? . . . Are you from San Francisco? . . . Do you stay at the Palace? . . . That's my hotel, you know. It was built for me. . . . Do you know Fred Sharon? When you go back, tell him Mrs. Terry sent you." Seven months later she died of bronchopneumonia.[43]

Adolph Sutro prospered in San Francisco long after his Comstock antagonist. At one time he owned one-twelfth of the acreage in the city. He developed one thousand acres of shoreline property called Sutro Heights, planted Sutro Forest, and built the Cliff House and below it the Sutro Baths, consisting of a museum, six pools, a promenade and an amphitheater. Sutro created a 300,000-volume library, the largest private collection in the United States, and donated twenty-six acres of midcity land to the University of California. In 1894 he was elected mayor of San Francisco, completing his term just before his death in 1898.[44]

Sharon's surviving daughter, Flora, lived her life among the landed gentry in England. Her country manor was the Hesketh family's Easton Neston estate, built by Christopher Wren. She was beautiful and reportedly the brightest of Sharon's children. One of her descendants, Lord Alexander Hesketh, served as whip in the House of Lords under Margaret Thatcher. Family legend holds that Flora engaged in her own secret affair, lasting for years, with King George V.[45]

Fred Sharon and his wife, Louise, spent the fourteen years after the trial living in leisurely fashion in Paris. Their California home in Sharon Heights (Menlo Park), referred to as their "cottage," included thirty-two rooms and thirty full-time gardeners. In 1910 they returned, and Fred spent his last five years overseeing the gardens. His life was made difficult by an addiction to cocaine.[46]

Sharon's son-in-law Newlands, the true heir to his legacy, established his home in Nevada in 1888, became one of its largest landowners, and in 1892 was elected its representative to the United States Congress. He died in 1917 while serving with distinction as a Nevada senator and a national statesman, one of the leaders of the Progressive Era. Although continuing to build the Sharon fortune, he was also largely responsible for what became known as the Newlands Reclamation Act, which contributed greatly to the growth and development of Nevada and the West.

The saga of the Sharon wealth traces in remarkable fashion America's story in the Gilded Age. William Sharon himself was a man of laissez faire "survival of the fittest" capitalism, building his wealth through monopoly and ruthless individualism. He engaged in a bitter struggle over twenty years to gain and maintain a fortune equal to any in the West. It came at inordinate cost, including the death of the partner who made it possible. Sharon's feats—conquering the Comstock, building an empire, and bringing the failed Bank of California back to life—are the stuff of legend. But in achieving those ends, he ignored his family, with whom he spent precious little time; acquired few friends; exhibited little spirituality; and championed no ideal. His life seems to have gained meaning solely from the acquisition of material wealth. In fighting to acquire half of it, Sarah Althea Hill attacked the one thing to which he was devoted. The trial caused the disaffection of his children and public scorn. Although believing that he could buy his way out, his nature was such that he endured humiliation rather than give up any part of his wealth.

Toward the end of Sharon's life, Judge John Currey talked to him concerning the ordeal: "In connection with his troubles with the Terry crowd, I have heard him express with feeling his care for his little grandchildren. He seemed to feel deeply the chagrin of this position on account of [the] little children."[47]

As he lay dying, Sharon demonstrated feelings for family and associates and displayed steadfast resolve and courage. But obituaries pointed out that his last years were embittered by the divorce litigation and that he was "keenly alive to the sensationalism" that impugned his name. More than once he complained that the marriage claim was a dagger in his heart. It tormented him to the end.[48]

Notes

Prologue

1. Gilman M. Ostrander, *Nevada: The Great Rotten Borough, 1859–1964* (New York: Knopf, 1966), 46.

2. The three most prominent early western economic historians make the point about the restoration's being an amazing feat: John S. Hittell, *The Commerce and Industries of the Pacific Coast* (San Francisco: A. L. Bancroft and Co., 1882), 420; Zoeth Skinner Eldredge, *History of California*, vol. 4 (New York: Century History, 1915), 440; Ira B. Cross, *Financing an Empire: Banking in California* (Chicago: S. J. Clark, 1927), 407.

3. See, for example, Robert E. Stewart Jr. and Mary Frances Stewart, *Adolph Sutro: A Biography* (Berkeley: Howell-North, 1962); Cecil G. Tilton, *William Chapman Ralston, Courageous Builder* (Boston: Christopher Publishing House, 1935); Julian Dana, *The Man Who Built San Francisco: A Study of Ralston's Journey with Banners* (New York: Macmillan Co., 1936); David Lavender, *Nothing Seemed Impossible* (Palo Alto: American West, 1975).

4. M. M. Matthews, *Ten Years in Nevada, or Life on the Pacific Coast* (1880; reprint, Lincoln: University of Nebraska Press, 1985), 202; *Territorial Enterprise*, February 27, 1864; Tilton, *William Chapman Ralston, Courageous Builder*, 138–39, 420.

5. *San Francisco Call*, November 14, 1885; Hubert Howe Bancroft, *The Works of Hubert Howe Bancroft*, vol. 7, *History of California, 1860–1890* (San Francisco: History Co., 1890), 331. The first five volumes of Bancroft's general California history were written by Henry L. Oak, the other two mostly by William Nemos and Mrs. F. F. Victor. Bancroft failed to give credit to the writers, referring to them merely as employees. California historian Walton Bean comments: "Oak was a better historian than his employer. . . . Bancroft's own historical style was florid, windy, and pontifical" (Walton Bean, *California: An Interpretive History* [New York: McGraw Hill Book Co., 1968], 255); John Currey to Col. Morrison, June 3, 1891, Sharon Family Papers, The Bancroft Library, University of California, Berkeley.

6. Reuben Lloyd, "Manuscript, 31 December 1886," Hubert Howe Bancroft

Collection, The Bancroft Library; C. C. Goodwin, *As I Remember Them* (Salt Lake City: Salt Lake Commercial Club, 1913), 131. The *San Francisco Examiner* of September 22, 1889, took a different perspective in a similar quote: "At times when convivial and surrounded by men who were even more of toadies than friends, he would speak of his achievements, and would say that Ralston was an overrated man. He would boast that his brain had conceived the schemes that made the money"; Eliot Lord, *Comstock Mining and Miners* (1883; reprint, Berkeley: Howell-North, 1959), 245.

7. Miriam Michelson, *The Wonderlode of Silver and Gold* (Boston: Stratford, 1934), 226.

8. Alexander Toponce, *Reminiscences of Alexander Toponce, Written by Himself* (1923; reprint, Norman: University of Oklahoma Press, 1971), 129–31.

9. Myron Angel, ed., *History of Nevada* (1881; reprint, Berkeley: Howell-North Books, 1958), 591.

10. Dan DeQuille (William Wright), *The Big Bonanza* (1877; reprint, Las Vegas: Nevada Publications, n.d.), 402.

11. DeQuille, *The Big Bonanza,* 403. The point that Sharon's actions were invaluable to the development of the Comstock is echoed in Lord, *Comstock Mining and Miners,* and Grant H. Smith, *The History of the Comstock Lode: 1850–1920* (1943; reprint, Reno: University of Nevada Press, 1998), as well as in Goodwin, *As I Remember Them.*

12. DeQuille, *The Big Bonanza,* 394–98.

13. Ambrose Bierce, *Black Beetles in Amber* (San Francisco: Western Authors, 1892), 25.

14. Richard Samuel West, *The San Francisco Wasp: An Illustrated History* (Easthampton, Mass.: Periodyssey Press, 2004), frontis., 204–5.

15. William M. Stewart, *Reminiscences of Senator William M. Stewart of Nevada,* ed. George Rothwell Brown (New York: Neale Publishing Co., 1908), 130, 340–41.

16. Adolph Sutro, "Autobiographical Notes," 1890, part 2, 5, The Bancroft Library.

17. Geo. Howard Morrison to H. H. Bancroft, June 13, 1891, Sharon Family Papers, The Bancroft Library.

Chapter One: Black Broadcloth

1. Hubert Howe Bancroft, *Chronicle of the Builders* (San Francisco: History Co., [1890?]), 24–33. The Bancroft account of Sharon's heritage and early life is

detailed and thorough. See also Tilton, *William Chapman Ralston, Courageous Builder,* 138–39; "Biographical Sketch of John D. Fry: Typescript [ca. 1890]," Hubert Howe Bancroft Collection, The Bancroft Library.

2. California Historical Society, *Sacramento, an Illustrated History: 1839 to 1874, from Sutter's Fort to Capital City* ([San Francisco]: 1973), 71–72.

3. J. D. Fry, quoted in a biographical sketch as part of an obituary for Sharon in the *San Francisco Call,* November 14, 1885.

4. Zoeth Skinner Eldredge, *The Beginnings of San Francisco: From the Expedition of Anza, 1774 to the City Charter of April 15, 1850 with Biographical and Other Notes* (New York: John C. Rankin Company, 1912), 5, 12, http://www.apub.com/sf50/sf/hbbegidx.htm (accessed May 6, 2002). Residents tried to fill the flooded streets using brush, tree limbs, and barrels of merchandise whose storage cost would have been prohibitive. (Eldredge's list of items included tons of wire sieves, iron, rolls of sheet lead, cement, and barrels of beef.)

5. See *San Francisco Gold Rush Chronology,* "*1849–1850,*" November 6 and 15, July 16 and 23, 1849 (Museum of The City of San Francisco), http://www.sfmuseum.org/hist/chron1.html (accessed May 2, 2002); Eldredge, *Beginnings of San Francisco,* 11–12; "The City of The Golden Gate," *Scribner's Monthly,* July 1875, in *Tales of California,* ed. Frank Oppel (Secaucus, N.J.: Castle Books, 1989), 8, 11.

6. Charles P. Kimball, *The San Francisco City Directory, September 1, 1850* (San Francisco: Journal of Commerce Press, 1850), 1, P–S, http://www.apub.com/sf50/sf/hd850a.htm (accessed May 6, 2002); Bancroft, *Chronicle of the Builders,* 41. There is an advertisement in the *San Francisco Alta,* December 21, 1851: "Henry S. Fitch & Co., real estate auctioneers, partners Henry S. Fitch, Wm. Sharon."

7. Bancroft, *Chronicle of the Builders,* 41; *San Francisco Chronicle,* November 14, 1885.

8. See Ronald Takaki, *A Different Mirror: A History of Multicultural America* (Boston: Little, Brown and Co., 1993), 180; John P. Young, *Journalism in California* (San Francisco: Chronicle Publishing Co., 1915), 18; Bancroft, *Chronicle of the Builders,* 41–42.

9. Frank Soule, John H. Gihon, M.D., and James Nisbet, *The Annals of San Francisco* (1855; reprint, Berkeley: Berkeley Hills Books, 1998), 305–7 and 286–87.

10. *San Francisco Gold Rush Chronology,* passim.

11. *Virginia Evening Chronicle,* October 24, 1874; Soule, Gihon, and Nisbet, *Annals of San Francisco,* 541–42.

12. B. E. Lloyd, *Lights and Shades in San Francisco* (1876; reprint, Berkeley: Berkeley Hills Books, 1999), 55; Bancroft, *Chronicle of the Builders*, 44.

13. *San Francisco Call*, November 14, 1885.

14. Young, *Journalism in California*, 59.

15. Alfred Bates, "Biography of William Sharon: And Material for Its Preparation, 1891," draft in the handwriting of Alfred Bates, Hubert Howe Bancroft Collection, The Bancroft Library.

16. Joseph L. King, *History of the San Francisco Stock and Exchange Board, by the Chairman, Jos. L. King* (San Francisco: J. L. King, 1910), 319, 362; Thomas Magee and E. P. Peckham, *San Francisco Call*, November 14, 1885. Stockjobbing such as this transaction was not limited to outsiders; similar actions by the market's brokers of the era earned them the sobriquet "the forty thieves."

17. See Bancroft, *Chronicle of the Builders*, 45. This fourth volume of the massive series of Bancroft histories contains vanity biographies dictated by the subjects or their families. (Bonanza millionaire James Fair was said to have paid fifteen thousand dollars for his to be written the way he wished. Leland Stanford's biography was prepared for publication but omitted when he refused to pay.) The Bancroft account differs from those of Ralston biographers, who believed that Ralston did not become acquainted with Sharon until their business association began in 1864. Although generally suspect because of its hagiographic nature, in this instance the Bancroft version is much less problematic. Ralston in 1858 married the niece and ward of Sharon's best friend. While Ralston was the prime mover in San Francisco's development through the '50s and into the '60s, Sharon was city alderman and a leading real-estate broker. Sharon was one of fifty-eight directors in the Ralston-financed Pacific Insurance Company. At the beginning of the Civil War, both worked to keep California in the Union. And they became full partners immediately upon Sharon's being hired by Ralston.

18. See Dana, *The Man Who Built San Francisco*, 388.

19. See the various Ralston biographies; *San Francisco Examiner*, September 22, 1889; Goodwin, *As I Remember Them*, 126.

20. B. E. Lloyd, *Lights and Shades in San Francisco*, 72–73; Lavender, *Nothing Seemed Impossible*, 149–51, 174–78.

21. Eldredge, *History of California*, 433–34.

22. See Thomas Bell, Statement, 1886, 1, in Hubert Howe Bancroft, "Biography of William C. Ralston Prepared for Chronicles of the Kings: And Materials Used in Its Preparation, 1886–1889," The Bancroft Library, University of California, Berkeley. Bank secretary Stephen Franklin commented: "In the early days of the Bank Wm. Mills was a good deal absent, arranging communications & corre-

spondents for the Bank Abroad" (Stephen Franklin, Biography of William Ralston, 1886, 2, in Hubert Howe Bancroft, "Biography of William C. Ralston Prepared for Chronicles of the Kings: And Materials Used in Its Preparation, 1886–1889," The Bancroft Library).

23. Neill C. Wilson, *401 California Street: The Story of The Bank of California, National Association and Its First 100 Years in the Financial Development of the Pacific Coast* (San Francisco: [The Bank of California?], 1964), 20–21; Lavender, *Nothing Seemed Impossible*, 179.

24. See Franklin, Biography of William Ralston, 1886, 6; Jerome A. Hart, *In Our Second Century: From an Editor's Notebook* (San Francisco: Pioneer Press, 1931), 44; *San Francisco Examiner,* September 22, 1889.

25. Mark Twain, *Roughing It* (1871; reprint, New York, Harper and Brothers, 1922), 12.

26. Mrs. Frank Leslie, *California: A Pleasure Trip from Gotham to the Golden Gate, April, May, June, 1877* (Nieuwkoop, Netherlands: B. De Graaf, 1972), chap. 32, 1, http://members.door.net/nbclumber/Leslie/Ch32.htm (accessed June 11, 2002); *New York Tribune,* August 27, 1875, in George Hinkle and Bliss Hinkle, *Sierra-Nevada Lakes* (1949; reprint, Reno: University of Nevada Press, 1987), 301.

27. Francis A Walker, *A Compendium of the Ninth Census (June 1, 1870), by Francis A. Walker, Superintendent of Census* (Washington, D.C.: Government Printing Office, 1872), 814.

28. *Gold Hill News,* October 21, 1872.

29. See James W. Nye, Governor and ex officio Superintendent of Indian Affairs, to Caleb B. Smith, Secretary of the Interior, July 19, 1861, *Annual Report of the Commissioner of Indian Affairs to the Secretary of the Interior for 1866 (ARCIA)* (Washington, D.C.: Government Printing Office, 1861), 111. The Paiutes engaged the whites in sporadic battle, including the "Paiute War of 1860," when they defeated an army of miners, killing forty-three. They were given limited reservation land at Pyramid Lake and on the Walker River. The Washoes, who "persistently refused all efforts to get them to join the Pai-Utes against the whites," were given no land. At the end of the twentieth century, Washoe tribal chair Brian Wallace explained, "Nineteenth century government agents determined the Washoe needed no reservation because they would soon be extinct." In fact, in his annual report in 1866 H. G. Parker, Nevada's superintendent of Indian Affairs, concluded: "There is no suitable place for a reservation in the bounds of their territory, and, in view of their rapidly diminishing numbers and the diseases to which they are subjected, none is required" (Brian Wallace, Tribal Chair, Washoe Tribe of Nevada and California, interview by the author, May 17, 1998;

H. G. Parker, Superintendent of Indian Affairs, Nevada, Walker River Indian Reserve, August 22, 1866, to D. N. Cooley, Commissioner, Washington D.C., *Annual Report of the Commissioner of Indian Affairs to the Secretary of the Interior [ARCIA] for 1866* [Washington, D.C.: Government Printing Office, 1866], 115–16). See also James F. Downs, *The Two Worlds of the Washo: An Indian Tribe of California and Nevada* (New York: Holt, Rinehart and Winston, 1966), 77.

30. Robert Lewers in Sam P. Davis, *The History of Nevada,* vol. 1 (Reno: Elms Publishing, 1913), 228, 590; Walker, *A Compendium of the Ninth Census,* 18, 20, 72–73.

31. Lord, *Comstock Mining and Miners,* 199. For a glimpse into living conditions for the Chinese, particularly Chinese women, see Sue Fawn Chung, "Their Changing World: Chinese Women on the Comstock, 1860–1910," in *Comstock Women: The Making of a Mining Community,* ed. Ronald M. James and C. Elizabeth Raymond (Reno: University of Nevada Press, 1998), 218–23, 228.

32. Ronald M. James, *The Roar and the Silence: A History of Virginia City and the Comstock Lode* (Reno: University of Nevada Press, 1998), 97–99, 153–55. The California mining law against minorities can be viewed at *San Francisco Gold Rush Chronology,* July 29, 1849. For a discussion of Nevada's first black rancher, see Grace Dangberg, *Carson Valley: Historical Sketches of Nevada's First Settlement* (Reno: Carson Valley Historical Society, 1979), 59–60. See also *Reno Gazette-Journal,* "Hot Sauce Bottle Offers Peek into Comstock's Past," June 28, 2002.

33. Lord, *Comstock Mining and Miners,* 199.

34. *Annual Mining Review and Stock Ledger* (San Francisco: Verdenal, Harrison, Murphy and Co., 1876), 15.

35. Alf Doten, *The Journals of Alfred Doten: 1849–1903,* vol. 2, ed. Walter Van Tilburg Clark (Reno: University of Nevada Press, 1973), 862, 934. The "superior class" comment is by editor Van Tilberg Clark.

36. Doten, *The Journals of Alfred Doten,* vol. 2, 905; George Williams III, *Rosa May: The Search For A Mining Camp Legend* (Riverside: Tree By The River, 1980) 130–33.

37. See Matthews, *Ten Years in Nevada, or Life on The Pacific Coast,* 193.

38. Angel, *History of Nevada,* 191–92.

Chapter Two: Gambling

1. See Charles Howard Shinn, *The Story of the Mine As Illustrated by the Great Comstock Lode of Nevada* (1910; reprint, Reno: University of Nevada Press, 1980),

162; Lord, *Comstock Mining and Miners,* 181; Smith, *History of the Comstock Lode,* 48.

2. *Virginia Daily Union,* May 13, 1864, in Smith, *History of the Comstock Lode,* 48–49.

3. W. H. Blauvelt, in Sam Davis, *The History of Nevada,* vol. 1, 628–30. Arrington's misfortune provided opportunity for Sharon. In July of 1865 two properties, one on A Street and one fronting on B Street, held jointly by the Arringtons, were sold to him for five thousand dollars (*Book of Deeds, Storey County Records, Nevada,* July 14, 1865, book Z, 359; George Morrison, n.d., 8, in Hubert Howe Bancroft, "Biography of William Sharon: And Material for Its Preparation," Hubert Howe Bancroft Collection, The Bancroft Library). See also Bancroft, *Chronicle of the Builders,* 50. Sharon associate C. C. Goodwin gives the time of Sharon's arrival as spring 1863, saying that he looked about for two or three days, wired Ralston that a real bank was needed, and "The result was that within a week thereafter Mr. Sharon opened a branch of the California Bank on The Comstock" (C. C. Goodwin, *The Story of The Comstock Lode: "Lest We Forget"* [Boston: Long, Pierce and Co., n.d.], 18–19). Goodwin, who got the information from Sharon years later, uses a time frame that seems condensed; he is mistaken about the year, as the bank opened in 1864.

4. George Lyman, *Ralston's Ring* (1937; reprint, New York: Ballantine Books, 1971), 38. G. H. Sharon is listed as a Virginia City assayer in the *Census of the State of Nevada 1875,* vol. 2, Storey County, 285.

5. Ferdinand Bacon Richtofen, *The Comstock Lode: Its Character, and the Probable Mode of its Continuance in Depth* (San Francisco: Towne and Bacon, 1866). Richtofen's exhaustive report, which investigated the geology of the Washoe range and the structure and nature of the vein, concluded that "the amount of nearly fifty million dollars which have been extracted from the Comstock lode, is but a small portion of the amount of silver awaiting future extractions" (73).

6. William Ashburner to Samuel Bowles, November 1865, in Samuel Bowles, *Across the Continent: A Summer's Journey to the Rocky Mountains, the Mormons, And the Pacific States with Speaker Colfax* (1866; reprint, Ann Arbor: University Microfilms, 1966), 449.

7. Goodwin, *As I Remember Them,* 127.

8. Bancroft, *Chronicle of the Builders,* 50–51.

9. E. S. Tibbey, Statement, 1886, 3–4, in Hubert Howe Bancroft, "Biography of William C. Ralston Prepared for Chronicles of the Kings," The Bancroft Library.

218   NOTES TO PAGES 24-26

10. *San Francisco Call,* November 14, 1885.

11. *The Oxford English Dictionary,* vol. 7 (1933; reprint, Oxford: Clarendon Press, 1970), 1061; David M. Hayano, *Poker Faces: The Life and Work of Professional Card Players* (Berkeley: University of California Press, 1982), 72.

12. Many sketches about Ralston give a variation of this anecdote. See, for example, *San Francisco Examiner,* September 22, 1899; Ira Cross, *Financing an Empire: Banking in California* (Chicago: S. J. Clark, 1927), 405.

13. In the book he edited on game theory, Martin Shubik commented: "Regardless of [your opponent's] general feelings toward you, in the narrow world of the poker game his interests and yours are opposed. By assuming the worst you are not ascribing any violently hostile intent to your opponent; you are merely observing that in the context of the situation, one man's poison is the other man's meat" (*Game Theory and Related Approaches to Social Behavior,* ed. Martin Shubik [New York: John Wiley and Sons, 1964], 31).

14. Besides ensuring the reclamation of the precept that all men are created equal, Nevada's statehood also ensured a flow of silver into the nation's coffers. "Yet, in spite of the services rendered to the nation," commented Sam Davis in 1913, "Congress, forgetful of the country's obligation to the Silver State, demonetized the white metal in 1873 and since then many eastern journals have gravely discussed the proposition of compelling Nevada to surrender her Statehood" (Sam Davis, *The History of Nevada,* vol. 1, 272).

15. Doten, *The Journals of Alfred Doten,* vol. 2, 814.

16. *Gold Hill News,* November 17, 1864.

17. Father Manogue would have to rebuild St. Mary's after the fire in 1875. The cost was "estimated roughly at $100,000.... On a marble slab inserted in the front doorway the story of the church and its builder is concisely told. 'Built in '68. Burned down in '75. Rebuilt in '76. P. Monogue, pastor'" (Sam Davis, *The History of Nevada,* vol. 1, 545).

18. Cave-ins occurred periodically thereafter until, in 1874, Alf Doten reported "a big crack ½ mile long, on the east and south side of Fort Homestead, in the ground—Caused by the whole of Gold Hill settling down into the mines" (Doten, *The Journals of Alfred Doten,* vol. 2, 931–32, 956, 1100, 1222). Grant Smith adds two anecdotes of the cave-ins. When the Wood & Goe store caved in, a young clerk who slept there had been at a hurdy-gurdy house. "If that was sinful, he said, he had rather be a sinner than buried in that hole." In the second cave-in at the site, the *Gold Hill News* reported that Superintendent Harvey Beckwith and his wife were sleeping when his house slid to the precipice. The paper received an indignant denial from Beckwith the next day saying he was not married, "there-

fore, he hastened to say that 'the lady was not his wife'" (Smith, *History of the Comstock Lode*, 90).

19. See *San Francisco Chronicle*, November 14, 1885; Lyman, *Ralston's Ring*, 41; Asbury Harpending, *The Great Diamond Hoax: And Other Stirring Incidents in the Life of Asbury Harpending*, ed. James H. Wilkins (San Francisco: James H. Barry, 1913), 131.

20. *San Francisco Examiner*, September 22, 1889; Neill C. Wilson, *401 California Street*, 30. Drury's regard for fiddle players seems to have been a minority opinion. Many Virginians believed there was an overabundance of them, as reflected in the oft-repeated anecdote, told here by Drury himself: "In one of the early playhouses on the Comstock, when a fight flared up in the gallery, a gigantic fellow was seen lifting an adversary above his head, ready to hurl him over the balustrade. Someone below was heard to yell, 'Don't waste him! Kill a fiddler with him!'" (J. Wells Drury, *An Editor on the Comstock* [1936; reprint, Reno: University of Nevada Press, 1984], 35).

21. Lucius Beebe and Charles Clegg, *U.S. West: The Saga of Wells Fargo* (New York: E. P. Dutton and Co., 1949), 100. Beebe identifies a right-hand stage box in Piper's Opera House as being reserved on opening nights for Sharon.

22. Toponce, *Reminiscences of Alexander Toponce*, 138–39.

23. *Territorial Enterprise*, September 4, 1874; Sam Davis, *The History of Nevada*, vol. 1, 630. Arnold and Blauvelt also conveyed to Sharon the Empire Mill and seventy-five acres of land in Six Mile Canyon for fifteen thousand dollars in July of 1866. There was a previous claim on the mill that led later to action in court, involving a suit against Sharon as well as Arnold and Blauvelt (*Book of Deeds, Storey County Records, Nevada*, July 6, 1866, book 26, 472).

24. The story of Bliss, partners, and company is best presented in Session S. Wheeler with William Bliss, *Tahoe Heritage: The Bliss Family of Glenbrook, Nevada* (Reno: University of Nevada Press, 1992). See also E. B. Scott, *The Saga of Lake Tahoe* (Crystal Bay, Lake Tahoe: Sierra-Tahoe Publishing Co., 1957), which is filled with references to the Bliss family's enterprises at Lake Tahoe. Yerington began working for Sharon after selling the Merrimac Mill to Sharon's Union Mill and Mining Company for forty thousand dollars, the same price he paid for it. Grace Dangberg, *Conflict on the Carson: A Study of Water Litigation in Western Nevada* (Minden, Nev.: Carson Valley Historical Society, 1975), 310.

25. Charles Wendte, *The Wider Fellowship; Memories, Friendships, and Endeavors for Religious Unity, 1844–1927*, vol. 1 (Boston: Beacon Press, 1927), 140.

26. W. H. Blauvelt in Sam Davis, *The History of Nevada*, vol. 1, 627. Blauvelt points out that the only exception to the 5 percent rate was Wells Fargo and

Company's agreement with the Mexican Mining Company, which was already set at 3 percent on coin given the middle of each month.

27. Sam Davis, *The History of Nevada*, vol. 1, 412–13. Adolph Sutro, "Speech of Adolph Sutro to the Miners of Nevada on the Sutro Tunnel and the Bank of California," 1870, The Bancroft Library.

28. Doten, *The Journals of Alfred Doten*, vol. 2, 831; Angel, *History of Nevada*, 271.

29. Bowles, *Across the Continent*, 353–54.

30. Goodwin, *The Story of The Comstock Lode*, 23.

31. *San Francisco Chronicle*, February 18, 1872.

32. Goodwin, *As I Remember Them*, 58; Shinn, *The Story of the Mine*, 163.

33. Goodwin, *As I Remember Them*, 58.

34. Bancroft, *Chronicle of the Builders*, 53–54.

35. Ashburner to Bowles in Bowles, *Across the Continent*, 446; Richtofen, *The Comstock Lode*, 70–71.

36. W.P.A. Writer's Project, *Individual Histories of the Mines of the Comstock*, a joint project of the W.P.A. Writer's Project and the Nevada State Bureau of Mines (Reno: Nevada State Bureau of Mines, 1942[?]), no. 56, "Yellow Jacket," 1, Special Collections Dept., Getchell Library, University of Nevada, Reno; Smith, *History of the Comstock Lode*, 91.

37. Blauvelt in Sam Davis, *The History of Nevada*, vol. 1, 630.

38. Angel, *History of Nevada*, 88–89; Doten, *The Journals of Alfred Doten*, vol. 2, 897; David Myrick, "Como," *Nevada Historical Society* 5, no. 2 (April–June 1962):18.

39. "Yellow Jacket Silver Mining Company Records 1861–1911," vol. 1, 1863, passim, Special Collections Dept., Getchell Library, University of Nevada, Reno.

40. "Yellow Jacket Silver Mining Company Records 1861–1911," vol. 1, August 4, 1864.

41. "Yellow Jacket Silver Mining Company Records 1861–1911," vol. 1, February 11, 1865, April 1, 1865. See Dangberg, *Conflict on the Carson*, 295–99, for a description of the Morgan Mill.

42. "Yellow Jacket Silver Mining Company Records 1861–1911," vol. 1, July 10, 1865.

43. "Yellow Jacket Silver Mining Company Records 1861–1911," vol. 1, July 9, 1866.

44. Adolph Sutro, "Closing Argument of Adolph Sutro, on the Bill Before Congress to Aid the Sutro Tunnel: Delivered Before the Committee on Mines

and Mining of the House of Representatives of the United States of America, Monday, April 22, 1872," 15, The Bancroft Library.

45. *Individual Histories of the Mines of the Comstock,* No. 56, "Yellow Jacket," 1–2.

46. Andrew Jackson Ralston, Statement, [1886?], 23, in Hubert Howe Bancroft, "Biography of William C. Ralston Prepared for Chronicles of the Kings," The Bancroft Library.

47. George Thomas Mayre Jr., *From '49 to '83 in California and Nevada: Chapters from the Life of George Thomas Marye, a Pioneer of '49* (San Francisco: A. M. Robertson, 1923), 93.

48. Sam Davis, *The History of Nevada,* vol. 1, 412–13.

49. Louis M. Hacker and Benjamin B. Kendrick, with the collaboration of Helene S. Zahler, *The United States Since 1865* (1932; reprint, New York: Appleton-Century-Crofts, 1949), 202.

50. See Matthew Josephson, *The Robber Barons: The Great American Capitalists, 1861–1901* (1934; reprint, New York: Harcourt, Brace and World, 1962), 5–20.

51. The handkerchief involved a scenerio wherein Drew would pull out his bandanna and a slip of paper would fall out of his pocket. Bystanders would fall on the paper as Drew left, apparently unaware that he had dropped it. The paper would have some buying order on it, and those who got it, thinking to get in on the action, would buy the stock that the devious Drew wanted to unload.

52. Lord, *Comstock Mining and Miners,* 248.

53. "Yellow Jacket Silver Mining Company Records 1861–1911," vol. 1, July 15, 1867.

54. *Virginia Evening Chronicle,* October 20, 1874. The *San Francisco Chronicle* had done an exposé two and a half years earlier, saying: "And so if no good rock was to be had, anything else that came first was sent—the mill would crush waste as well as the richest ore, and one paid as much as the others to those who crushed it. It sometimes happened, of course, that this business brought the mines into debt and then the Trustees would LEVY AN ASSESSMENT to pay the mill bill" (*San Francisco Chronicle,* February 18, 1872).

55. Smith, *History of the Comstock Lode,* 91, table on 310–11.

56. Joe Goodman in Michelson, *The Wonderlode of Silver and Gold,* 190.

57. See John D. Fry, "John D. Fry Biographical Sketch: Typescript [ca. 1890?]," The Bancroft Library; *San Francisco Chronicle,* May 20, 1875.

58. Sam Davis, *The History of Nevada,* vol. 1, 413–14.

59. See John M. Townley, "Reclamation in Nevada 1850-1904" (Ph.D. diss., University of Nevada, Reno, 1976), 208-11; Dangberg, *Conflict on the Carson,* 17-27.

60. Zeke Edgecomb, Sharon's first water marshall, in Dangberg, *Conflict on the Carson,* 27.

61. Townley, *Reclamation in Nevada, 1850-1904,* 213.

62. Dangberg, *Conflict on the Carson,* 74-75. For comments about Judge Whitman, see Doten, *The Journals of Alfred Doten,* vol. 2, 840, 871, 895, 897, and vol. 3, 1593; Goodwin in Sam Davis, *The History of Nevada,* vol. 1, 301. Regarding his position with the Virginia & Truckee Railroad, see, for example, "Minute Book, Virginia & Truckee Railroad Company," August 4, 1881–May 9, 1882, Special Collections Dept., Getchell Library, University of Nevada, Reno.

63. *Virginia Evening Chronicle,* October 20, October 5, October 6, 1874. Needless to say, the excerpts are also prima facie evidence of the era's laxness concerning slander and libel.

64. D. O. Mills, in *Lizzie F. Ralston et al., Plaintiffs, vs. William Sharon and J. D. Fry, Defendants . . . Deposition of D. O. Mills,* September 5, 1881, 80-81, The Bancroft Library.

65. Goodwin, *The Story of the Comstock Lode,* 18-19.

66. See The Committee on Mines and Mining of the House of Representatives of the United States, *Report of the Commissioners and Evidence Taken by the Committee on Mines and Mining of the House of Representatives of the United States, in Regard to the Sutro Tunnel, Together with the Arguments and Report of the Committee, Recommending a Loan by the Government in Aid of the Construction of Said Work* (Washington, D.C.: M'Gill and Witherow, 1872), 687-88, in Special Collections Dept., Getchell Library, University of Nevada, Reno.

67. *Territorial Enterprise,* September 29, 1867.

68. William S. Bliss, "Biography of D. L. Bliss," [n.d.], The Bancroft Library. George Wharton James, *The Lake of the Sky: Lake Tahoe In the High Sierras of California and Nevada* (1915; reprint, Pasadena: Radiant Life Press, 1921), 203, provides a description of a famous Tahoe boat used to haul lumber: "The principal vessel for this purpose at the time I first visited Tahoe in 1881 was an iron tug, called the Meteor. It was built in 1876 at Wilmington, Delaware, by Harlan, Hollingsworth & Co., then taken apart, shipped by rail to Carson City and hauled by teams to Lake Tahoe. It was a propeller, eighty feet long and ten feet beam, and cost $18,000." In 1939 the *Meteor,* heralded at the time of its launching as the fastest boat on the American continent, steamed into Lake Tahoe for the last time, being consigned to its depths on April 21 by the Bliss family (E. B. Scott,

The Saga of Lake Tahoe, vol. 2 [Crystal Bay, Lake Tahoe: Sierra-Tahoe Publishing Co., 1973], 92).

69. DeQuille, *The Big Bonanza*, 177–78; Bowles, *Across the Continent*, 165; Smith, *History of the Comstock Lode*, 247.

70. As related in Rodman Paul, *Mining Frontiers of the Far West 1848–1880* (New York: Holt, Rinehart, and Winston, 1963) 72–73; J. Ross Browne to Lucy [Browne], April 23, 1860, in *J. Ross Browne: His Letters, Journals and Writings*, ed. Lina Fergusson Browne (Albuquerque: University of New Mexico Press, 1969), 240.

71. Lord, *Comstock Mining and Miners*, 262.

72. *Territorial Enterprise*, February 17, 1869, in Lord, *Comstock Mining and Miners*, 260, 262.

73. Oscar Lewis, *Silver Kings: The Lives and Times of Mackay, Fair, Flood and O'Brien, Lords of the Nevada Comstock Lode* (1947; reprint, New York: Ballantine, 1971), 107.

74. John Debo Galloway, "Early Engineering Works Contributory to the Comstock," *University of Nevada Bulletin*, vol. 41, no. 5, Nevada State Bureau of Mines and the Mackay School of Mines, June 1947, 67; DeQuille, *The Big Bonanza*, 170–73; George Wharton James, *The Lake of The Sky*, 260; Lewis, *Silver Kings*, 107.

Chapter Three: The Virginia & Truckee

1. Robert Clifton Wittemore, *Makers of the American Mind* (New York: William Morrow and Co., 1964), 309–26; William Graham Sumner, "The Absurd Effort to Make the World Over," in *Words That Made American History Since the Civil War*, ed. Richard N Current and John A Garraty (Boston: Little, Brown and Co., 1962), 116–27.

2. Quoted in William D. Rowley, *Reclaiming the Arid West: The Career of Francis G. Newlands* (Bloomington: Indiana University Press, 1996), 18.

3. Sam Davis, *The History of Nevada*, vol 1, 588–91.

4. B. Silliman, *Report on the Empire Mill and Mining Co. of Gold Hill, on the Comstock Lode, in Nevada* (San Francisco: Wm. P. Harrison and Co., 1864), 20.

5. Angel, *History of Nevada*, 505, 610.

6. Lord, *Comstock Mining and Miners*, 235.

7. William C. Ralston to Oriental Bank Corporation in London, May 4, 1866, in Angel, *History of Nevada*, 505; Robert E. Stewart and Stewart, *Adolph Sutro*, 47–48; Shinn, *The Story of the Mine*, 196.

8. Robert E. Stewart and Stewart, *Adolph Sutro*, 56–57; see also Lord, *Com-*

stock Mining and Miners, 236; Smith, *History of the Comstock Lode,* 109; Lyman, *Ralston's Ring,* 65–66.

9. Ashburner to Bowles, in Bowles, *Across the Continent,* 452.

10. Smith, *History of the Comstock Lode,* 109–10.

11. Angel, *History of Nevada,* 506.

12. Lavender, *Nothing Seemed Impossible,* 232; Robert E. Stewart and Stewart, *Adolph Sutro,* 60.

13. Sutro, "Autobiographical Notes," part 2, 4; part 6, 16.

14. Sutro, "Autobiographical Notes," part 2, 6; Sutro, "Closing Argument," 15.

15. Shinn, *The Story of the Mine,* 199.

16. Angel, *History of Nevada,* 280

17. Nevada historian Ronald M. James, in contrasting the rapid progress of building the road connecting the mines and the mills to the "almost lazily" constructed links for passenger travel and the transcontinental connection in Reno, illustrated Sharon's priorities. After the initial tie facilitated the movement of ore to the mills, "the rest was luxury" (Ronald M. James, *The Roar and the Silence,* 81).

18. *Territorial Enterprise,* April 9, 1869.

19. Lord, *Comstock Mining and Miners,* 251.

20. "Minute Book, Virginia & Truckee Railroad Company," January 9, 1869, 6–7.

21. "Minute Book, Virginia & Truckee Railroad Company," December 13, 1869, 27–32; Angel, *History of Nevada,* 280–81; Smith, *History of the Comstock Lode,* 123–24.

22. *Territorial Enterprise,* April 9, 1869.

23. Smith, *History of the Comstock Lode,* 124.

24. *Virginia Evening Chronicle,* October 20, 1872.

25. John Conness, Washington, D.C., to William C. Ralston, January 10, 1869, in "William Chapman Ralston Correspondence, 1864–1875," The Bancroft Library.

26. Sam Davis, *The History of Nevada,* vol. 1, 592; Galloway, "Early Engineering Works Contributory to the Comstock," 53; Lyman, *Ralston's Ring,* 110–11.

27. *Gold Hill News,* September 29, 1869; Richard E. Lingenfelter, *The Hardrock Miners: A History of the Mining Labor Movement in the American West, 1863–1893* (Berkeley: University of California Press, 1974), 56.

28. Howard Zinn, *A People's History of the United States* (1980; reprint, New York: HarperPerennial, 1990), 229–31.

29. Guy Louis Rocha, "The Many Images of the Comstock Miners' Union,"

http://www.nevadalabor.com/rocha.html (accessed May 17, 2002); *Territorial Enterprise*, August 23, 1865; Lingenfelter, *The Hardrock Miners*, 39.

30. *Gold Hill News*, September 29, 1869. William I. Cummings, Virginia City sheriff, was said to have issued only a feeble protest in ordering the miners to desist and disperse. His action was perhaps predictable, given his having previously served as president of the Gold Hill Miners' Union (Lingenfelter, *The Hardrock Miners*, 56).

31. *Gold Hill News*, September 30, 1869.

32. Michelson, *The Wonderlode of Silver and Gold*, 194–96.

33. *San Francisco Chronicle*, November 14, 1885.

34. For a discussion of racism's central role in the era's academic reasoning and its use to justify fundamentally inegalitarian societies with egalitarian philosophies, see E. J. Hobsbawm, *The Age of Capital: 1848–1875* (1975; reprint, New York: New American Library, 1979), 288–99.

35. *Gold Hill News*, November 13, 1869.

36. Lord, *Comstock Mining and Miners*, 254–56.

37. *Annual Mining Review and Stock Ledger*, 13; "Minute Book, Virginia & Truckee Railroad Company," July 11, 1870, 39.

38. Brooke D. Mordy and Donald L. McCaughey, *Nevada Historical Sites* (n.p.: University of Nevada System, 1968), 243. Eventually at least forty miles of spur tracks would be built, connecting various mines and mills to the road.

39. *Appendix to the Journal of the Sixth Session of the Legislature of the State of Nevada* (Carson City: Charles A. V. Putnam, State Printer, 1873), 21.

40. Lord, *Comstock Mining and Miners*, 254.

41. Lyman, *Ralston's Ring*, 110.

42. *The People's Tribune* (Virginia City), January 1870.

43. Ibid.

44. *Annual Mining Review and Stock Ledger*, 15.

45. See "Mark Hopkins Transportation Collection," vol. 10, 181, Stanford University Library; *Appendix to the Journal of the Sixth Session of the Legislature of Nevada*, 20.

46. Smith, *History of the Comstock Lode*, 124.

47. Hubert Howe Bancroft, *The Works of Hubert H. Bancroft*, vol. 25, *History of Nevada, Colorado and Wyoming, 1540–1888* (San Francisco: History Co., 1890), 238.

48. Angel, *History of Nevada*, 282.

49. Shinn, *The Story of the Mine*, 168.

50. *Territorial Enterprise*, January 3, 1873. Correspondence between Jones

and William Ralston reveals that it was Jones who was involved in planning for a rival railroad. See J. P. Jones to William Ralston, August 18, 1872, in "Ralston Correspondence"; Sam Davis, *The History of Nevada,* vol. 1, 419.

Chapter Four: The Lamb

1. Issac Lawrence Requa, "Notes Relating to the Development of the Comstock. Typescript. Information Concerning the Development of the Mining Operations, the 'Combination Shaft' and Machinery, and His Own Association with the Area," San Francisco, 1887, in Hubert Howe Bancroft Collection, The Bancroft Library.

2. DeQuille, *The Big Bonanza,* 310–11; *Territorial Enterprise,* March 22, 1873.

3. Concerning the nineteenth-century American, Henry Steele Commager commented: "Whatever promised to increase wealth was automatically regarded as good, and the American was tolerant, therefore, of speculation, advertising, deforestation, and the exploitation of natural resources, and bore patiently with the worst manifestations of industrialism" (Henry Steele Commager, *The American Mind: An Interpretation of American Thought and Character Since the 1880s* [1950; New Haven: Yale University Press, 1966], 7).

4. H. R. Linderman, *Report of the Director of the Mint to the Secretary of the Treasury for the Fiscal Year Ended June 30, 1875* (Washington D.C.: Government Printing Office, 1875), 20.

5. Lord, *Comstock Mining and Miners,* 265. It is not fair to judge nineteenth-century actions by twenty-first-century standards. Still, it is interesting to note the region's losses against the gains of mining the Comstock Lode, including: the resources removed from the state of Nevada (Eldrege [*History of California,* vol. 4, 251] noted: "Most of the 340,000,000 in gold and silver which the lode produced within twenty years after it was discovered, was poured into California and remained there"); the mining-induced pollution of air and the poisoning of soil and rivers, whose beds to this day harbor mercury and other poisons; the clear-cutting of forests and resultant damage to lakes and streams; the ruination of the ecological system, which had supported Native American cultures for millennia; the exploitation of Chinese workers, blacks, and women; the breaking of investors by fraudulent mine assessments and stock manipulations; the losses to taxpayers forced to subsidize private concerns; and the damages to the quality of life incurred by subsequent generations.

6. In the 1870 Nevada census, the space under the columns "Real Estate" and "Personal Estate" were left blank for most individuals on the Comstock. A few

citizens listed their assets of a couple of hundred or a thousand dollars. Joseph Goodman, owner of the *Territorial Enterprise,* listed ten thousand dollars in real estate and a personal estate of five thousand dollars. Yellow Jacket president and superintendent John B. Winters had five thousand dollars in real estate and the fabulous personal estate sum of fifty thousand dollars. William Sharon reported five hundred thousand dollars in real estate and a one-hundred-thousand-dollar personal estate (*Nevada 1870 U.S. Census,* National Archives and Record Service, General Services Administration [Washington, D.C.: National Archives Microfilm Publications, 1965], microcopy 593, roll 835, vol. 1 (313–592A), Storey, Washoe, and White Pine Counties, 141).

7. Doten, *The Journals of Alfred Doten,* vol. 2, 1055.

8. *Gold Hill News,* September 29, 1869.

9. *Territorial Enterprise,* February 23, 1868.

10. Doten, *The Journals of Alfred Doten,* vol. 2, 980. This summary was written by journals' editor Clark, taken from Wiegand's card published in the *Territorial Enterprise* and the *Gold Hill News.*

11. Doten, *The Journals of Alfred Doten,* vol. 2, 982.

12. *San Francisco Gold Rush Chronology, 1855–1856,* October 12, 1856, and November 13, 1856, Museum of The City of San Francisco, http://www.sf museum.org/hist/chron4.html (accessed May 2, 2002); George H. Tinkham, *California: Men and Events* (Stockton, Calif.: Record Publishing Co., 1915), 196.

13. Twain, *Roughing It,* vol. 2, 315. The account by Twain uses Wiegand's statement about an assault on him from the *Territorial Enterprise* with Twain's ironic comments interspersed. It is the last of three articles in the appendix (the first two deal with the Mormons). The appendix may have been added to *Roughing It* to increase bulk, so customers buying the book of an unknown author would at least feel they were getting quantity for their purchase—a common practice in the era. Part C is introduced: "Long as it is, it is well worth reading, for it is the richest specimen of journalistic literature the history of America can furnish, perhaps." When living in Nevada some years earlier, Twain was a friend of Wiegand's antagonist, John B. Winters.

14. Conrad Wiegand, Letter to the Editor, *Territorial Enterprise,* January 20, 1870.

15. *The People's Tribune,* January 1870.

16. Ibid.

17. Ibid.

18. *Gold Hill News,* January 13, 1870.

19. *The People's Tribune,* February 1870.

20. This entire account is from Wiegand's statement printed in the *Territorial Enterprise*, January 20, 1870.

21. *Gold Hill News*, January 17, 1870.

22. *Territorial Enterprise*, January 20, 1870.

23. *Gold Hill News*, January 19, 1870.

24. *A Compendium of the Ninth Census*, June 1, 1870, 940.

25. *The People's Tribune*, February 1870.

26. Richard E. Lingenfelter, with an introduction by David F. Myrick, *1858–1958, The Newspapers of Nevada: A History and Bibliography* (San Francisco; John Howell—Books, 1964), 55.

27. Wells Drury in Sam Davis, *The History of Nevada*, vol. 1, 479.

28. Michelson, *The Wonderlode of Silver and Gold*, 189.

29. Michelson, *The Wonderlode of Silver and Gold*, 189–90.

30. *Territorial Enterprise*, January 5, 1873.

31. "Exhibit No. 1, Affidavit of H. Symons," March 26, 1873, Comstock Lode (Nev.) Cipher Books, Special Collections Dept., Getchell Library, University of Nevada, Reno.

32. Doten, *The Journals of Alfred Doten*, vol. 2, 1364.

Chapter Five: Conflicts

1. Galloway, "Early Engineering Works Contributory to the Comstock," 34.

2. George D. Oliver, as told by Scott, *The Saga of Lake Tahoe*, vol. 1, 279.

3. It is interesting to note that Sharon competed fiercely in pastimes—cockfighting, poker, horse racing—that, if won, served as magnifications of the ego. Anthropologist Clifford Geertz studied cockfighting in Bali, noting that the bloody drama combines aroused human masculinity with base destructiveness. He discusses the psychological identification of the men with their cocks (and notes that the double entendre is deliberate—the same in Balinese as in English): "It is not only apparently cocks that are fighting there. Actually it is men" (Clifford Geertz, "Deep Play: Notes on the Balinese Cockfight," *The Interpretation of Cultures* [New York: Basic Books, 1973], 412–53).

4. Scott, *The Saga of Lake Tahoe*, vol. 1, 269; see also Galloway, "Early Engineering Works Contributory to the Comstock," 34.

5. Currey to Morrison, June 3, 1891, in Sharon Family Papers.

6. Goodwin, *The Story of The Comstock Lode*, 20. How much money Sharon loaned Ralston is not clear. In his later book, *As I Remember Them*, Goodwin says: "Four years previously Mr. Sharon had loaned [Ralston] $4,000,000, in just

such an emergency" (106), but in this anecdote Sharon only says he had that amount in the bank when Ralston needed $3,000,000.

7. Goodwin, *As I Remember Them*, 161–62.

8. Mayre, *From '49 to '83 in California and Nevada*, 91–92, 175–76.

9. Lavender, *Nothing Seemed Impossible*, 268, in "Ralston Correspondence."

10. *Virginia Evening Chronicle*, October 20, 1872.

11. Ferol Egan, *Last Bonanza Kings: The Bourns of San Francisco* (Reno: University of Nevada Press, 1998), 39, 33, 45.

12. *Book of Deeds, Storey County Records, Nevada*, October 15, 1866, book 26, 672.

13. *Territorial Enterprise*, October 26, 1866, August 4, 1871, January 28, 1872.

14. Lord, *Comstock Mining and Miners*, 255–58, from Report of O. D. Wheeler, Special Agent Tenth Census, "Flumes and Fluming Operations in Western Nevada"; John S. Hittell, *The Commerce and Industries of the Pacific Coast*, 420.

15. Angel, *History of Nevada*, 190–91; Milton S. Gould, *A Cast of Hawks* (La Jolla, Calif.: Copley Books, 1985), 169. In 1882 historian John S. Hittell identified Haines as the inventor, commenting: "Whether the law gives [Haines] the profit of his invention or not, the industrial historian must give him the credit." Hittell, *The Commerce and Industries of the Pacific Coast*, 420.

16. C. B. Glasscock, *Lucky Baldwin: The Story of an Unconventional Success* (1933; reprint, Reno: Silver Syndicate Press, 1993), 177–78.

17. See Angel, *History of Nevada*, 122–26.

18. Ibid.

19. Lewis, *Silver Kings*, 33.

20. Tilton, *William Chapman Ralston, Courageous Builder*, 224–25.

21. Ibid.; Smith, *History of the Comstock Lode*, 117; Lewis, *Silver Kings*, 33–34.

22. Tilton, *William Chapman Ralston, Courageous Builder*, 231; *San Francisco Call*, November 14, 1885.

23. Sam Davis, *The History of Nevada*, vol. 1, 415.

24. Lewis, *Silver Kings*, 119.

25. *Individual Histories of the Mines of the Comstock*, No. 56, "Yellow Jacket," 2.

26. Glasscock, *Lucky Baldwin*, 187.

27. *Territorial Enterprise*, April 8, 1869. In the *Enterprise* under "Local News" was the announcement by the Northwestern Mutual Life Insurance Company: "We would call the attention of the public to the advertisement of this Company in our columns. . . . The sad calamity that has fallen upon us, in the burning of three of our principal mines, coupled with the death of some of our

inhabitants, brings to our mind the uncertainty of human life. We say to one and all, make a provision for those dependent on you for support, by securing a policy."

28. James V. Comerford in Sam Davis, *The History of Nevada,* vol. 2, 1001. Comerford, in 1913, mentions without further comment: "It was claimed at the time that Senator Sharon instigated the work of firing the mine to depress the stock." See also Doten, *The Journals of Alfred Doten,* vol 2, 1044.

29. *Gold Hill News,* July 20, 1869. On July 24 a *News* article on the Yellow Jacket concluded, "There's a good time coming, wait a little longer."

30. Robert E. Stewart and Stewart, *Adolph Sutro,* 73–74.

31. C. A. Luckhardt to R. W. Raymond, September 20, 1868, in "General Description and Report on the Comstock Vein," Special Collections Dept., Getchell Library, University of Nevada, Reno.

32. Samuel Hooper to William C. Ralston, September 5, 1869, in "Ralston Correspondence."

33. Sutro, in "Autobiographical Notes," part 6, 17.

34. *Gold Hill News,* July 2, 1869.

35. Sutro, "Closing Argument," 26.

36. Robert E. Stewart and Stewart, *Adolph Sutro,* 75–76.

37. Broadside [187?], The Bancroft Library. This item is a generic sample of the posters Sutro used to announce his speeches; it has the place and date left blank, to be filled in before being posted.

38. Shinn, *The Story of the Mine,* 200–201.

39. Lyman, *Ralston's Ring,* 142; Shinn, *The Story of the Mine,* 201–2.

40. *Report of the Commissioners and Evidence Taken by the Committee on Mines and Mining,* 2–15.

41. Ibid., 55–56.

42. Sutro, in "Autobiographical Notes," part 6, 20.

43. *Report of the Commissioners and Evidence Taken by the Committee on Mines and Mining,* 155–56.

44. Ibid., 166–67, 175–76.

45. Ibid., 343.

46. Ibid., 526–27.

47. Ibid., 551.

48. Ibid., 679, 687–88.

49. Sutro, "Autobiographical Notes," part 1, 13.

50. Hittell, *The Commerce and Industries of the Pacific Coast,* 413.

51. Alfred Bates, "J. P. Jones," (n.d.), manuscript in the handwriting of Alfred Bates in Hubert Howe Bancroft Collection, The Bancroft Library.

52. Lord, *Comstock Mining and Miners*, 282–83.

53. Ibid., 279.

54. Joseph L. King, *History of the San Francisco Stock and Exchange Board*, 47; Lord, *Comstock Mining and Miners*, 284.

55. *Report of the Commissioners and Evidence Taken by the Committee on Mines and Mining*, 174–75; Bancroft, *Chronicle of the Builders*, vol. 4, 41; Smith, *History of the Comstock Lode*, 130, 141.

Chapter Six: Hurly-Burly

1. James B. Fry, the provost marshal general who headed the War Department in the Civil War, wrote Ralston in 1869, enclosing a newspaper clipping regarding representative government. Fry noted that "the writer has expressed better than I could some of the views I advanced when the subject of Sharon's taking a Senatorship was up while I was at your house" (General James B. Fry, Louisville, to William Ralston, October 24, 1869, in "Ralston Correspondence").

2. Angel, *History of Nevada*, 89–90.

3. *Elko Independent*, September 24, 1870.

4. Angel, *History of Nevada*, 90.

5. See "Second Biennial Message of H. G. Blasdel, Governor of Nevada. Delivered to the Legislature, January, 1869," 10, in *The Journal of the Senate during the Fourth Session of the Legislature of the State of Nevada, 1869* (Carson City: Henry R. Mighels, State Printer, 1869). After discussing the three campaigns involving Sharon, Sam Davis stated: "From the beginning Nevada sent its wealthy men to the Senate of the United States. This earned the State the name of the 'Rotten Borough' and this name seems destined to cling to it" (Sam Davis, *The History of Nevada*, vol. 1, 423).

6. Effie Mona Mack, "James Warren Nye," *Nevada Historical Society* 4, nos. 3–4 (July–December 1961):54–56.

7. *Territorial Enterprise*, May 10, 1870.

8. Smith, *History of the Comstock Lode*, 132.

9. *San Francisco Chronicle*, February 16, 1872.

10. Ibid., February 18, 1872.

11. Ibid.

12. Sharon dumped stocks for reasons other than attacking competitors.

Joseph L. King, stock-market president, said: "Whenever the market became dull, so that neither operators nor speculating brokers were active, Mr. Sharon would give Mr. Sherwood a large selling order that would be termed a 'settler.' Occasionally, such an order would be to sell 2000 shares of six or seven of the principal stocks, the result being to break the prices of everything on the list, and thus induce all speculators to buy at what would be deemed low prices. A break in prices from $3 to $10 a share in Ophir, Chollar, Belcher, Crown Point, Yellow Jacket, Savage or Overman would turn the whole street into buyers, in which case prices would rise again, when all the stock purchased could be sold at a profit" (King, *History of the San Francisco Stock and Exchange Board,* 135–36).

13. Lyman, *Ralston's Ring,* 207.

14. *San Francisco Call,* May 16, 1872, in Tilton, *William Chapman Ralston, Courageous Builder,* 277.

15. Doten, *The Journals of Alfred Doten,* vol. 2, 1164.

16. *Territorial Enterprise,* May 9, 1872.

17. Ibid., May 10, 1872. Even William Ralston made a statement that "unless Sharon could exonerate himself from the charges against him, either he or [Ralston and Mills] must leave the Bank of California" (*Territorial Enterprise,* May 9, 1872). The statement was never acted upon.

18. *Gold Hill News,* May 10, May 13, 1872; *Territorial Enterprise,* May 11, 1872.

19. *Territorial Enterprise,* May 14, 1872.

20. Doten, *The Journals of Alfred Doten,* vol. 2, 1159; *Gold Hill News,* May 30, 1872.

21. Doten, *The Journals of Alfred Doten,* vol. 2, 115.

22. *Territorial Enterprise,* May 31, 1872.

23. *Gold Hill News,* May 31, 1872.

24. Doten, *The Journals of Alfred Doten,* vol. 2, 1166.

25. *Territorial Enterprise,* June 16, 1872.

26. *Gold Hill News,* June 17, 1872; *Territorial Enterprise,* June 19, 1872.

27. *Territorial Enterprise,* June 20, 1872.

28. Ibid., June 22, 1872.

29. Ibid., July 18, 1872.

30. J. P. Jones to William Ralston, August 18, 1872, in "Ralston Correspondence." The Ralston-Jones relationship would evolve into a strong association, as evinced by a telegram from Jones two years later: "Have drawn on you for ten thousand dollars will explain and pay when I see you in July" (Telegram, John P. Jones to W. C. Ralston, June 8, 1874, in "Ralston Correspondence").

31. See Doug Henwood, *Wall Street: How It Works and for Whom, 1997* (London: Verso, 1998), 4.

32. *Book of Deeds, Storey County Records, Nevada,* March 24, 1874, book 38, 422; *Nevada 1870 U.S. Census,* 383.

33. C. C. Goodwin in Angel, *History of Nevada,* 322. See also E. T. H. Bunje, F. J. Schmitz, and H. Penn, *Journals of the Golden Gate, 1846–1936* (Berkeley: University of California Press, 1936), 26–27; Sam Davis, *The History of Nevada,* vol. 2, 709.

34. Goodwin, *As I Remember Them,* 189.

35. Russell R. Elliot, *Servant of Power: A Political Biography of Senator William M. Stewart* (Reno: University of Nevada Press, 1983), 80–82; Ostrander, *Nevada: The Great Rotten Borough,* 70; William M. Stewart, *Reminiscences,* 261.

36. Takaki, *A Different Mirror,* 278; Matthews, *Ten Years in Nevada, or Life on the Pacific Coast,* 169.

37. Robert E. Stewart and Stewart, *Adolph Sutro,* 122–23; Doten, *The Journals of Alfred Doten,* vol. 2, 1226 (from the *Gold Hill News,* May 18, 1874); vol. 2, 1234 (from the *Gold Hill News,* August 19, 1874).

38. S. O. Houghton to W. C. Ralston, April 10, 1874; Jno. Hager to Ralston, San Francisco, April 16, 1874; McCrellish to WCR, May 21, 1874; H. R. Linderman to Ralston, June 10, 1874, all in "Ralston Correspondence." Senator Hager is an interesting study in his own right. He had studied at Princeton and had a taste for letters, translating at least one medieval hymn from the Latin for a periodical. He was a judge in early San Francisco and presided in the notorious case of Charles Cora, accused of killing a U.S. marshall. There was no witness, his instructions to the jury were said to have been "clear and unbiased," and the trial ended in a hung jury. Cora was remanded to prison, but in its inaugural action the San Francisco Vigilance Committee took him by force, tried him, and hanged him. A Mr. Cohen provided another anecdote: On the day set to sentence a murderer, Hager could not be found. "Finally a policeman said to the sheriff, 'If you want to find Hager he is in a bagnio at the corner of Washington and Dupont streets. If you go up there you will find him. They went down there and found him; that man was brought down, reeking with the moral filth and fumes of that den of prostitution, to sentence a human being to death. Not even the performance of that sacred and solemn duty could keep him from indulging in his dissipation and licentiousness, for which he was so well known when he was on the bench" (Mr. Cohen in "John Sharpenstein Hager, Biographical Sketch," 1887, The Bancroft Library).

39. This was the Reverend T. H. McGrath who, in a lecture at the Opera House, denounced men offering to buy votes and politicos who were bringing in unregistered workers to vote (Francis Phelps Weisenburger, *Idol of the West: The Fabulous Career of Rollin Mallory Daggett* [Syracuse: Syracuse University, 1965], 97). For more on McGrath, see Doten, *The Journals of Alfred Doten,* vol. 2, 1207; Angel, *History of Nevada,* 194–95, 213.

40. *Daily Independent,* September 23, 1874, July 20, 1874.

41. Smith, *History of the Comstock Lode,* 163n.

42. Angel, *History of Nevada,* 91; see also Harry M. Gorham, *My Memories of the Comstock* (Los Angeles: Suttonhouse, 1939), 106.

43. *Territorial Enterprise,* August 26, 1874.

44. Chris Carlsson, "The 8-Hour Movement," http://www.shapingsf.org/exine/labor/8hour/main.html (accessed May 9, 2002); *Virginia Evening Chronicle,* October 24, 1874.

45. Angel, *History of Nevada,* 595.

46. Sam Davis, *The History of Nevada,* vol. 1, 451; Smith, *History of the Comstock Lode,* 112n. Regarding Fitch's political fortunes, Nevada Historian Eric N. Moody commented: "His convictions and public stances tended to shift in accordance with changing circumstances, and eventually too many people heard him speak with equal spellbinding eloquence on both sides of an issue" (Eric N. Moody, *Southern Gentleman of Nevada Politics: Vail N. Pittman* [Reno: University of Nevada Press, 1974], viii).

47. *Virginia Evening Chronicle,* October 24, 1874. For another version of this anecdote, see Sam Davis, *The History of Nevada,* vol. 1, 450–51.

48. Doten, *The Journals of Alfred Doten,* vol. 2, 1238; see also Smith, *History of the Comstock Lode,* 112; Angel, *History of Nevada,* 93.

49. Rowley, *Reclaiming the Arid West: The Career of Francis G. Newlands,* 18; B. E. Lloyd, *Lights and Shades in San Francisco,* 109.

50. *San Francisco Chronicle,* November 20, 1874.

51. Julia Cooley Altrocchi, *The Spectacular San Franciscans* (New York: E. P. Dutton and Co., 1949), 189; B. E. Lloyd, *Lights and Shades in San Francisco,* 110.

52. *Territorial Enterprise,* November 24, 1874.

53. *Book of Deeds, Storey County Records, Nevada,* January 9, 1875, book 37, 243–57; May 14, 1875, book 36, 559–60; June 5, 1876, book 39, 522; September 19, 1876, book 40, 328–29.

54. *Virginia Evening Chronicle,* January 4, 1875.

55. Fred H. Hart, "Biography—Sharon, William: Description of Physical Appearance, Written by Fred H Hart, Under Pseud. of Toby Green," *Gold Hill*

News, January 7, 1875, in Special Collections Dept., Getchell Library, University of Nevada, Reno.

56. *Gold Hill News,* January 6, 1875.

57. *San Francisco Alta,* January 14, 1875. His proposal for specie payments and the abandonment of the system of subsidies echoes the 1872 Liberal Republican platform in reaction to the Radical Republicans' Southern Policy and Grant administration scandals. See "Liberal Republican Party Platform: Cincinnati, Ohio, May 1, 1872," in *Documents of American History,* ed. Henry Steele Commager (1934; reprint, New York: Meredith Publishing Co., 1963), 520–21.

58. *San Francisco Alta,* January 13, 14, 1875; *Territorial Enterprise,* January 14, 1875.

59. Sam Davis, *The History of Nevada,* vol. 1, 421; Sam Davis, in Ostrander, *Nevada: The Great Rotten Borough,* 73.

60. *Territorial Enterprise,* January 13, 1875.

61. *Virginia Evening Chronicle,* January 5, 1875.

Chapter Seven: The Ophir Debacle

1. See "Jefferson's First Inaugural Address, 4 March 1801," *Documents of American History,* 188; Robert A. Lively, "The American System: A Review Article," *The Shaping of Twentieth-Century America: Interpretive Articles,* ed. Richard M. Abrams and Lawrence W. Levine (Boston: Little, Brown and Co., 1965), 4–5; Samuel Eliot Morison and Henry Steele Commager, *The Growth of the American Republic,* vol. 1 (1930; reprint, New York: Oxford University Press, 1958), 338–46; Vernon L. Parrington, *Main Currents in American Thought,* vol. 2, *The Romantic Revolution in America, 1800–1860* (New York; Harcourt, Brace and World, 1927), xii; Kevin Phillips, *Wealth and Democracy: A Political History of the American Rich* (New York: Broadway Books, 2002), 28.

2. Stuart Bruchey, "Economic Growth and Change to 1860," in *Interpreting American History: Conversations with Historians,* ed. John A. Garraty (New York: Macmillan Co., 1970), vol. I, 180–81.

3. Alfred A. Cohen, in Dana, *The Man Who Built San Francisco,* 379–81.

4. Eldredge, *History of California,* vol. 4, 440–41; Cross, *Financing an Empire: Banking in California,* 404.

5. Mills, in *Ralston vs. Sharon and Fry,* 105–8. Information on the relationship between Ralston and Mills from Mills's perspective is found throughout the manuscript, especially 1–171; Henry D. Bacon, Statement, n.d., in Hubert Howe

Bancroft, "Biography of William C. Ralston Prepared for Chronicles of the Kings," The Bancroft Library; Bell, Statement, 1886, 2.

6. Goodwin, *As I Remember Them*, 104.

7. Dana, *The Man Who Built San Francisco*, 385–86.

8. Mills, in *Ralston versus Sharon and Fry*, 80–81; Bell, 1886, Statement, 3.

9. Henry Lewis King, Statement, 1887, 12, The Bancroft Library; "Largest Hotel in the United States Now Going Up Here" and "Squeezing Sharon," *San Francisco Real Estate Circular*, December 1873, online Museum of the City of San Francisco, http://www.sfmuseum.org/hist1/1873.html (accessed October 31, 2001).

10. Bancroft, *Chronicle of the Builders*, 63.

11. Eldredge, *History of California*, 437. Ralston found after purchasing the ranch alluded to that the oak in the heavily wooded property was not suited to creating the planking the hotel needed.

12. Smith, *History of the Comstock Lode*, 138.

13. Professor R. E. Rogers in Linderman, *Annual Report of the Director of the United States Mint to the Secretary of the Treasury for the Fiscal Year Ended June 30, 1875*, 82.

14. Smith, *History of the Comstock Lode*, 148–49.

15. Lord, *Comstock Mining and Miners*, 311.

16. Josephson, *The Robber Barons*, 56–58.

17. Mills, in *Ralston vs. Sharon and Fry*, 72–101; King, *History of the San Francisco Stock and Exchange Board*, 135–36.

18. This account follows information from Smith, *History of the Comstock Lode*, 162–64, and the *San Francisco Call*, November 14, 1885. The *Call*'s source was "a prominent stock operator and State Senator." Of secondary sources, Smith's research regarding Comstock mines is the most comprehensive. C. B. Glasscock relates several anecdotes regarding the Ophir at or about the time of Sharon's efforts to buy it, including the tale of a stockholder's meeting that was held while Baldwin controlled the mine. Stalling while awaiting an injunction to stop an attempt to replace Superintendent Curtis, Baldwin knocked the mine president under a table and "verbally and physically" sparred with others. The accuracy of this and other Ophir tales is suspect; Glasscock points out that its records were destroyed in the 1906 San Francisco fire and its history is rife with contradictions. He comments further on Baldwin himself, as regarded autobiographical anecdotes: "His memory was like his temper. It flared" (Glasscock, *Lucky Baldwin*, 142, 156–64).

19. *San Francisco Chronicle*, May 20, 1875.

20. Smith, *History of the Comstock Lode,* 82. Smith points out further that once Mackay's Bonanza Firm took control in 1877, "A narrow east–west vein was found on the 1900 level, from which two dividends of $108,000 each were paid" (82).

21. Angel, *History of Nevada,* 90; Doten commented that a DeLong lecture on Japan was "one of the very best and finest lectures I ever listened to" (Doten, *The Journals of Alfred Doten,* vol. 2, 1249).

22. Charles E. DeLong to Mrs. Elida DeLong, January 31, 1875.

23. Regarding the rumor, see George Lyttleton Upshur, *As I Recall Them: Memories of Crowded Years* (New York: Wilson-Erickson, 1936), 118.

Chapter Eight: Failure

1. Angel, *History of Nevada,* 126.
2. Ibid.
3. "Old Man" [H. R. Linderman] to [William C.] R[alston], March 16, 1875, (marked *Private*), in "Ralston Correspondence." Leland Stanford commented on the gold crisis in the *San Francisco Alta,* September 8, 1875. For a discussion of wheat farming in California from the 1860s to the 1890s, see Bean, *California: An Interpretive History,* 271–72.
4. *San Francisco Chronicle,* May 20, 1875.
5. Wendte, *The Wider Fellowship,* 146; Andrew Jackson Ralston, Statement, [1886?], 33.
6. Bell, Statement, 1886, 2–3; see also Bacon, Statement, n.d.
7. Albert W. Atwood, *Francis G. Newlands: A Builder of the Nation* (n.p.: Newlands Co., 1969), 13.
8. Mills, in *Ralston versus Sharon and Fry,* 93–96, 170–71.
9. Ibid. Nogues also charged that on January 31 of 1869 Sharon and Company was overdrawn by more than $250,000 in the Virginia City branch (236); Lord, *Comstock Mining and Miners,* 279; Atwood, *Francis G. Newlands: A Builder of the Nation,* 13; Bell, Statement, 1886, 5. Others associated with the bank took a tack similar to that of Sharon. Nogues asked D. O. Mills, under oath, if he had known that the bank was "kiting"—that is, drawing checks before money was deposited to cover them. Mills responded: "I could not say that I did." The attorney suggested: "After it failed—after this thunder clap came on you?" Mills then agreed: "We found then that it had been weak for some time" (Mills, in *Ralston versus Sharon and Fry,* 171).
10. Eldredge, *History of California,* 437; Cross, *Financing an Empire: Banking in California,* 403.

238 NOTES TO PAGES 113-116

11. Reuben Lloyd, "Manuscript, 31 December 1886."

12. Oscar Lewis and Carrol D. Hall, *Bonanza Inn: America's First Luxury Hotel* (New York: Doubleday and Co., 1956), 14; Amelia Ransome Neville, *The Fantastic City: Memoirs of the Social and Romantic Life of Old San Francisco*, ed. and rev., Virginia Brastow (Boston and New York: Houghton Mifflin Co., 1932).

13. Henry Lewis King, Statement, 1887; Neville, *The Fantastic City*, 202.

14. Dana, *The Man Who Built San Francisco*, 347-48.

15. Bell, Statement, 1886, 5. Bell does not give the figure of overissued stock, saying merely that it had been issued to a very large extent. The figures come from T. H. Rearden, [Opinion] in *The Superior Court of the City and County of San Francisco . . . The Odd Fellows Savings Bank vs. William Sharon*, December 19, 1884, 6, 7, 10, The Bancroft Library.

16. H. Schussler, Affidavit, in *The Circuit Court of the United States, Ninth Judicial Circuit, Northern District of California. In Equity. Spring Valley Water Company, vs. The City and County of San Francisco*, June 20, 1908, The Bancroft Library; Bell, Statement, 1886, 3; see also Lavender, *Nothing Seemed Impossible*, 370-71; Grey Brechin, *Imperial San Francisco: Urban Power, Earthly Ruin* (Berkeley: University of California Press, 1999), 85-89.

17. Tilton, *William Chapman Ralston, Courageous Builder*, 354.

18. Bell, Statement, 1886, 4-5; Tilton, *William Chapman Ralston, Courageous Builder*, 352, 390-91.

19. Rearden, in *The Odd Fellows Savings Bank vs. William Sharon*, 7, 10.

20. Tilton, *William Chapman Ralston, Courageous Builder*, 339.

21. Upshur, *As I Recall Them*, 92-93; Smith, *History of the Comstock Lode*, 188.

22. See Bacon, Statement. Bacon said Mills quit the bank presidency because he feared it would fail.

23. Mills, in *Ralston versus Sharon and Fry*, 92, 120-21.

24. *San Francisco Alta*, September 5, 1875, in Tilton, *William Chapman Ralston, Courageous Builder*, 352. Tilton comments, "Mills never saw fit to comment."

25. See John Bruce, *Gaudy Century: The Story of San Francisco's Hundred Years of Robust Journalism* (New York: Random House, 1948), 76.

26. Mills, in *Ralston versus Sharon and Fry*, 290.

27. *San Francisco Call*, August 19, August 23-26, 1875. The September 22, 1889, issue of the *San Francisco Examiner* said the *Call* and the *Bulletin* had an ulterior motive in their assaults: "Two newspapers owned by one firm attacked and vilified his memory. In life Ralston had opposed a scheme to subsidize the St.

Louis and San Francisco Railway, in which the proprietors of these papers were interested to the extent of a million and they never forgave him. He opposed the subsidy because he was interested in the Colorado, a rival road which was built without subsidy." The *Call* and the *Bulletin* insisted throughout that they were merely being honest in presenting issues to prevent the citizens from being plundered by the Bank Ring.

28. Upshur, *As I Recall Them*, 92–93; Eldredge, *History of California*, 438.

29. Harpending, *The Great Diamond Hoax*, 274; Grant Smith commented: "As a matter of fact, both Mackay and Flood admired Ralston and had no personal differences with him. Sharon they disliked, to put it mildly" (Smith, *History of the Comstock Lode*, 189).

30. Upshur, *As I Recall Them*, 92; Eldredge, *History of California*, 437–38; Tilton, *William Chapman Ralston, Courageous Builder*, 95; Lavender, *Nothing Seemed Impossible*, 288–92, 327–28.

31. Upshur, *As I Recall Them*, 93–94. For an account of the 1869 ploy, see Harpending, *The Great Diamond Hoax*, 135–38.

32. King, *History of the San Francisco Stock and Exchange Board*, 103–5.

33. Upshur, *As I Recall Them*, 103.

34. Franklin, Biography of William Ralston, 1886, 8; Bell, Statement, 1886, 4.

35. King, *History of the San Francisco Stock and Exchange Board*, 102. King listed the amount of Baldwin's account at $1 million; others put it at $2 million. Afterward Baldwin was the bank's largest creditor at $1,700,000, giving credence to the second number (Tilton, *William Chapman Ralston, Courageous Builder*, 399).

36. *San Francisco Call*, August 28, 1875.

37. King, *History of the San Francisco Stock and Exchange Board*, 101.

38. Hart, *In Our Second Century*, 48; King, *History of the San Francisco Stock and Exchange Board*, 105.

39. King, *History of the San Francisco Stock and Exchange Board*, 105–7.

40. King, *History of the San Francisco Stock and Exchange Board*, 107–8.

41. *San Francisco Alta*, August 27, 1875. The $4 million figure to move the wheat, mentioned by Ralston, was later calculated by Ira Cross to have been $5 million (Cross, *Financing an Empire: Banking in California*, 398).

42. Hart, *In Our Second Century*, 51.

43. Mills, in *Ralston versus Sharon and Fry*, 227–28.

44. C.F.S. to the Editor of the *San Francisco Chronicle*, in "Ralston Correspondence"; Franklin, Biography of William Ralston, 1886, 15.

45. *Territorial Enterprise,* August 27, 1875, in Gordon E. Oliver, "The History of Early Banking in Nevada, 1859–1900" (M.B.A. thesis, University of Nevada, 1983), 33.

46. *San Francisco Alta,* August 29, 1875.

47. Mills, in *Ralston versus Sharon and Fry,* 251, 254.

48. Bell, Statement, 1886, 4.

49. *San Francisco Call,* August 28, 1875.

50. Reuben Lloyd, "Manuscript, 31 December 1886"; *San Francisco Alta,* August 29, 1875; *San Francisco Chronicle,* November 14, 1885.

51. *San Francisco Call,* August 28, 1875. C. C. Goodwin said that when Mills asked for Ralston's resignation, he did so in his "mathematically correct business way" (Goodwin, *As I Remember Them,* 104).

52. Upshur, *As I Recall Them,* 94.

53. John Pitman to Mrs. Bertha Ralston Bright, January 5, 1903, in Gertrude Atherton, *California: An Intimate History* (1914; reprint, New York: Horace Liveright, 1927), 280.

54. *San Francisco Call,* August 29, 1875; *Gold Hill News,* August 28, 1875.

55. B. E. Lloyd, *Lights and Shades in San Francisco,* 114.

56. Doten, *The Journals of Alfred Doten,* vol. 2, 1257.

57. *San Francisco Examiner,* September 22, 1889.

58. Tibbey, Statement, 1886, 4.

59. Atherton, *California: An Intimate History,* 279. Gertrude Atherton relates the same anecdote in *My San Francisco* (Indianapolis: Bobbs-Merrill Co., 1946), 213, and it is often repeated in Ralston biographies and histories of the era.

60. Tilton, *William Chapman Ralston, Courageous Builder,* 406. See also Charles Caldwell Dobie, *San Francisco: A Pageant* (New York: D. Appleton-Century Co., 1943), 150.

61. Tilton, *William Chapman Ralston, Courageous Builder,* 406; B. E. Lloyd, *Lights and Shades in San Francisco,* 193–94.

62. *San Francisco Chronicle,* August 30, 1875; George H. Morrison, Statement, n.d. Morrison collected notes on the life of Ralston from A. J. Ralston, E. S. Tibbey, A. B. Forbes, Thomas Bell, and Stephen Franklin as well as the Sharon family.

63. *San Francisco Alta,* September 8, 1875.

64. *San Francisco Chronicle,* August 30, 1875.

65. Mills, in *Ralston versus Sharon and Fry,* 290.

66. Charles Foreman, "Statement from Charles Foreman," [1887?], Hubert Howe Bancroft Collection, The Bancroft Library.

67. Pitman, Letter, in Atherton, *An Intimate History of California*, 280. Pitman also calls the *Call* and *Bulletin* to task for being involved in "dirty work." But his quarrel with them was in regard to their "foulest lie," accusing Ralston of suicide. Pitman believed the death was due to "cramp produced by his heated condition and very cold water."

68. See Dobie, *San Francisco*, 149–50; Sam Davis, *The History of Nevada*, vol. 1, 417–19.

69. Lewis, *Silver Kings*, 120–21, 182–83.

70. Gould saved only himself during the "Black Friday" hysteria in September 1869. After cornering the gold market, Gould drove it until selling just before the government threw millions in gold on the market, breaking the price. The crash buried brokers, including Gould's own agents, his associates, and his partner, Jim Fisk. Carnegie did not help Thomas Scott, his original benefactor, when Scott was losing his fortune, nor did he help his partner Kloman, upon whose mechanical skill their steel company had been built, in 1873. Instead Carnegie acquired Kloman's share, eliminating him from the business. Josephson, *The Robber Barons*, 144–48, 177.

Chapter Nine: Rebirth

1. *Carson Valley News*, September 4, 1875; D. O. Mills to H. M. Yerington, August 27, 1875, in "Ralston Correspondence." There is an addendum to this note saying that it is not in Mills's handwriting, nor is his name signed. It is included here because the content is relevent and there seems to be no motive for forgery. Moreover, in the stress and turmoil of that moment such a note might likely be dictated and unsigned.

2. Cross, *Financing an Empire: Banking in California*, 404; Hart, *In Our Second Century*, 51; Rearden, in *The Odd Fellows Savings Bank vs. William Sharon*, 4.

3. Thomas Edwin Farish, *The Gold Hunters of California* (Chicago: M. A. Donohue and Co., 1904), 204; *San Francisco Alta*, September 29, 1875. Regarding oversight, in 1884 Judge T. H. Rearden found: "The directors of the bank had (as directors always have done since corporations were founded, and possibly always will do) been guilty of grave neglect in the performance of their duties of office" (Rearden, in *The Odd Fellows Savings Bank vs. William Sharon*, 4).

4. Reuben Lloyd, "Manuscript, 31 December 1886."

5. Ibid.; *San Francisco Alta*, August 28, 1875; Chris Carlsson, "Shaping San

Francisco," http://www.shapingsf.org/exine/afamerican/earlyorg.html (accessed May 9, 2002).

6. *San Francisco Alta,* August 29, 1875; *San Francisco Bulletin,* August 27, 1875, in Tilton, *William Chapman Ralston, Courageous Builder,* 362; Bell, Statement, 1886, 4.

7. Mills, in *Ralston versus Sharon and Fry,* 141.

8. *San Francisco Examiner,* September 22, 1889.

9. Reuben Lloyd, "Manuscript, 31 December 1886."

10. Eldredge, *History of California,* 442; Mills, in *Ralston versus Sharon and Fry,* 46, 145–47.

11. Mills, in *Ralston versus Sharon and Fry,* 154.

12. Ibid., 103.

13. Eldredge, *History of California,* 444.

14. Reuben Lloyd, "Manuscript, December 31, 1886"; Goodwin, *As I Remember Them,* 130.

15. *San Francisco Chronicle,* November 14, 1885.

16. Eldredge, *History of California,* 442–43.

17. *San Francisco Chronicle,* October 3, 1875, in Tilton, *William Chapman Ralston, Courageous Builder,* 397–99.

18. Tilton, *William Chapman Ralston, Courageous Builder,* 340; Coll Deane to Judge T. H. Reardon, December 22, 1884, Hubert Howe Bancroft Collection, The Bancroft Library.

19. Tilton, *William Chapman Ralston, Courageous Builder,* 399; Hart, *In Our Second Century,* 50–51.

20. Bell, Statement, 1886, 5–6.

21. Eldredge, *History of California,* 443; Rearden, in *The Odd Fellows Savings Bank vs. William Sharon,* 15–16.

22. King, *History of the San Francisco Stock and Exchange Board,* 112.

23. King, *History of the San Francisco Stock and Exchange Board,* 111–12.

24. Mills, in *Ralston versus Sharon and Fry,* 280–81.

25. *Gold Hill News,* September 6, 1875.

26. *San Francisco Chronicle,* September 5, 1875.

27. *San Francisco Alta,* January 25, 1876.

28. Eldredge, *History of California,* 443–44.

29. Harpending, *The Great Diamond Hoax,* 273, 275.

30. Charles Lee Tilden, in Dana, *The Man Who Built San Francisco,* 386–87.

31. Tilton, *William Chapman Ralston, Courageous Builder,* 419.

Chapter Ten: Settling Up

1. By January 16, 1876, 46,342 of the 50,000 shares had paid the assessment (*San Francisco Alta*, January 18, 1876).

2. *San Francisco Chronicle*, October 2, 1875.

3. Ibid., October 3, 1875.

4. Cross, *Financing an Empire: Banking in California*, 407.

5. See Tilton, *William Chapman Ralston, Courageous Builder*, 260, 316, 322.

6. Neville, *The Fantastic City*, 203–4; Tilton, *William Chapman Ralston, Courageous Builder*, 409–10; *San Francisco Chronicle*, October 3, 1875.

7. Jake Highton, *Nevada Newspaper Days: A History of Journalism in the Silver State* (Stockton, Calif.: Heritage West Books, 1990), 75. Regarding the fire, the *Territorial Enterprise* reported: "The occupants of the house were generally a rowdy set of men and women, and it is said that some kind of drunken carouse was going on among them until about 2 o'clock yesterday morning. The house had been complained of as disorderly and a nuisance, and it was a great mistake that it was not closed at that time" (*Territorial Enterprise*, October 27, 1875).

8. *Gold Hill News*, October 26, 1875; *Territorial Enterprise*, October 27, 1875. Goodwin told of John Mackay's directing fire-fighting work when an elderly woman approached him: "'Oh, Mr. Mackay, the church is on fire!' All the answer that he vouchsafed was, 'D—n the church, we can build another if we can keep the fire from going down these shafts!'" Mackay later gave $150,000 to relieve those suffering the fire's effects and rebuild the church (Goodwin, *As I Remember Them*, 161).

9. Smith, *History of the Comstock Lode*, 193–94, 197.

10. *San Francisco Chronicle*, November 27, 1877.

11. Lavender, *Nothing Seemed Impossible*, 262–64; *San Francisco Chronicle*, November 27, 1877.

12. *San Francisco Alta*, September 30, 1875. Regarding his children's inheritance, Ralston explains in the will: "I hereby intentionally omit to make any bequests whatever to any of my children, because they will be the natural heirs of my said wife, and during her lifetime they will need no other protection or provision than will be supplied by her affection for them" (Tilton, *William Chapman Ralston, Courageous Builder*, 458).

13. Tilton, *William Chapman Ralston, Courageous Builder*, 456, chap. xvi, n.9.

14. Tilton, *William Chapman Ralston, Courageous Builder*, 418.

15. Mills, in *Ralston versus Sharon and Fry,* 292–93.

16. Altrocchi, *The Spectacular San Franciscans,* 187. In 1870 a guest wrote: "It has been my fortune to enjoy the hospitality of some of England's proudest nobles, as well as to visit the grand old castles of France and Germany, and the villas and palaces of Italy; but I have seldom seen evidences of a higher taste, culture and refinement than were presented in your fine mansion and grounds" (M. P. Jewett to W. C. Ralston, October 17, 1870, in "Ralston Correspondence").

17. *San Francisco Alta,* September 30, 1875; Tilton, *William Chapman Ralston, Courageous Builder,* 420.

18. Lewis and Hall, *Bonanza Inn: America's First Luxury Hotel,* 57–58.

19. Neville, *The Fantastic City,* 205; *Territorial Enterprise,* December 27, 1876.

20. Mills, in *Ralston versus Sharon and Fry,* 102–3, 114.

21. Newspaper clippings, June 10, 1884, in Bancroft, "Biography of William Sharon."

22. Mills, in *Ralston versus Sharon and Fry,* 64, 70 (this line of questioning began on page 30).

23. David Oliver Sr. to Mrs. Arthur Page [Emilita Ralston, daughter of W. C. Ralston], [A Statement of Arguments in Favor of W. C. Ralston], [19]42, in "Ralston Correspondence." Oliver, born in 1861, was the son of a California pioneer. His manuscript contains his arguments, as suggested by Mrs. Page, and he gives her permission to use the manuscript in any way she might. See also Andrew Jackson Ralston, Statement, [1886?], 33; Franklin, Biography of William Ralston, 1886, 15.

24. Mills, in *Ralston versus Sharon and Fry,* 70.

25. Tilton, *William Chapman Ralston, Courageous Builder,* 416.

26. Newspaper clippings, October 8, 1880, in Bancroft, "Biography of William Sharon"; Alexander D. Sharon was named as codefendant because he "held certain real estate in trust for plaintiff"; *San Francisco Alta,* October 9, 1880.

27. *San Francisco Alta,* October 9, 1880.

28. Newspaper clippings, December 23, 26, 1880, in Bancroft, "Biography of William Sharon."

29. Newspaper clippings, March 12, 1883, in Bancroft, "Biography of William Sharon." Magnates in the West were decidedly lacking in chivalry as regarded the widows of partners. Sharon's peers, Huntington, Crocker, and Stanford, were about to become embroiled in similar litigation. Mrs. David D. Colton, widow of their business associate, filed suit in the spring of 1882 claiming she was tricked into turning over a million dollars worth of her husband's stocks and securities to

the corporation. The deal allowed her to collect interest on two hundred Southern Pacific bonds for a ten-year period. When the time elapsed, those bonds, too, reverted to the company. Interestingly, her advisor when she agreed to the deal was railroad attorney S. M. Wilson, the longtime Bank of California attorney. After eight years of litigation, the court ruled for the railroad. During the trial, the notorious "Colton letters," illustrating how the railroad men bribed and bullied Washington legislators and the press, became public. This denied them open access to congressmen, who, now fearing their constituents' reaction, contributed to the defeat of a funding bill that would have postponed for years the railroad's payment of original subsidy bond—costing its owners millions (Oscar Lewis, *The Big Four* [1938; New York: Ballantine Books, 1971], 221–31).

30. Newspaper clippings, March 12, 1883, in Bancroft, "Biography of William Sharon." The suit was reinstated in Federal Court on October 11, 1887. The case, called "one of the most famous in the history of California," restated Lizzie's contentions that Ralston's liabilities were much less than his estate, that Sharon's actions had been "false and fraudulent in every particular," and that at her husband's death her executors claimed to have examined estate books and papers when they had not. By this time Sharon was deceased. On July 11, 1892, Judge Hawley of the U.S. Circuit Court dismissed the case. Since all parties of the suit were citizens of California, he found, a U.S. court had no jurisdiction. The following year a Ralston niece put in a claim for title to properties worth over $1 million, but Newlands, as attorney for the Sharon estate, quickly filed countersuits quelling the action (Newspaper clippings, January 6, 1894, in Bancroft, "Biography of William Sharon"). As for Lizzie, she moved to Georgetown in the Northern California foothills, where her sons developed a mine. The mother reportedly enjoyed the mountains and her books, dying, at age ninety-two, on November 30, 1929 (Millie Robbins, *Tales of Love and Hate In Old San Francisco* [San Francisco: Chronicle Books, 1971], 40–41).

31. Rearden, in *The Odd Fellows Savings Bank vs. William Sharon*, 13–14.

32. Ibid., 15.

33. Ibid., 18–25.

34. Cited in Dana, *The Man Who Built San Francisco*, 386–88.

35. David Smith Terry, in *S. A. Sharon, Plaintiff and Respondent, vs. F. W. Sharon, Executor of William Sharon, Appellant. Respondent's Brief in Reply, D. S. Terry, Attorney for Respondant. W. H. S. Barnes, Attorney for Appellant*, 1887, 13, The Bancroft Library; *San Francisco Alta*, September 8, 1875; *San Francisco Examiner*, September 22, 1889; *San Francisco Call*, November 6, 1885.

Chapter Eleven: An Ill-Fitting Toga

1. *Territorial Enterprise*, February 12, 1876.

2. United States Congress, *Senate Journal*, 44th Congress, 1st sess., December 6, 1875, 240.

3. *Territorial Enterprise*, May 14, 1876.

4. See Abram S. Hewitt, "Secret History of the Disputed Election, 1876–77," in *History of U.S. Political Parties*, vol. 2, *1860–1910: The Gilded Age of Politics*, ed. Arthur M. Schlesinger, Jr. (New York: Chelsea House Publishers, 1973), 964–66; Samuel Eliot Morison, *The Oxford History of the American People*, vol. 3, *1869–1963* (1965; reprint, New York: Mentor Book, 1972), 38; Governor Daniel H. Chamberlain to William Lloyd Garrison, June 11, 1877, in Commager, *Documents of American History*, 546.

5. *Territorial Enterprise*, December 6, 1876, in *San Francisco Chronicle*, December 4, 1876.

6. *Territorial Enterprise*, December 6, 1876.

7. *Chicago Times*, January 2, 1877, in *Territorial Enterprise*, January 9, 1877.

8. United States Congress, *Senate Journal*, 44th Congress, 2d sess., 1876–77, passim.

9. *Territorial Enterprise*, May 14, 1876.

10. Mark Twain, "The Dutch Nick Massacre; The Latest Sensation," 1863, in *The Complete Humorous Sketches and Tales of Mark Twain*, ed. Charles Neider (New York: Doubleday and Co., 1961), 719–20. For a description of the tumult created by the article, see Lucius Beebe, *Comstock Commotion: The Story of the Territorial Enterprise and Virginia City News* (Stanford: Stanford University Press, 1954), 69–70.

11. Hermann Schussler, "Affidavit."

12. See, for example, Brechin, *Imperial San Francisco*, 79–80.

13. Schussler, "Affidavit," 19–20.

14. *San Francisco Chronicle*, December 4, 1876, in *Territorial Enterprise*, December 6, 1876.

15. Bean, *California: An Interpretive History*, 238; William Lilley III, "The Early Career of Francis G. Newlands, 1848–1897" (Ph.D. diss., Yale University, New Haven, Conn., 1965), in Brechin, *Imperial San Francisco*, n. 335.

16. Young, *Journalism in California*, 147.

17. In 1923 Spring Valley's franchise would be revoked and, after years of battle at the national level resulting in the damming and flooding of "Little Yosemite," Hetch Hetchy Valley, for use as a reservoir, the company's monopolistic service was broken.

18. *San Francisco Chronicle,* November 27, 1877.

19. *New York Tribune,* November 26, 1877, in *San Francisco Chronicle,* November 27, 1877.

20. Young, *Journalism in California,* 93; A. E. Wagstaff, *Life of David S. Terry: Presenting An Authentic, Impartial and Vivid Hisory of His Eventful Life and Tragic Death* (San Francisco: Continental Publishing Co., 1892), 258, 278; Jerome Hart, "The Sand Lot And Kearneyism," *In Our Second Century,* http://www.sfmuseum.org/hist2/kearneyism.html (accessed June 10, 2002); Bean, *California: An Interpretive History,* 240-41.

21. United States Congress, *Senate Journal,* 45th Congress, 3d sess., 1880-81, passim.

22. Angel, *History of Nevada,* 290; Bean, *California: An Interpretive History,* 308. Bean's discussion of "Politics in the Era of Railroad Domination," (298-311) presents an overview of California's problem in the last third of the nineteenth century. For a discussion of Central Pacific rate discrimination in Nevada, see Angel, *History of Nevada,* 275-80; for a twentieth-century perspective, see Russell R. Elliott, with the assistance of William D. Rowley, *History of Nevada* (1973; reprint, Lincoln: University of Nebraska Press, 1987), 157-64. Dale L. Morgan explained Central Pacific's argument for back-haul rates as well as Nevada's argument against them: "The railroad justification was that water competition had to be met, and with no water competition Nevada should pay higher rates; moreover, handling charges were less for bulk shipments, and it was to the railroad's convenience to ship in bulk to its San Francisco terminal and transship from there. Nevada might argue that if the railroad could haul goods to the Pacific and then back three or four hundred miles, and still meet water competition, there was no justification for the back haul, while if water competition so far undercut rail profits on the transcontinental haul as to force operations at a loss, there was no reason why the inland provinces should be taxed for the benefit of coastal areas" (Dale L. Morgan, *The Humboldt: Highroad of the West* [New York and Toronto: Farrar and Rinehart, 1943; reprint, Lincoln: University of Nebraska Press, 1985], 310).

23. Lewis, *The Big Four,* passim; Elliott, *History of Nevada,* 159-61; Tinkham, *California: Men and Events,* 212.

24. Dolores Waldorf Bryant, in John Taylor Waldorf, *A Kid on the Comstock: Reminicences of a Virginia City Childhood* (1970; reprint, Reno: University of Nevada Press, 1984), 10.

25. F. E. Fisk, The Dalles, Oregon, April 12, 1881, in Angel, *History of Nevada,* 290-91.

26. See "Ralston Correspondence."

27. Neville, *The Fantastic City*, 205.

28. Altrocchi, *The Spectacular San Franciscans*, 213.

29. Neville, *The Fantastic City*, 205; *San Francisco Call*, November 14, 1885; *San Francisco Examiner*, September 22, 1889.

30. *Carson Valley News*, December 19, 1879. Leadville was the incredibly rich mining town in Colorado where Jones was pursuing interests. On October 31 the *Carson Valley News* again ridiculed Sharon, printing a story of his dining at a literary club in New York. "At the table [Sharon] quoted from history, and a little man at his right joined the issue on the question. Sharron [*sic*] waxed a little warm, and insinuated that his opponent might be a clever sort of a man, but history wasn't his forte. After dinner Sharron remarked to a friend: 'Who is that little cuss there who disputed my dates?' 'Bancroft, the historian.'"

31. *Carson Valley News*, January 9, 1880.

32. United States Congress, *Senate Journal*, 46th Cong., 2d sess., 1879–80, passim; *San Francisco Alta*, March 12, 1880.

33. Sam Davis, *The History of Nevada*, vol. 1, 422.

34. Lewis, *Silver Kings*, 94–95.

35. *Territorial Enterprise*, August 8, 1880.

36. Ibid., August 19, 1880.

37. Ibid., August 27, 1880.

38. Ibid., August 31, 1880.

39. Sharon family legend regarding their initial meeting has Sarah dropping her handkerchief at the elevator of the Palace Hotel, the senator retrieving it and inviting her for a drink (William Francis Sharon, grandson of Senator Sharon's nephew, interview by the author, July 5, 2002).

40. Robert H. Kroninger, *Sarah & the Senator* (Berkeley: Howell-North, 1964), 53; Helen Holdredge, *Mammy Pleasant's Partner* (New York: G. P. Putnam's Sons, 1954), 231.

41. Kroninger, *Sarah & the Senator*, 53.

42. Newspaper clippings, September 30, 1880, in Bancroft, "Biography of William Sharon."

43. Kroninger, *Sarah & the Senator*, 56.

44. Doten, *The Journals of Alfred Doten*, vol. 2, 1373; Sam Davis, *The History of Nevada*, vol. 1, 422–23.

45. Gorham, *My Memories of the Comstock*, 106–7.

46. Neville, *The Fantastic City*, 206; Altrocchi, *The Spectacular San Franciscans*, 222–23.

47. Newspaper clippings, June 10, 1884, in Bancroft, "Biography of William Sharon"; Altrocchi, *The Spectacular San Franciscans,* 224.

48. Rowley, *Reclaiming the Arid West: The Career of Francis G. Newlands,* 16; Ambrose Bierce, *The Wasp,* January 15, 1881, 3–5; Altrocchi, *The Spectacular San Franciscans,* 224; newspaper clippings, June 1, 1884, in Bancroft, "Biography of William Sharon."

49. Neville, *The Fantastic City,* 206.

50. United States Congress, *Senate Journal,* 46th Cong., 3d sess., 1880–81, passim.

51. Elliott, *History of Nevada,* 164.

Chapter Twelve: The Rose

1. B. E. Lloyd, *Lights and Shades in San Francisco,* 66.

2. Ibid., 108.

3. Bancroft, "Biography of William Sharon"; *San Francisco Chronicle,* November 14, 1885.

4. Francis Newlands in Bancroft, "Biography of William Sharon."

5. Lewis and Hall, *Bonanza Inn: America's First Luxury Hotel,* 71–75.

6. Atwood, *Francis G. Newlands,* 21–22, 11–12.

7. *San Francisco Chronicle,* November 14, 1885; *San Francisco Call,* November 14, 1885.

8. Rowley, *Reclaiming the Arid West: The Career of Francis G. Newlands,* 23–31; see also Bean, *California: An Interpretive History,* 278–80; Brechin, *Imperial San Francisco,* 102–4.

9. *San Francisco Call,* November 14, 1885.

10. Newspaper clippings, September and October 1883, in Bancroft, "Biography of William Sharon."

11. Newspaper clippings, February 6, April 16, June 1, 1884, in Bancroft, "Biography of William Sharon"; Kroninger, *Sarah & the Senator,* 126.

12. Ambrose Bierce's description was earthier: "Sharon was a Senator in dreams and a nuzzler after hot dugs by instinct" (in Gould, *A Cast of Hawks,* 256); Dana, *The Man Who Built San Francisco,* 245.

13. *San Francisco Call,* November 14, 1885; Scott, *The Saga of Lake Tahoe,* vol. I, 269; Dana, *The Man Who Built San Francisco,* 340.

14. Kroninger, *Sarah & the Senator,* 19–20, 25–26.

15. Women suffrage was propagandized as supported only by free-love advo-

cates, communists, and anarchists. In the mid-nineteenth century, the *Philadelphia Public Ledger and Daily Transcript* proclaimed that the ladies of Philadelphia wished to maintain their rights "as wives, belles, virgins and mothers, and not as women" (*Women in Gilded Age America,* http//www.elon.edu/bisset/currentsem/123GildedAgeWomen.htm [accessed December 29, 2003]).

16. Newspaper clippings, September 9, 16, 17, 1883, in Bancroft, "Biography of William Sharon."

17. Newspaper clippings, October 4, 6, 1883, in Bancroft, "Biography of William Sharon."

18. Rowley, *Reclaiming the Arid West: The Career of Francis G. Newlands,* 35.

19. Roche, in Abrams and Levine, *The Shaping of Twentieth-Century America,* 131; Wittemore, *Makers of the American Mind,* 309–26; Phillips, *Wealth and Democracy,* 42–43; Josephson, *The Robber Barons,* 105, 157, 198, 210–12; Gould, *A Cast of Hawks,* 154.

20. Gould, *A Cast of Hawks,* 196, 327.

21. Kroninger, *Sarah & the Senator,* 20.

22. Newspaper clippings, October 6, 1883, in Bancroft, "Biography of William Sharon."

23. Kroninger, *Sarah & the Senator,* 20.

24. *San Francisco Bulletin,* October 4, 1883, in Lewis and Hall, *Bonanza Inn: America's First Luxury Hotel,* 121–23; information on Morgan Hill, http://www.morgan-hill.ca.gov/html/about/history.asp (accessed February 22, 2002).

25. Newspaper clippings [correspondence of the *New York Sun*], April 25, 1884, in Bancroft, "Biography of William Sharon"; *San Francisco Bulletin,* October 4, 1883, in Lewis and Hall, *Bonanza Inn: America's First Luxury Hotel,* 122.

26. Gould, *A Cast of Hawks,* 196; Kroninger, *Sarah & the Senator,* 23.

27. *San Francisco Alta,* June 1, 1884; B. E. Lloyd, *Lights and Shades in San Francisco,* 153, 159.

28. Newspaper clippings, October 20, 1883, in Bancroft, "Biography of William Sharon"; Kroninger, *Sarah & the Senator,* 25.

29. Newspaper clippings, October 20, 1883, in Bancroft, "Biography of William Sharon."

30. Lewis and Hall, *Bonanza Inn: America's First Luxury Hotel,* 133; Kroninger, *Sarah & the Senator,* 25; Newspaper clippings, October 22, 1883, in Bancroft, "Biography of William Sharon."

31. Kroninger, *Sarah & the Senator,* 28–31.

32. See Michelson, *The Wonderlode of Silver and Gold,* 189, 194–96; Goodwin, *As I Remember Them,* 162, 129–30.

33. Goodwin, *As I Remember Them*, 33–34.

34. Newspaper clippings, November 24, 1883, in Bancroft, "Biography of William Sharon."

35. Kroninger, *Sarah & the Senator*, 36–37.

36. Ibid., 38–41.

37. Ibid., 43–44; Newspaper clippings, February 6, 1884, in Bancroft, "Biography of William Sharon."

38. Kroninger, *Sarah & the Senator*, 166.

39. Newspaper clippings, March 10, 1884, in Bancroft, "Biography of William Sharon"; *San Francisco Alta*, June 1, 1884.

Chapter Thirteen: In Superior Court

1. Kroninger, *Sarah & the Senator*, 48–51; Gould, *A Cast of Hawks*, 208–9; *San Francisco Chronicle*, March 11, 1884.

2. *San Francisco Chronicle*, March 11, 1884.

3. Kroninger, *Sarah & the Senator*, 54–55.

4. Ibid., 55.

5. Ibid., 56–58; Lewis and Hall, *Bonanza Inn: America's First Luxury Hotel*, 139.

6. Gould, *A Cast of Hawks*, 223.

7. Ibid., 224–25.

8. Newspaper clippings, April 16, 1884, in Bancroft, "Biography of William Sharon."

9. Lewis and Hall, *Bonanza Inn: America's First Luxury Hotel*, 135–36.

10. *Sharon v. Sharon*, 79 Cal., 660 (1889).

11. Kroninger, *Sarah & the Senator*, 59–60.

12. *San Francisco Alta*, June 1, 1884.

13. Kroninger, *Sarah & the Senator*, 60–64; Newspaper clippings, March 20, 1884, in Bancroft, "Biography of William Sharon."

14. Kroninger, *Sarah & the Senator*, 65.

15. Ibid., 66–67.

16. Gould, *A Cast of Hawks*, 237; B. E. Lloyd, *Lights and Shades in San Francisco*, 65–66.

17. Oscar Lewis, *Bay Window Bohemia* (New York: Doubleday and Co., 1956), 90–91; Irwin Will, *The City That Was* (New York: B. W. Huebsch, 1906), 32–34.

18. Kroninger, *Sarah & the Senator*, 67.

19. Gould, *A Cast of Hawks*, 236, 186; Kroninger, *Sarah & the Senator*, 99.

20. Kroninger, *Sarah & the Senator*, 68, 47.

21. See, for example, Wagstaff, *Life of David S. Terry;* David A. Williams, *David C. Broderick: A Political Portrait* (San Marino, Calif.: Huntington Library, 1969); Irving Stone, *Men to Match My Mountains: The Opening of the Far West, 1840–1900* (New York: Doubleday and Co., 1956), 211.

22. Kroninger, *Sarah & the Senator*, 73.

23. See Holdredge, *Mammy Pleasant* (New York: G. P. Putnam's Sons, 1953) and *Mammy's Partner*. For a reasoned overview, see Lynn M. Hudson, *The Making of "Mammy Pleasant": A Black Entrepreneur in Nineteenth-Century San Francisco* (Urbana and Chicago: University of Illinois Press, 2003); Sushiel Bibbs, "Mary Ellen Pleasant: Mother of Civil Rights in California," http://www.geocities.com/mepleasant.geo/map.html (accessed August 11, 2002).

24. Neville, *The Fantastic City*, 126.

25. Newspaper clippings, July 12, 1884, in Bancroft, "Biography of William Sharon."

26. Kroninger, *Sarah & the Senator*, 74–75; Hudson, *The Making of "Mammy Pleasant*," 70–77.

27. Newspaper clippings, July 12, 1884, April 20, 1884, in Bancroft, "Biography of William Sharon."

28. Newspaper clippings, July 12, 1884, in Bancroft, "Biography of William Sharon"; Kroninger, *Sarah & the Senator*, 86–87.

29. Newspaper clippings, July 12, April 13, 1884, in Bancroft, "Biography of William Sharon."

30. Kroninger, *Sarah & the Senator*, 90, 134; Gould, *A Cast of Hawks*, 237.

31. Newspaper clippings, April 9, 19, 20, 1884, in Bancroft, "Biography of William Sharon."

32. Altrocchi, *The Spectacular San Franciscans*, 250; see, for example, Annegret Ogden, "'Give Up That Filthy Habit—Cocaine,'" *Californians* (March–April 1988), 10–49.; newspaper clippings, March 20, 1885, in Bancroft, "Biography of William Sharon."

33. Newspaper clippings, April 9, 19, 20, 1884, in Bancroft, "Biography of William Sharon."

34. Newspaper clippings, April 9, 19, 20, 1884, in Bancroft, "Biography of William Sharon."

35. *Territorial Enterprise*, December 27, 1876, January 9, 1877; see also Kroninger, *Sarah & the Senator*, 100–101; Lewis and Hall, *Bonanza Inn*, 182; Gould, *A Cast of Hawks*, 178, 227, 258.

36. Newspaper clippings, April 26, 1884, in Bancroft, "Biography of William Sharon."

37. Ibid.

38. Kroninger, *Sarah & the Senator,* 101.

39. Ibid., 102–3.

40. Ibid., 104–12.

41. Ibid., 114–15.

42. Newspaper clippings, June 1, 1884, in Bancroft, "Biography of William Sharon."

43. Newspaper clippings, June 1, 1884, in Bancroft, "Biography of William Sharon."

44. Kroninger, *Sarah & the Senator,* 121.

45. Newspaper clippings, June 1, 1884, in Bancroft, "Biography of William Sharon."

46. Ibid.

47. Newspaper clippings, April 16, 1884, in Bancroft, "Biography of William Sharon."

48. Ibid.

49. Kroninger, *Sarah & the Senator,* 125.

50. Newspaper clippings, June 1, 1884, in Bancroft, "Biography of William Sharon."

51. Ibid.

52. *San Francisco Chronicle,* November 14, 1885.

53. Newspaper clippings, June 1, 1884, in Bancroft, "Biography of William Sharon."

Chapter Fourteen: Pressing On

1. Gorham, *My Memories of the Comstock,* 106. Harry Gorham, who was Jones's descendent, commented on the reconciliation: "I have to give Sharon credit for carrying out his part without dispute and without anything that approached unfriendliness as long as he lived."

2. Newspaper clippings, June 1, 1884, in Bancroft, "Biography of William Sharon."

3. Wagstaff, *Life of David S. Terry,* 396–97.

4. Tinkham, *California: Men and Events,* 294–95.

5. Ibid., 295; Bancroft, *Chronicle of the Builders,* 92–93.

6. Newspaper clippings, June 23, 1884, in Bancroft, "Biography of William Sharon."

7. Ibid., July 12, 1884.

8. Ibid., August 11, 1884; William Henry Linow Barnes, in *William Sharon, Complainant, vs. Sara Althea Hill, Respondent in Equity: Closing Argument for Complainant,* 1887, 87–88, The Bancroft Library.

9. Kroninger, *Sarah & the Senator,* 136–37.

10. Newspaper clippings, August 8, 1884, in Bancroft, "Biography of William Sharon."

11. Kroninger, *Sarah & the Senator,* 135–37.

12. Newspaper clippings, June 18, 1884, in Bancroft, "Biography of William Sharon."

13. *San Francisco Chronicle,* August 13, 1884; Transcript of Argument of W. H. L. Barnes, in *Sharon vs. Sharon,* in Hudson, *The Making of "Mammy Pleasant,"* 70–73.

14. Terry, *Argument of David S. Terry,* 12, 89; Barnes, *William Sharon, Complainant,* vs. *Sara Althea Hill, Respondent,* 7.

Chapter Fifteen: Bitter End

1. See Kroninger, *Sarah & the Senator,* 205. Sawyer favored farmers in a famous 1884 decision that prohibited hydraulic mining operations from dumping their tailings into rivers. It appears surprising that Sawyer found against the large mining interests, since he was generally known for utilizing unorthodox interpretations to grant corporations expansive powers. It is less surprising when we discover that among those who opposed the mines were the steamship and railroad companies.

2. *Sharon* v. *Hill,* 20 F. 1, 2 (1884); *Sharon* v. *Hill,* 22 F. 28, 29 (1884).

3. Kroninger, *Sarah & the Senator,* 143–45; newspaper clippings, December 24, 1884, in Bancroft, "Biography of William Sharon."

4. Terry, *Argument of David S. Terry,* "Note," n.p.

5. Newspaper clippings, December 24, 1884, in Bancroft, "Biography of William Sharon"; Kroninger, *Sarah & the Senator,* 147.

6. Newspaper clippings, December 25, 1884, in Bancroft, "Biography of William Sharon."

7. Ibid.

8. Kroninger, *Sarah & the Senator,* 157–58.

9. *Sharon* v. *Sharon,* 67 Cal. 185 (1886).

10. See William M. Stewart, *Reminiscences,* 274–75; William M. Stewart to [William F.] Herrin, March 11, [188]8, 1, in "William M. Stewart Papers," Nevada Historical Society, Reno, Nevada.

11. Kroninger, *Sarah & the Senator,* 166.

12. *San Francisco Chronicle,* March 28, 1885.

13. Kroninger, *Sarah & the Senator,* 167.

14. Ibid., 172.

15. Newspaper clippings, March 15, 1885, in Bancroft, "Biography of William Sharon."

16. Bierce, *The Wasp,* March 21, 1885.

17. Newspaper clippings, March 20, 1885, in Bancroft, "Biography of William Sharon."

18. *San Francisco Chronicle,* March 28, 1885, April 1, 1885; Kroninger, *Sarah & the Senator,* 167–69.

19. *Fresno Democrat,* April 24, 1885.

20. See *Sharon v. Sharon,* 67 Cal., 185; Kroninger, *Sarah & the Senator,* 163–64.

21. William Stewart, in *Sarah A. Sharon, Plaintiff, vs. William Sharon, Defendant: Argument of Wm. M. Stewart on Motion for Alimony and Counsel Fees, In the Superior Court of the State of California, In and for the City and County of San Francisco, Department No. 2,* n.d., 2–10, The Bancroft Library. O. P. Evans and William F. Herrin assisted William Stewart. Herrin, Stewart's partner, would eventually take over management of the entire case. Owing to this case and another that grew from it, Herrin later became the chief attorney for the Sharon estate and Spring Valley Water and went on to head the Southern Pacific Railroad's legal department for seventeen years. Journalist and reformer Franklin Hichborn often criticized the corrupting force of Herrin's politics, "but he also described him as 'perhaps the ablest man I ever met.'" Bean, *California: An Interpretive History,* 306–8.

22. Barnes, in *William Sharon vs. Sara Althea Hill,* 1887, 59–60, The Bancroft Library; Kroninger, *Sarah & the Senator,* 175–77.

23. Lewis and Hall, *Bonanza Inn,* 180.

24. *San Francisco Call,* November 5, 6, 1885; *San Francisco Chronicle,* November 14, 1885; Bancroft, *Chronicles of the Builders,* 77.

25. *San Francisco Call,* November 6, 1885.

26. Gould, *A Cast of Hawks,* 258.

27. Ibid.; *San Francisco Chronicle,* November 6, 1885.

28. *San Francisco Chronicle,* November 7, 1885.

29. *San Francisco Call,* November 7, 1885.

30. *San Francisco Chronicle,* November 7, 1885.

31. Ibid., November 14, 1885.

Chapter Sixteen: Resolutions

1. *San Francisco Chronicle,* November 14, 1885.

2. *San Francisco Call,* November 6, 17, 1885.

3. Ibid.; *San Francisco Chronicle,* November 17, 1885. The papers listed those who attended and those who sent floral tributes. It is interesting to note associates who were not mentioned among attendees or as having sent flowers: Nevadans Alf Doten, Rollin Daggett, and John Mackay; Sharon's attorney, William Stewart; San Franciscans James Fair, James Flood, Leland Stanford, Lucky Baldwin, Thomas Bell, and Reuben Lloyd; and New York partner, D. O. Mills.

4. Andrew Carnegie, "The Gospel of Wealth," in Current and Garraty, *Words That Made American History Since The Civil War,* 212–22.

5. The William Hammond Hall Building was severely damaged in the 1909 earthquake and again in a fire in 1978. The site is now home to the Sharon Art Studio.

6. On one occasion in March 1868, Ralston invited the judge to dine with him and meet General Irvin McDowell, visiting from headquarters of the Department of the East. A month later U.S. senator C. J. Hutchison wrote a "Strictly Confidential" letter notifying Ralston that Deady was almost certain to be appointed to the new U.S. judgeship in Oregon. In 1869 Ralston acted as Deady's agent, taking Deady's checks in the amount of several thousand dollars to purchase and hold bonds for him until they could be sent north by steamer. See the summaries of letters to Matthew P. Deady, "Ralston Correspondence." (The originals are in the Oregon Historical Society.)

7. Kroninger, *Sarah & the Senator,* 180.

8. Ibid., 181–82.

9. Ibid., 184.

10. Ibid., 180–85.

11. Gould, *A Cast of Hawks,* 271–73.

12. *San Francisco Call,* January 16, 1886.

13. Wagstaff, *Life of David S. Terry,* 316–17; Kroninger, *Sarah & the Senator,* 190.

14. *San Francisco Call,* February 4, 1886.

15. Rowley, *Reclaiming the Arid West,* 20, 37.

16. Ibid., 37.

17. Francis Newlands, Virginia City, February 3, 1887, to Fred Sharon, Paris, Sharon Family Papers. A year later Stewart wrote Herrin saying much the same thing, emphasizing that "delays are dangerous. . . . The danger is that some proceeding will be inaugurated before this will be done" (William M. Stewart to [William F.] Herrin, March 11, [188]8, 3, "William M. Stewart Papers").

18. The case involved an attorney who pressured a widow's son into assigning him half of a ten-thousand-dollar debt that he collected on her behalf. Tyler, acting at the widow's behest, told the attorney he, Tyler, should hold the money. Once he received it, he refused to return it. He forced the attorney to drag the case through the courts in an attempt to collect. When the attorney won his judgment, Tyler claimed to be insolvent, as did his appeal sureties (who were required to pay if Tyler did not). When the case was brought before the Supreme Court, the attorney asked that Tyler be disbarred on the grounds he had violated duties acting as his lawyer. Tyler argued that he had been acting as the widow's lawyer, not the attorney's. He produced a receipt given the attorney when the money was exchanged, which stated that Tyler was acting for the widow. Except for one dissenting judge, the Supreme Court looked past that fact, finding Tyler guilty of breach of an attorney's duties. Few observers thought his offenses were serious enough to warrant expulsion from the profession. Kroninger remarked: "The sins were generally thought to be venial, if not trivial, and the popular sentiment in his favor was enhanced by a feeling that [the plaintiff], in making a very great profit at the expense of the widow and her profligate son, was much more to be censured than was Tyler" (Kroninger, *Sarah & the Senator,* 191–93).

19. Terry, *Argument of David S. Terry,* 7.

20. Kroninger, *Sarah & the Senator,* 194–95.

21. *Sharon v. Sharon,* 75 Cal. 1 (1889).

22. Kroninger, *Sarah & the Senator,* 199–200.

23. *Cunningham v. Neagle,* 135 U.S. 1 (1890).

24. Rowley, *Reclaiming the Arid West: The Career of Francis G. Newlands,* 39.

25. Tinkham, *California: Men and Events,* 294–95.

26. Gould, *A Cast of Hawks,* 279; Tinkham 318n.

27. *Cunningham v. Neagle,* 135 U.S. 1.

28. Ibid.

29. Ibid.

30. Ibid.; Kroninger, *Sarah & the Senator,* 202.

31. Kroninger, *Sarah & the Senator*, 203–6.

32. Newspaper clippings, May 3, 1889, in Bancroft, "Biography of William Sharon."

33. Francis Newlands to Fred Sharon, June 10, 1889, in Sharon Family Papers; Kroninger, *Sarah & the Senator*, 209–12.

34. *Sharon v. Sharon*, 79 Cal. 663 (1889).

35. Newspaper clippings, July 17, 1889, in Bancroft, "Biography of William Sharon."

36. Wagstaff, *Life of David S. Terry*, 314–15.

37. *Cunningham v. Neagle*, 135 U.S., 1.

38. Ibid.; Kroninger, *Sarah & the Senator*, 213–14.

39. *Cunningham v. Neagle*, 135 U.S., 1; *San Francisco Examiner*, August 15, 1889.

40. Kroninger, *Sarah & the Senator*, 228.

41. Barnes, in *William Sharon, Complainant, vs. Sara Althea Hill, Respondent*, 14.

42. Gould, *A Cast of Hawks*, 336.

43. Lewis and Hall, *Bonanza Inn*, 212–14.

44. See "Adolph Sutro (1830–1898)," Virtual Museum of the City of San Francisco, http://www.sfmuseum.org/bio/adolph.html (accessed December 28, 2003).

45. William Francis Sharon, interview by the author, July 5, 2002.

46. Ogden, "Give Up That Filthy Habit," 10–49. Ogden writes that Louise no longer touched the drug and on May 22, 1896, wrote Fred pleading with him "to give up that filthy habit—cocaine." Louise told him that the French consul had visited, and she said: "He thought you were looking so thin and so ill—All who have seen you of late say the same thing and I know your condition of sleepless nights and miserable days is due entirely to cocaine."

47. Currey to Morrison, June 3, 1891, in Sharon Family Papers.

48. *San Francisco Call*, November 14, 1885; *San Francisco Chronicle*, November 14, 1885.

Bibliography

Abrams, Richard M., and Lawrence W. Levine. *The Shaping of Twentieth-Century America: Interpretive Articles.* Boston: Little, Brown and Co., 1965.

Altrocchi, Julia Cooley. *The Spectacular San Franciscans.* New York: E. P. Dutton and Co., 1949.

Angel, Myron, ed. *History of Nevada.* 1881. Reprint, Berkeley: Howell-North Books, 1958.

Annual Mining Review and Stock Ledger. San Francisco: Verdenal, Harrison, Murphy and Co., 1876.

Annual Report of the Commissioner of Indian Affairs to the Secretary of the Interior (ARCIA) for 1861. Washington, D.C.: Government Printing Office, 1861.

Annual Report of the Commissioner of Indian Affairs to the Secretary of the Interior (ARCIA) for 1866. Washington, D.C.: Government Printing Office, 1866.

Armstrong, Leroy, and J. O Denny. *Financial California.* San Francisco: The Coast Banker Publishing Co., 1916.

Atherton, Gertrude. *California: An Intimate History.* Rev. ed. New York: Horace Liveright, 1927.

———. *My San Francisco.* Indianapolis: Bobbs-Merrill Co., 1946.

Atwood, Albert W. *Francis G. Newlands: A Builder of the Nation.* N.p.: Newlands Co., 1969.

Bancroft, Hubert Howe. "Biography of William C. Ralston Prepared for Chronicles of the Kings: And Materials Used in Its Preparation, 1886–1889." Hubert Howe Bancroft Collection. The Bancroft Library, University of California, Berkeley.

———. "Biography of William Sharon: And Material for Its Preparation, 1886–1889." Sharon Family Papers. Hubert Howe Bancroft Collection. The Bancroft Library, University of California, Berkeley.

———. *Chronicle of the Builders.* San Francisco: History Company, [1890?].

———. *The Works of Hubert H. Bancroft,* vol. 7, *History of California, 1860–1890.* San Francisco: The History Company, 1890.

———. *The Works of Hubert H. Bancroft*, vol. 25, *History of Nevada, Colorado and Wyoming 1540–1888*. San Francisco: The History Company, 1890.

Barnes, William Henry Linow. *William Sharon, Complainant, vs. Sara Althea Hill, Respondent in Equity: Closing Argument for Complainant*. 1887. The Bancroft Library, University of California, Berkeley.

Bates, Alfred. "Biography of Francis G. Newlands." Manuscript in the handwriting of Alfred Bates. Sharon Family Papers. Hubert Howe Bancroft Collection. The Bancroft Library, University of California, Berkeley.

———. "Biography of William Sharon and Material for Its Preparation, 1891." Hubert Howe Bancroft Collection. The Bancroft Library, University of California, Berkeley.

———. "J. P. Jones." N.d. Manuscript in the handwriting of Alfred Bates. Hubert Howe Bancroft Collection. The Bancroft Library, University of California, Berkeley.

Bean, Walton. *California: An Interpretive History*. New York: McGraw Hill Book Co., 1968.

Beebe, Lucius. *Comstock Commotion: The Story of the Territorial Enterprise and Virginia City News*. Stanford: Stanford University Press, 1954.

Beebe, Lucius, and Charles Clegg. *Legends of the Comstock Lode*. Stanford: Stanford University Press, 1950.

———. *U.S. West: The Saga of Wells Fargo*. New York: E. P. Dutton and Co., 1949.

Berkove, Lawrence I. "Joe Goodman, In His Own Write." *Nevada Magazine*, January/February 2001, 16–19.

Bethel, John D. *A General Business and Mining Directory of Storey, Lyon, Ormsby and Washoe Counties, Nevada*. Virginia City, Nev.: John D. Bethel and Co., 1875.

Bibbs, Sushiel. "Mary Ellen Pleasant: Mother of Civil Rights in California." http://www.geocities.com/mepleasant.geo/map.html (accessed August 11, 2002).

Bierce, Ambrose. *Black Beetles in Amber*. San Francisco: Western Authors, 1892.

———. *The Wasp*, January 3, 1885, 3–5.

———. *The Wasp*, March 21, 1885, 4–5.

Bliss, William S. "Biography of D. L. Bliss." N.d. Hubert Howe Bancroft Collection. The Bancroft Library, University of California, Berkeley.

Books of Deeds, Storey County Records, Nevada. Books 26, 27, 36, 37, 39, 40, and Z. Story County Court House, Virginia City, Nev.

Bowles, Samuel. *Across the Continent: A Summer's Journey to the Rocky Mountains, the Mormons, and the Pacific States with Speaker Colfax*. 1866. Reprint, Ann Arbor: University Microfilms, 1966.

Brechin, Grey. *Imperial San Francisco: Urban Power, Earthly Ruin.* Berkeley: University of California Press, 1999.

Browne, J. Ross. *A Peep at Washoe and Washoe Revisited.* Reprinted from *Crusoe's Island, California and Washoe* (New York: Harper and Brothers, 1864), *The Apache Country; A Tour Through Arizona and Sonora* (New York: Harper and Brothers, 1869), and *Harper's Weekly,* February 1863. Reprint, Balboa Island, Calif.: Paisano Press, 1959.

Browne, Lina Fergusson, ed. *J. Ross Browne: His Letters, Journals and Writings.* Albuquerque: University of New Mexico Press, 1969.

Bruce, John. *Gaudy Century: The Story of San Francisco's Hundred Years of Robust Journalism.* New York: Random House, 1948.

Bunje, E. T. H., F. J. Schmitz, and H. Penn. *Journals of the Golden Gate, 1846–1936.* Berkeley: University of California Press, 1936.

California Historical Society. *Sacramento, an Illustrated History: 1839 to 1874, from Sutter's Fort to Capital City.* [San Francisco], 1973.

Carlsson, Chris. "The 8-Hour Movement." http://www.shapingsf.org/exine/labor/8hour/main.html (accessed May 9, 2002).

———. "Shaping San Francisco." http://www.shapingsf.org/exine/afamerican/earlyorg.html(accessed May 9, 2002).

Cash, W. J. *The Mind of the South.* New York: Vintage Books, 1941.

Chatteriee, Pratap. "The Gold Rush Legacy: Greed, Pollution and Genocide." http://www.earthisland.org/ejounrnal/spring98/sp98g_wr.html (accessed June 14, 2002).

"The Children's Playground and Sharon Lodge." http://www.sfpix.com/park/Archives/Playground/ (accessed May 17, 2002).

Colbert, David, ed. *Eyewitness to the American West.* New York: Penguin Putnam, 1998.

"Collection of Legal Briefs Relating to Legal Action of William Sharon, Plaintiff-Respondent, vs. Matthew Nunan, Defendant-Appellant." 1881. The Bancroft Library, University of California, Berkeley.

Commager, Henry Steele. *The American Mind: An Interpretation of American Thought and Character Since the 1880s.* 1950. Reprint, New Haven: Yale University Press, 1966.

———, ed. *Documents of American History.* 1934. 7th ed., New York: Meredith Publishing Co., 1963.

———. *The Era of Reform, 1830–1860.* Princeton: D. Van Nostrand, 1960.

Committee on Mines and Mining of the House of Representatives of the United States. *Report of the Commissioners and Evidence Taken by the Committee on*

Mines and Mining of the House of Representatives of the United States, in Regard to the Sutro Tunnel, Together with the Arguments and Report of the Committee, Recommending a Loan by the Government in Aid of the Construction of Said Work. Washington, D.C.: M'Gill and Witherow, 1872.

A Compendium of the Ninth Census (June 1, 1870). Washington, D.C.: Government Printing Office, 1870.

Conwell, Russell H. "Acres of Diamonds." http:www.temple.edu/documentation/heritage/speech.html (accessed July 14, 2002).

Cross, Ira. *Financing an Empire: Banking in California.* Chicago: S. J. Clark, 1927.

Cunningham v. Neagle, 135 U.S. 1 (1890).

Current, Richard N., and John A. Garraty, eds. *Words That Made American History, Since the Civil War.* 2d ed. Boston, Toronto: Little, Brown and Company, 1962.

Dana, Julian. *The Man Who Built San Francisco: A Study of Ralston's Journey with Banners.* New York: Macmillan Co., 1936.

Dangberg, Grace. *Conflict on the Carson: A Study of Water Litigation in Western Nevada.* Minden, Nev.: Carson Valley Historical Society, 1975.

Davis, Sam P. *The History of Nevada.* Reno: Elms Publishing, 1913.

Davis, William Heath. "Appendix I: Chinese in California." *Seventy-five Years in San Francisco.* 1929. [Original edition, named *Sixty Years in California,* 1889.] Reprint, San Francisco: John Howell, 1929. http://www.zpub.com/sf50/sf/hb75yap3.htm (accessed May 6, 2002).

DeQuille, Dan [William Wright]. *The Big Bonanza.* 1876. Reprint, Las Vegas: Nevada Publications, n.d.

de Russailh, Albert Benard. *Albert Benard de Russailh's Last Adventure: San Francisco in 1851.* Translated by Clarkson Crane. San Francisco: Westgate Press, 1931. http://www.shapingsf.org/ezine/womens/1851/main.html (accessed May 14, 2002).

Dobie, Charles Caldwell. *San Francisco: A Pageant.* New York: D. Appleton-Century Co., 1943.

Doten, Alf. *The Journals of Alfred Doten: 1849–1903.* Edited by Walter Van Tilburg Clark. Reno: University of Nevada Press, 1973.

Downs, James F. *The Two Worlds of the Washo: An Indian Tribe of California and Nevada.* New York: Holt, Rinehart and Winston, 1966.

Driggs, Don W. *The Constitution of the State of Nevada: A Commentary.* Carson City: Nevada State Printing Office, 1961.

Drury, J. Wells. *An Editor on the Comstock.* 1936. Reprint, Reno: University of Nevada Press, 1984.

Egan, Ferol. *Last Bonanza Kings: The Bourns of San Francisco.* Reno: University of Nevada Press, 1998.

Eldredge, Zoeth Skinner. *The Beginnings of San Francisco: From the Expedition of Anza, 1774, to the City Charter of April 15, 1850, with Biographical and Other Notes.* New York: John C. Rankin Co., 1912. http://www.apub.com/sf50/sf/hbbegidx.htm (accessed May 6, 2002).

———. *History of California.* New York: Century History, 1915.

Elko Independent, September 24, 1870.

Elliott, Russell R., with the assistance of William D. Rowley. *History of Nevada.* Lincoln: University of Nebraska Press, 1987.

Exhibit No. 1, Affidavit of H. Symons. March 26, 1873. Comstock Lode (Nev.) Cipher Books. Special Collections Dept., Getchell Library, University of Nevada, Reno.

Farish, Thomas Edwin. *The Gold Hunters of California.* Chicago: M. A. Donohue and Co., 1904.

Field, Stephen Johnson. "Correspondence, 1860–1895." The Bancroft Library, University of California, Berkeley.

Foreman, Charles. "Statement from Charles Foreman." [1887?], n.p. Hubert Howe Bancroft Collection, The Bancroft Library, University of California, Berkeley.

Fresno Democrat, April 24, 1886.

Fry, John D. "John D. Fry Biographical Sketch: Typescript [ca. 1890?]." Hubert Howe Bancroft Collection. The Bancroft Library, University of California, Berkeley.

Galloway, John Debo. *Early Engineering Works Contributory to the Comstock.* University of Nevada Bulletin, vol. 41, no. 5. Nevada State Bureau of Mines and the Mackay School of Mines, June 1947.

Gardner, David. "Sharon Cottage" (Worldwide, 1998). http://www.lightight.com/GGP/mem_images/Mem4P32.html (accessed May 17, 2002).

Garraty, John A. *Interpreting American History: Conversations with Historians.* New York: Macmillan Co., 1970.

Geertz, Clifford. *The Interpretation of Cultures.* New York: Basic Books, 1973.

Glasscock, C. B. *The Big Bonanza,* Indianapolis: Bobbs-Merrill, 1931.

———. *Lucky Baldwin: The Story of an Unconventional Success.* N.d. Reprint, Reno: Silver Syndicate Press, 1993.

Gold Hill News, November 17, 1864–October 26, 1875.

Goodwin, C. C. *As I Remember Them.* Salt Lake City: Salt Lake Commercial Club, 1913.

———. *The Story of the Comstock Lode: "Lest We Forget."* Boston: Long, Pierce and Co., n.d.

Gorham, Harry M. *My Memories of the Comstock.* Los Angeles: Suttonhouse, 1939.

Gould, Milton S. *A Cast of Hawks.* La Jolla, Calif.: Copley Books, 1985.

Gracey, Robert. "Recollections of Virginia City from May, 1860." Paper delivered at the Twentieth Century Club, February 10, 1911.

Hacker Louis M., and Benjamin B. Kendrick, with the collaboration of Helene S. Zahler. *The United States Since 1865.* 1932. 4th ed., reprint, New York: Appleton-Century-Crofts, 1949.

Harpending, Asbury. *The Great Diamond Hoax: And Other Stirring Incidents in the Life of Asbury Harpending.* San Francisco: James H. Barry, 1913.

Hart, Jerome A. *In Our Second Century: From an Editor's Notebook.* San Francisco: Pioneer Press, 1931.

Hayano, David M. *Poker Faces: The Life and Work of Professional Card Players.* Berkeley: University of California Press, 1982.

Henwood, Doug. *Wall Street: How It Works and for Whom.* London: Verso, 1998.

Highton, Jake. *Nevada Newspaper Days: A History of Journalism in the Silver State.* Stockton, Calif.: Heritage West Books, 1990.

Hinkle, George, and Bliss Hinkle. *Sierra-Nevada Lakes.* 1949. Reprint, Reno: University of Nevada Press, 1987.

Hittell, John S. *The Commerce and Industries of the Pacific Coast.* San Francisco: A. L. Bancroft and Co., 1882.

Hobsbawm, E. J. *The Age of Capital: 1848–1875.* New York: New American Library, 1979.

Holdredge, Helen. *Mammy Pleasant.* New York: G. P. Putnam's Sons, 1953.

———. *Mammy Pleasant's Partner.* New York: G. P. Putnam's Sons, 1954.

Howard, Thomas Frederick. *Sierra Crossing: First Roads to California.* Berkeley: University of California Press, 1998.

Hudson, Lynn M. *The Making of "Mammy Pleasant": A Black Entrepreneur in Nineteenth-Century San Francisco.* Urbana and Chicago: University of Illinois Press, 2003.

Hulse, James W. *The Nevada Adventure: A History.* 1965. 6th ed., reprint, Reno: University of Nevada Press, 1990.

James, George Wharton. *The Lake of the Sky: Lake Tahoe in the High Sierras of California and Nevada.* 1915. 2d ed., Pasadena, Calif.: Radiant Life Press, 1921.

James, Ronald M. *The Roar and the Silence: A History of Virginia City and the Comstock Lode.* Reno: University of Nevada Press, 1998.

James, Ronald M., and Elizabeth Raymond, eds. *Comstock Women: The Making of a Mining Community.* Reno: University of Nevada Press, 1998.

Josephson, Matthew. *The Robber Barons: The Great American Capitalists, 1861–1901.* 1934. Reprint, New York: Harvest Book, 1962.

Judah, Theodore. "A Practical Plan For Building the Pacific Railroad." Washington, D.C.: Museum of the City of San Francisco, Henry Polkinhorn, Printer, 1857. http://www.sfmuseum.org/hist4/practical.html (accessed May 22, 2002).

Kelly, J. Wells. *First Directory of Nevada Territory.* San Francisco: 1862.

Kimball, Charles P. *The San Francisco City Directory: September 1, 1850.* San Francisco: Journal of Commerce Press, 1850. http://www.apub.com/sf50/sf/hd850a.html (accessed May 6, 2002).

King, Joseph L. *History of the San Francisco Stock and Exchange Board, by the Chairman, Jos. L. King.* San Francisco: J. L. King, 1910.

Kroninger, Robert H. *Sarah & the Senator.* Berkeley: Howell-North, 1964.

Lavender, David. *Nothing Seemed Impossible.* Palo Alto: American West, 1975.

Leadabrand, Russ. "North of Bishop." http://www.owensvalleyhistory.com/bishop_residents/north_of_bishop.pdf (accessed June 11, 2002).

Leopold, Richard W., and Arthur S Link. *Problems in American History.* Englewood Cliffs, N.J.: Prentice-Hall, 1957.

Leslie, Mrs. Frank. *California: A Pleasure Trip from Gotham to the Golden Gate, April, May, June, 1877.* Reprint, Nieuwkoop, Netherlands: B. De Graaf, 1972. http://members.door.net/nbclumber/Leslie/Ch32.htm (accessed June 11, 2002).

Lewis, Oscar. *Bay Window Bohemia.* New York: Doubleday and Co., 1956.

———. *The Big Four.* 1938. Reprint, New York: Ballantine Books, Comstock Edition, 1971.

———. *Silver Kings: The Lives and Times of Mackay, Fair, Flood and O'Brien, Lords of the Nevada Comstock Lode.* 1947. Reprint, New York: Ballantine, Comstock Edition, 1971.

Lewis, Oscar, and Carroll D. Hall. *Bonanza Inn: America's First Luxury Hotel.* New York: Alfred A. Knopf, 1940.

Linderman, H. R. *Report of the Director of the Mint to the Secretary of the Trea-*

sury for the Fiscal Year Ended June 30, 1875. Washington, D.C.: Government Printing Office, 1875.

Lingenfelter, Richard E. *The Hardrock Miners: A History of the Mining Labor Movement in the American West, 1863–1893.* Berkeley: University of California Press, 1974.

——, with an introduction by David F. Myrick. *1858–1958, The Newspapers of Nevada: A History and Bibliography.* San Francisco; John Howell-Books, 1964.

Lizzie F. Ralston et al., Plaintiffs, vs. William Sharon and J. D. Fry, Defendants . . . Deposition of D. O. Mills. 1881. The Bancroft Library, University of California, Berkeley.

Lloyd, B. E. *Lights and Shades in San Francisco.* San Francisco: A. L. Bancroft and Co., 1876. Facsimile ed., Berkeley: Berkeley Hills Books, 1999.

Lloyd, Reuben. "Manuscript, 31 December 1886." Hubert Howe Bancroft Collection, The Bancroft Library, University of California, Berkeley.

Lord, Eliot. *Comstock Mining and Miners.* 1883. Reprint, Berkeley: Howell-North, 1959.

Luckhardt, C. A. "General Description and Report on the Comstock Vein." Special Collections Dept., Getchell Library, University of Nevada, Reno.

Lyman, George. *Ralston's Ring.* 1937. Reprint, New York: Ballantine Books, Comstock Edition, 1971.

——. *The Saga of the Comstock Lode.* New York: Charles Scribner's Sons, 1934.

Lyttleton, George. *As I Recall Them: Memories of Crowded Years.* New York: Wilson-Erickson, 1936.

Mack, Effie Mona. "James Warren Nye." *Nevada Historical Society* 4, nos. 3–4 (July–December 1961): 54–56.

Marye, George Thomas, Jr. *From '49 to '83 in California and Nevada: Chapters from the Life of George Thomas Marye, a Pioneer of '49.* San Francisco: A. M. Robertson, 1923.

Matthews, M. M. *Ten Years in Nevada, or Life on the Pacific Coast.* 1880. Reprint, Lincoln: University of Nebraska Press, 1985.

McDonald, Douglas, *The Legend of Julia Bulette and the Red Light Ladies of Nevada.* Edited by Stanley Paher. Las Vegas: Nevada Publications, 1980.

Michelson, Miriam. *The Wonderlode of Silver and Gold.* Boston: Stratford, 1934.

Moody, Eric N. *Southern Gentleman of Nevada Politics: Vail N. Pittman.* Reno: University of Nevada Press, 1974.

Mordy, Brooke D., and Donald L. McCaughey. *Nevada Historical Sites.* N.p.: University of Nevada System, 1968.

Morgan, Dale L. *The Humboldt: Highroad of the West.* 1943. Reprint, Lincoln: University of Nebraska Press, 1985.

Morison, Samuel Eliot. *The Oxford History of the American People.* Vol. 2. 1965. Reprint, New York: Mentor Book, New American Library, 1972.

Morison, Samuel Eliot, and Henry Steele Commager. *The Growth of The American Republic.* 2 vols. 1930. Revision and reprint, New York: Oxford University Press, 1958.

Myrick, David. *Nevada Historical Society,* vol. 5, no. 2 (April–June 1962): 3–27.

Nevada State Railroad Museum, "V & T coach No. 17 (Former V & T No. 25). http://www.nsrm-friends.org/nsrm32.htm (accessed May 17, 2002).

Neville, Amelia Ransome. *The Fantastic City: Memoirs of the Social and Romantic Life of Old San Francisco.* Edited and revised by Virginia Brastow. Boston and New York: Houghton Mifflin Co., 1932.

Ogden, Annegret. "'Give Up That Filthy Habit—Cocaine.'" *Californians* (March–April 1988): 10–49.

Oliver, Gordon E. "The History of Early Banking in Nevada, 1859–1900." Master's thesis, University of Nevada, 1983.

Oppel, Frank, ed. *Tales of California.* Secaucus, N.J.: Castle Books, 1989.

Ostrander, Gilman M. *Nevada: The Great Rotten Borough, 1859–1964.* New York: Knopf, 1966.

Parrington, Vernon L. *Main Currents in American Thought.* Vol. 2, *The Romantic Revolution in America, 1800–1860.* New York: Harcourt, Brace and World, Harvest Book, 1927.

Paul, Rodman. *Mining Frontiers of the Far West, 1848–1880.* New York: Holt, Rinehart, and Winston, 1963.

The People's Tribune (Virginia City), January–February 1870.

Phillips, Kevin. *Wealth and Democracy: A Political History of the American Rich.* New York: Broadway Books, 2002.

Powell, John J. *Nevada: The Land of Silver.* San Francisco: Bacon and Co., 1876.

Quiett, Glenn Chesney. *They Built the West: An Epic of Rails and Cities.* New York: D. Appleton-Century Co., 1934.

Ralston, William Chapman. "William Chapman Ralston Correspondence, 1864–1875." The Bancroft Library, University of California, Berkeley.

Regents of the University of California. "Biographies." University of California History Digital Archives. http://www.sunsite.berkeley.edu/uchistory/general history/overview/regents/biographies_a.html (accessed April 4, 2002).

Requa, Issac Lawrence. "Notes Relating to the Development of the Comstock. Typescript. Information Concerning the Development of the Mining Operations, the 'Combination Shaft' and Machinery, and His Own Association with the Area." San Francisco, 1887. Hubert Howe Bancroft Collection, The Bancroft Library, University of California, Berkeley.

Richtofen, Ferdinand Bacon. *The Comstock Lode: Its Character, and the Probable Mode of Its Contiuence in Depth*. San Francisco: Towne and Bacon, 1866.

Robbins, Millie. *Tales of Love and Hate in Old San Francisco*. San Francisco: Chronicle Books, 1971.

Rocha, Guy Louis. "The Many Images of the Comstock Miners' Union." http://www.nevadalabor.com/rocha.html (accessed May 17, 2002).

Rowley, William D. *Reclaiming the Arid West: The Career of Francis G. Newlands*. Bloomington: Indiana University Press, 1996.

San Francisco Alta, December 21, 1851–November 14, 1885.

San Francisco Call, May 9, 1972–February 4, 1886.

San Francisco Chronicle, February 16, 1872–November 17, 1885.

San Francisco Examiner, August 15, 1889–September 22, 1889.

San Francisco Gold Rush Chronology, 1849–1850. November 6, 1849. Museum of the City of San Francisco. http://www.sfmuseum.org/hist/chron1.html (accessed May 2, 2002).

San Francisco Gold Rush Chronology, 1855–1856. October 12 and November 13, 1856. Museum of The City of San Francisco. http://www.sfmuseum.org/hist/chron4.html (accessed May 2, 2002).

Sarah A Sharon, Plaintiff, vs. William Sharon, Defendant: Argument of Wm. M. Stewart on Motion for Alimony and Counsel Fees. In the Superior Court of the State of California, In and for the City and County of San Francisco, Department no. 2. N.d. The Bancroft Library, University of California, Berkeley.

Schlesinger, Arthur M., Jr., ed. *History of U.S. Political Parties,* vol. 2, *1860–1910: The Gilded Age of Politics.* New York: Chelsea House Publishers, 1973.

Schussler, Hermann. Affidavit. *The Circuit Court of the United States, Ninth Judicial Circuit, Northern District of California. In Equity. Spring Valley Water Company, vs. the City and County of San Francisco.* June 20, 1908. The Bancroft Library, University of California, Berkeley.

Scott, E. B. *The Saga of Lake Tahoe.* Crystal Bay, Lake Tahoe: Sierra-Tahoe Publishing Co., 1957.

———. *The Saga of Lake Tahoe, Vol. 2.* Crystal Bay, Lake Tahoe: Sierra-Tahoe Publishing Co., 1973.

Sharon Family Papers. Hubert Howe Bancroft Collection. The Bancroft Library, University of California, Berkeley.

Sharon v. Hill, 20 F. 1 (1884).

Sharon v. *Hill*, 22 F. 28 (1884).

Sharon v. *Sharon*, 67 Cal. 185 (1886).

Sharon v. *Sharon*, 79 Cal. 660 (1889).

Sharon v. *Sharon*, 79 Cal. 663 (1889).

Sherman, William T. *Memoirs of General W. T. Sherman.* New York: C. I. Webster and Co., 1891.

Shinn, Charles Howard. *The Story of the Mine As illustrated by the Great Comstock Lode of Nevada.* 1910. Reprint, Reno: University of Nevada Press, 1980.

Shubik, Martin, ed. *Game Theory and Related Approaches to Social Behavior.* New York: John Wiley and Sons, 1964.

Silliman, B. *Report on the Empire Mill and Mining Co. of Gold Hill, on the Comstock Lode, in Nevada.* San Francisco: William P. Harrison and Co., 1864.

Smith, Grant H. *The History of the Comstock Lode: 1850–1920.* 1943. Reprint, Reno: University of Nevada Press, 1998.

Soule, Frank, John H. Gihon, M.D., and James Nisbet. *The Annals of San Francisco.* New York: D. Appleton and Co., 1855. Facsimile ed., Berkeley: Berkeley Hills Books, 1998.

Stewart, Robert E., Jr., and Mary Frances Stewart. *Adolph Sutro: A Biography.* Berkeley: Howell-North, 1962.

Stewart, William M. "William M. Stewart Papers." Nevada Historical Society, Reno, Nevada.

———. *Reminiscences of Senator William M. Stewart of Nevada.* Edited by George Rothwell Brown. New York: Neale Publishing Co., 1908.

Stone, Irving. *Men to Match My Mountains: The Opening of the Far West, 1840–1900.* New York: Doubleday and Co., 1956.

The Superior Court of the City and County of San Francisco . . . The Odd Fellows Savings Bank vs. William Sharon. December 19, 1884. The Bancroft Library, University of California, Berkeley.

Sutro, Adolph. "Autobiographical Notes." 1890. The Bancroft Library, University of California, Berkeley.

———. "Closing Argument of Adolph Sutro, on the Bill Before Congress to Aid the Sutro Tunnel: Delivered Before the Committee on Mines and Mining of the House of Representatives of the United States of America, Monday, April 22, 1872." The Bancroft Library, University of California, Berkeley.

———. "Speech of Adolph Sutro to the Miners of Nevada on the Sutro Tunnel and the Bank of California." 1870. The Bancroft Library, University of California, Berkeley.

Takaki, Ronald. *A Different Mirror: A History of Multicultural America.* Boston: Little, Brown and Co., 1993.

Tawney, R. H. *Religion and the Rise of Capitalism.* New York: Harcourt, Brace and World, 1926.

Territorial Enterprise, February 27, 1864–August 31, 1880.

Terry, David Smith. *S. A. Sharon, Plaintiff and Respondent, vs. F. W. Sharon, Executor of William Sharon, Apellant. Respondent's Brief in Reply, D. S. Terry, Attorney for Respondent. W. H. S. Barnes, Attorney for Apellant.* 1887. The Bancroft Library, University of California, Berkeley.

Thompson, Bruce R., U.S. District Judge. *Alpine Decree.* October 28, 1980, Alpine County Library, Alpine County, California.

Thompson, Judy Ann. "Historical Archaeology in Virginia City, Nevada: A Case Study of the 90-H Block (Chinese)." Master's thesis, University of Nevada, 1992.

Tilton, Cecil G. *William Chapman Ralston, Courageous Builder.* Boston: Christopher Publishing House, 1935.

Tinkham, George H. *California: Men and Events.* Stockton, Calif.: Record Publishing Co., 1915.

Toponce, Alexander. *Reminiscences of Alexander Toponce, Written by Himself.* 1923. Reprint, Norman: University of Oklahoma Press, 1971.

Townley, John M. "Reclamation in Nevada, 1850–1904," Ph.D. diss., University of Nevada, February 1976.

Twain, Mark. "The Dutch Nick Massacre: The Latest Sensation." *The Complete Humorous Sketches and Tales of Mark Twain.* Edited by Charles Neider. New York: Doubleday and Co., 1961.

———. *Roughing It.* 2 vols. New York: Books, Inc., 1913, by arrangement with Harper and Brothers, New York, 1871.

United States Congress. *House Congressional Record,* 55th Congress, 3d sess., December 16, 1898.

———. *Senate Journal.* 44th Congress, 1st sess., December 6, 1875.

———. *Senate Journal.* 44th Congress, 2d sess., 1876–77.

———. *Senate Journal.* 45th Congress, 3d sess., 1878–79.

———. *Senate Journal.* 46th Congress, 2d sess., 1879–80.

———. *Senate Journal.* 46th Congress, 3d sess., 1880–81.

———, Senate. *Learning About the Senate, "Series of Historical Minutes: Former Slave Presides."* http://www.senate.gov/learning/min-4m.html (accessed February 10, 2002).

———, Senate. *Memorial Addresses: Delivered in the Senate of the United States, 65th Congress.* Washington, D.C.: Joint Congressional Committee on Printing, 1920.

Upshur, George Lyttleton. *As I Recall Them: Memories of Crowded Years.* New York: Wilson-Erickson, 1936.

Virginia & Truckee Railroad Company. "Minute Book, Virginia & Truckee Railroad Company." March 2, 1868. Special Collections Dept., Getchell Library, University of Nevada, Reno.

———. "Minute Book, Virginia & Truckee Railroad Company." August 4, 1881– May 9, 1882. Special Collections Dept., Getchell Library, University of Nevada, Reno.

Virginia Evening Chronicle, October 20, 1872–January 5, 1875.

Wagstaff, A. E. *Life of David S. Terry: Presenting an Authentic, Impartial and Vivid History of His Eventful Life and Tragic Death.* San Francisco: Continental Publishing Co., 1892.

Waldorf, John Taylor. *A Kid on the Comstock: Reminicences of a Virginia City Childhood.* 1968. Reprint, Reno: University of Nevada Press, Vintage West Series, 1984.

Walker, Francis A. *A Compendium of the Ninth Census (June 1, 1870), by Francis A. Walker, Superintendent of Census.* Washington, D.C.: Government Printing Office, 1872.

Weisenburger, Francis Phelps. *Idol of the West: The Fabulous Career of Rolin Mallory Daggett.* Syracuse, N.Y.: Syracuse University Press, 1965.

Wendte, Charles. *The Wider Fellowship: Memories, Friendships, and Endeavors for Religious Unity, 1844–1927.* Vol. 1. Boston: Beacon Press, 1927.

West, Richard Samuel. *The San Francisco Wasp: An Illustrated History.* Easthampton, Mass.: Periodyssey Press, 2004.

Western Americana Auction #11. "Wm. Sharon Silver Presentation Ingot." November 3, 2001, Reno, 917.5. http://www.holabird.org/americana2002/ archive/Auction11/ingots.htm (accessed June 11, 2002).

Wheeler, Session S., with William Bliss. *Tahoe Heritage: The Bliss Family of Glenbrook Nevada.* Reno: University of Nevada Press, 1992.

Will, Irwin. *The City That Was.* New York: B. W. Huebsch, 1906.

Williams, David A. *David C. Broderick: A Political Portrait.* San Marino, Calif.: The Huntington Library, 1969.

Wilson, Neill C. *401 California Street: The Story of the Bank of California, National Association, and Its First 100 Years in the Financial Development of the Pacific Coast.* San Francisco: [The Bank of California?], 1964.

Wittemore, Robert Clifton. *Makers of the American Mind.* New York: William Morrow and Co., 1964.

w.p.a. Writer's Project. *Individual Histories of the Mines of the Comstock.* A joint project of the W.P.A. Writer's Project and the Nevada State Bureau of Mines. Reno: Nevada State Bureau of Mines, 1942[?].

"Yellow Jacket Silver Mining Company Records, 1861–1911." Vol. 1. Special Collections Dept., Getchell Library, University of Nevada, Reno.

Yohalem, Betty. *"I Remember . . ." Stories and Pictures of El Dorado County Pioneer Families.* Placerville, Calif.: El Dorado County Chamber of Commerce, 1977.

Young, John P. *Journalism in California.* San Francisco: Chronicle Publishing Co., 1915.

Zinn, Howard. *A People's History of the United States.* 1980. Reprint, New York: HarperPerennial, 1990.

Index

Ludwig, John D., 36
Lyman, George, 23, 87
Lynch, Philip, 61, 61–65

Mackay, John: against Sharon, 83, 164;
as a Bonanza King, 1, 2, 40, 123;
Consolidated Virginia mine and,
106; and dislike of Sharon, 116,
239n29; fire of 1875 and, 135,
243n8; Hale & Norcross mine and,
2, 72–73; Ophir mine and, 237n20;
Ralston and, 116, 239n29; Sharon's
cipher stolen by, 72; Sharon's
funeral and, 256n3; Sharon's loan
to, 67; Sharon's milling operations
and, 73, 82; taxation on mines and,
110; threat to Virginia & Truckee
Railroad by, 54–55; Virginia and
Gold Hill Water Company and, 40
Malloy, Maria. *See* Sharon, Maria
Manogue, Father Patrick, 26, 74,
218n17
Market Street (San Francisco), 157
Marshall, John, 186, 207
Matthews, Mrs. M. M., 3
Maynard's Block (Gold Hill), 100
Mayre, George, Jr., 33, 67
Mayre, George, Sr., 67
McAllister, Hall, 8
McCrellish, Fred, 95
McEwen, Arthur, 149, 153
McGill, James, 97
McGrath, Reverend T. H., 234n39
McLane, Louis, 16
Menken, Adah Issacs, 26
Metropolitan Orchestra, 156
Mexican-American War, 173
Mexican mine, 35
Miller, Beverly, 12
Millionaire's Row, 38

Mills, Darius Ogden (D. O.): Bank of
California collapse and, 115, 117–18,
119, 120, 122, 238n24; Bank of California revival and, 125, 127–30;
Bank Ring and, 108; confrontation
of Ralston and Sharon by, 29–30;
Coll Deane on, 128; and his disas-
sociation from Ralston, 123–24;
dowry provided by, 156; exposure
of Ralston's finances and, 122; as
president of Bank of California,
16, 29–30, 37, 214–15n22, 237n9,
238n22; purchase of Ralston stocks
and, 115; Ralston and, 138, 240n51;
Lizzie Ralston and, 137, 138; request
for Ralston's resignation and, 119,
120, 122; resignation of, 104, 159;
and resumption of bank presidency,
127; on Sharon, 37, 125, 126; Sharon
and, 127, 137, 138; Sharon's funeral
and, 256n3; Leland Stanford on,
122; Union Mill and Mining Com-
pany and, 33, 40; Virginia & Truc-
kee Railroad and, 7, 53, 115, 125
Mills, Edgar, 150
Mineral Statistics, 75
Miners Union, 50
Mining Review, 53
Mission Dolores, 13
Mitchell, H. K., 96, 100
Monk, Hank, 66
Montgomery Real Estate Company.
See *New Montgomery Street Real
Estate Company*
Moody, Eric, 234n46
Morgan, Dale L., 247n22
Morgan, Pierpont, 111
Morgan Hill (Calif.), 162
Morgan Mill, 31, 34
Morrison, George H., 122, 153, 240n62

(*continued*)

nese laborers and, 48–49, 143; Civil
War and, 14; Clara (daughter) and,
98–99, 110, 158; comparison of
Ralston and, 2; conflict between
Jones and, 81–83, 86, 87–89, 97,
155, 184–85; congressional
committee's visit and, 75; consistent litigation and, 69–70; control
of mines by, 2; John Currey on, 3,
209; Rollin Daggett and, 93; Sam
Davis on, 101–2; "Dear Wife" letters
and, 160, 170, 179, 182, 195; death of,
196; Charles DeLong on, 109; Dan
DeQuille on, 5–6; described as
"King," 4, 20, 42, 84; descriptions
of, 5, 10, 15; disposition of fortune
of, 195, 198, 200; divorce scandal
and, 177, 193, 209; divorce testimony of, 180–85, 187, 192; dona-
tions by, 3, 198; Alf Doten and, 65,
94–95; dowry provided by, 156;
drinking water and, 39–40; early life
of, 10; employees and, 3, 126, 137;
endorsement of Sutro by, 43;
Stephen Field and friendship of,
161–62, 202; financial assistance by,
67; Flora (daughter) and, 151, 155–
56, 177, 196; foreclosures on mills
by, 29–30, 32, 38; Frederick (son)
and, 176–77, 195–96, 200; John Fry
and, 10–11, 15, 139, 196; funeral of,
197; the Gilded Age and, 2, 33–34,
160, 208; Glenbrook House and,
66; *Gold Hill News* and financial
aid from, 85, 95; *Gold Hill News*'s
editorial support of, 85, 90–92, 95;
granddaughter on, 158; U. S. Grant
and, 150–51; Hale & Norcross mine
and, 71–73; Alvinza Hayward and,
81–83, 86–87; Sarah Hill and accusations against, 160; Sarah Hill and

initial meeting of, 154–55, 180,
248n39; Sarah Hill at Belmont and,
169, 181, 183; Sarah Hill on, 169–73,
195, 207; hindrance of Sutro tunnel
by, 2, 44–45, 75, 76, 77–81; ill health
of, 9, 10, 158; intelligence of, 3, 9;
jests and stories about, 4–5, 25–26,
66–67, 85–86; last illness of, 194–
96; loss of Crown Point by, 81–83;
and the marriage document, 160,
164–65, 182, 195; marriage of, 13,
98–99, 110; D. O. Mills and, 125,
127–28, 129–30, 137–38; D. O.
Mills's opposition to, 29–30, 138;
mining stock swindle against, 14–
15; monopolistic practices of, 3, 33–
34, 38, 39, 55, 70; W. M. Neilson
and, 164, 178–79, 186; Francis
Newlands and, 195–96, 198, 200,
208; Francis Newlands on, 8, 158;
obituaries for, 197; Odd Fellows
Bank and, 129, 132; Ophir mine
management by, 107–8, 111; Ophir
mine swindle by, 107–9; Palace
Hotel and, 105–6, 112, 113–14, 126,
137–38; Palace Hotel as residence
of, 137, 157–58; Palace Hotel opening and, 133–35; partnership of
Ralston and, 15, 17, 105, 112, 119,
126, 209, 212n6; *The People's Tribune* and charges against, 59–60;
perception of deceit by, 69, 70;
personal attacks on Sutro and, 95;
philosophical discourse by, 158;
poker and, 24–25, 158; railroad
bribes and, 149–50; railroad taxes
manipulated by, 47, 52–54; on
Ralston, 106, 129; Lizzie Ralston
and, 136–40; Ralston and horse
race with, 67; Ralston estate and,
127–32, 136–41, 142, 144, 159;
Ralston's assistance from, 32, 36,